Prince William County, Virginia
Deed Book Abstracts
1794-1796

Ruth and Sam Sparacio

The Antient Press Collection
from

Colonial Roots
Millsboro, Delaware
2016

Colonial Roots

Helping You Grow Your Family Tree

ISBN 978-1-68034-237-6

CONTENTS

[this page intentionally blank]

(This book is a continuation of Prince William County Deed Book Y, 1791-1796. Pages 1 - 380 of Prince William County Deed Book Y appeared in our book, Deed Abstracts of Prince William County, Virginia (1791-1794).

pp.   (On margin: Examd. & Deld. GEORGE LANE April 26th 1797; N. COX.)
380-   THIS INDENTURE made this the Twenty seventh day of April in year of our Lord
382   one thousand seven hundred and ninety four Between SAMUEL TEBBS of County
        of Prince William of one part and JESSE EWELL JUNR. of County aforesaid of
other part; Witnesseth that SAMUEL TEBBS in consideration of the sumof One hundred
and Twelve pounds, Ten shillings current money of Virginia to him in hand paid by
JESSE EWELL JUNR. hath bargained sold and delivered unto JESSE EWELL JUNR. all that
part of the Lott laid down in a plan and Survey by the number Fifty Nine, which was
conveyed by WILLOUGHBY TEBBS and NATHL. HEDGMAN TRIPLETT to JOHN POPE by Deeds
of Lease and Release dated the seventeenth and eighteenth days of May one thousand
seven hundred and Eighty five & by JOHN POPE to said SAMUEL TEBBS by Deed of Bargain and Sale dated the second day of May one thousand seven hundred and ninety one;
which several Deeds are duly recorded among the Record of the County Court aforesaid;
which part of the lott hereby conveyed is bounded; Begining at the intersection of
PRINCES to FAIRFAX STREETS thence with PRINCES STREET to that part of the said lott
conveyed by JOHN POPE to a certain WILLIAM TYLER, thence runing with TYLERs line
eighty feet thence at right angles with said TYLERs line and parallel with the aforesaid
PRINCES STREET to FAIRFAX STREET thence with said Street to the begining; To have
and to hold the part of the lott hereby conveyed and every appurtenances to the same
in any wise appertaining unto JESSE EWELL JUNR. his heirs; And SAMUEL TEBBS his
heirs the bargained premises unto JESSE EWELL JUNR. his heirs do by these presents
warrant and defend against the claim of all persons; In Witness whereof said SAMUEL
TEBBS has hereunto set his hand and affixed his seal the day and year above written
Signed Sealed and Delivered in presence of
        JOHN DAROCH,   SAMUEL TEBBS
        JAMES McDONALD,   HENRY C. DADE
  At a Court continued and held for Prince William County the 6th day of May 1794
This Deed from SAMUEL TEBBS to JESSE EWELL JUNR. was proved by the Oaths of the
witnesses and ordered to be recorded   Test R. GRAHAM, Cl Cur

pp.   (On margin: Exd. & Deld. JOHN WATSON the 20th day of Septr: 1796, J. WILLIAMS)
382-   THIS INDENTURE made the Thirtieth day of June one thousand seven hundred
386   and ninety four Between RODHAM BLANCETT and JANE his Wife of Prince Wil-
        liam County of one part and WILLIAM SMITH of same County of other part;
Whereas RODHAM BLANCETT and JANE his Wife did on the ninth day of November one
thousand seven hundred and ninety two execute a Deed of Conveyance to WILLIAM
SMITH for two tracts of land in the aforesaid County, one of which tracts WILLIAM
HUGHES & MARGARET his Wife by a certain Deed bearing date the ( ) day of September
1781 and duly recorded among the Records of the County Court aforesaid, did convey to
said RODHAM BLANCETT for one hundred and thirty three acres; And whereas the
boundaries of the said One hundred and thirty three acres as expressed in the aforesaid
Deeds of Conveyance are erronious and inconsistent with the true intent thereof and

WILLIAM HUGHS and MARGARET his Wife did by Deed bearing date the 29th day of June 1793 and proved by two witnesses in the County Court aforesaid grant and confirm to RODHAM BLANCETT the aforementioned one hundred and thirty three acres of land; Now This Indenture Witnesseth that RODHAM BLANCETT and JANE his Wife as well to secure the title of the aforesaid tract of land to WILLIAM SMITH as for the sum of Two hundred pounds current money of Virginia to them in hand paid by WILLIAM SMITH by these presents do bargain sell and confirm unto WILLIAM SMITH his heirs all that tract of land lying in County aforesaid containing One hundred and Thirty three acres which tract is part of a tract of land originally granted to a certain THOMAS HOOPER, who conveyed to a certain JOHN COMBS, who conveyed to aforesaid WM. HUGHS, the tract of land hereby conveyed is bounded; Begining at a Poplar standing on South side of BULL RUN corner to ROBERT SPITTLE and runing with his line So. 68 Wt. 125 po: to a red Oak another corner of SPITTLE, thence So. 35 3/4 E. 180 poles to a white Oak, corner to the original Patent, thence with the line of the Old Patent So. 72 1/2 Et. 66 poles to a small Hicory on the bank of BULL RUN, thence up the said Run according to the several meanders thereof to the begining, including One hundred and thirty three acres but is said courses should contain a greater quantity the said SMITH is to have the same, And all houses profits and appurtenances to the same in any wise appertaining; To have and to hold the tract of land with its appurtenances unto WILLIAM SMITH his heirs; And RODHAM BLANCETT and JANE his Wife their heirs do by these presents warrant and defend the tract of land unto WILLIAM SMITH against the claim of all persons; In Witness whereof they the said RODHAM BLANCETT and JANE his Wife have hereunto set their hands and affixed their seals the day and year first within written
Sealed and Delivered in presence of
        JOHN WILLIAMS, THOMAS CHAPMAN,   RODHAM BLANCETT
        ASA BLANCETT, PHILIP DAWE   JANE BLANCETT
  The Commonwealth of Virginia to ALEXANDER LITHGOW, WILLIAM BARNES and JOHN LAWSON Gentlemen, Greeting, Whereas (the Commission for the privy Examination of JANE, the Wife of RODHAM BLANCETT); Witness ROBERT GRAHAM, Clerk of our said Court the 30th day of June in the 18th year of the Commonwealth 1794
  Prince William County, to wit; In Obedience to the within, we the subscribers have caused to come before us the within named JANE BLANCETT and have examined her privily (the return of the execution of the privy Examination of JANE BLANCETT); Given under our hands and seals this 30th day of June 1794   ALEXANDER LITHGOW
                                                              WM. BARNES

  At a Court held for Prince William County the 7th day of July 1794
This Deed from RODHAM BLANCETT and JANE his Wife to WILLIAM SMITH (a Dedimus for the privy examination of the feme being returned executed) was proved by the Oaths of ASA BLANCETT, PHILIP DAWE, THOMAS CHAPMAN and JOHN WILLIAMS and admitted to Record   Test ROBERT GRAHAM, Cl Cur

pp.   THIS INDENTURE made this twenty 5th day of January in the year of our Lord
386-   one thousand seven hundred and ninety four Between JAMES FOLEY of County
388   of Prince William and MARY his Wife of one part and PHILIP DAWE of same
          County of other part. Whereas JAMES FOLEY as an Attorney in fact for MASON FOLEY of NORTH CAROLINA together with his Wife, MARY, hath made a Deed bearing equal date with these presents to PHILIP DAWE for One hundred and Fifty three and three quarter acres of land situated in aforesaid County as in said Deed will fully appear, Now This Indenture Witnesseth that JAMES FOLEY and MARY his Wife in order to secure the title of the land conveyed by the aforesaid Deed and in consideration of the sum of Ten pounds current money to them in hand paid by PHILIP DAWE, by these pre-

sents do bargain and sell lunto PHILIP DAWE his heirs One hundred and Fifty three and
three quarter acres of land in County of Prince William, being part of a tract of land
which was conveyed to JAMES FOLEY by a certain JOHN FOLEY by Deed bearing date the
second day of October one thousand seven hundred and ninety two and duly recorded in
the County of Prince William which One hundred and fifty three acres and three quarters of an acre of land hereby conveyed is to be laid off in one body whenever required
by PHILIP DAWE his heirs on either end of the aforesaid tract which PHILIP DAWE his
heirs shall think convenient, And all houses profits commodites and appurtenances to
said One hundred and Fifty three and three quarter acres of land hereby granted unto
PHILIP DAWE his heirs, Provided always nevertheless that if JAMES FOLEY his heirs
shall on or before the first day of November one thousand seven hundred and ninety
four next obtain a writing under the hand and seal of his Brother, MASON FOLEY,
attested by three witnesses at lease and proved by them or acknowledged by MASON
FOLEY before any two Justices of the Peace in the County and State wherein said MASON
FOLEY lives, which said Justices are to be certified to be such by the Clerk of the County
Court wherein said MASON FOLEY resides under his hand and seal of the County confirming a certain Letter of Attorney mde by him to JAMES FOLEY (bearing date the fifth
day of November one thousand seven hundred and Seventy one and duly recorded
among the Records of the County Court of Prince William on the same day) impowering
JAMES FOLEY in his name (among other things) to sell a certain tract of land containing One hundred and fifty three and three quarters acres of land which land was
originally granted by the Proprietor of the Northern Neck of Virginia to a certain JOHN
WALLIS and is the same land mentioned in the deed to have been conveyed by JAMES
FOLEY as Attorney in fact for MASON FOLEY to PHILIP DAWE. In Witness whereof the
said JAMES FOLEY and MARY his Wife have hereunto set their hands and seals the day
and year first within written
Sealed and Delivered in the presence of
    WALKER TURNER, ASA BLANCETT,   JAMES FOLEY
    THOMAS CHAPMAN, JOHN WILLIAMS,   MARY FOLEY
    W. SMITH
  At a Court held for Prince William County the 7th day of July 1794
This Deed from JAMES FOLEY and MARY his Wife to PHILIP DAWE was proved by the
Oaths of WM: SMITH, THOMAS CHAPMAN and ASA BLANCETT and admitted to Record
          Test ROBERT GRAHAM, Cl Cur

pp.   KNOW ALL MEN by these presents that I ROBERT SEWELL of County of PRINCE
389-   GEORGE in the State of MARYLAND in consideration of the sum of Four hundred
390   and three pounds one shilling and seven pence current money of Virginia to
       me in hand paid by JOHN GIBSON, Merchant, of Prince William County, by these
presents do release acquit and discharge JOHN GIBSON his heirs from all right title and
demand in Law or Equity which I have unto seven hundred and twenty four acres of
land conveyed to JOHN GIBSON by Deed bearing date the 26th day of November 1793 by
JOHN TAYLOE Esquire to whom the same was conveyed by JOHN TAYLOE THORNTON by
Deed bearing date the 21st day of January 1793, which Seven hundred and twenty four
acres of land is part of a tract of land containing Nine hundred and Fifty four acres
which by Deed of Mortgage bearing date the fourth day of May one thousand seven
hundred and ninety two was conveyed to me ROBERT SEWELL by JOHN TAYLOE THORN-
TON to secure the payment of Four hundred and three pounds one shilling and seven
pence current money of Virginia due from JOHN TAYLOE THORNTON to me said ROBERT
SEWELL by Bond dated the 4th day of May 1792, In Witness whereof I have hereunto set
my hand and affixed my seal the second day of July one thousand seven hundred and

ninety four
Sealed and Delivered in presence of
     DANIEL CARROLL BRENT,   ROBERT SEWALL
     ALEXR: HENDERSON,   JAS: LORIMER,
     JOHN WILLIAMS,   J: SPENCE
  At a Court held for Prince William County the 7th day of July 1794]
This Deed of Release from ROBERT SEWALL to JOHN GIBSON was proved by the Oaths of
ALEXANDER HENDERSON, JOHN SPENCE and JOHN WILLIAMS and admitted to Record
          Test ROBERT GRAHAM, Cl Cur

pp.   THIS INDENTURE made the twenty fourth day of June in the year Seventeen
390-   hundred and ninety four Between MARK MATHEWS MANKIN of County of Prince
392   William, Farmer, of one part and PETER TRONE of same County, Blacksmith, of the
       other part; Witnesseth that MARK MATHEWS MANKIN in consideration of the
sum of Onehundred and sixty ( ) pounds current money of Virginia to him in hand paid
by PETER TRONE, by these presents doth bargain and sell unto PETER TRONE and to his
heirs One hundred and sixty acres of land situate on NEABSCO RUN in said County being
the tract whreon said MARK MATHEWS MANKIN now lives, together with all houses
orchards improvements and appurtenances to the same belonging; the same being part
of Two hundred and Sixty acres of land laid of to the said MARK MATHEWS MANKIN in
right of his Mother, JANE WOOD, whom it became due under the Will of her Father, JOHN
WOOD of CHARLES County in MARYLAND registered in the year 1716 and is part of a
tract of Two thousand nine hundred and sixty acres granted to HENRY WALKER on the
15th of January in the year 1677, and by HENRY WALKER on the 14th day of May in the
year 1678 was assigned to aforesaid JOHN WOOD, who repatented the same in the Proprietors Office on 13th day of March 1695, and after conveying parts thereof by Deeds
of Gift (which are recorded in STAFFORD County in April 1706), divided the remainder
by Will as before recited among his Children in consequence whereof the said MARK
MATHEWS MANKIN came into possession of the Two hundred and sixty acres herein
before mentioned in the year seventeen hundred and Seventy one and in the year 1791
conveyed One hundred acres part thereof to a certain THOMAS LAWSON as will appear
by Deed recorded in County of Prince William; To have and to hold the parcel of land
continuing One hundred and sixty acres complete (according to the bounds now claimed
andheld by said MARK MATHEWS MANKIN) unto PETER TRONE his heirs freed and
exonerated from all incumbrances, And MARK MATHEWS MANKIN against the claim of
all persons shall warrant and by these presents defend; In Witness whereof said MARK
MATHEWS MANKIN hath hereunto set his hand and seal the day and year first within
written
Signed Sealed and Delivered in the presence of
     JOHN GIBSON,   MARK MATHEWS MANKIN
     HANSON RENO,
   · P. HANSBROUGH JR., JAMES LORIMORE
Received of PETER TRONE the sum of One hundred and Eight pounds current money of
Virginia being the consideration paiable by him on the perfection of the foregoing
Deed. Witness my hand this 24th June 1794
     (same witnesses)   MARK MATHEWS MANKIN
  At a Court held for Prince William County the seventh day of July 1794
This Deed with the Receipt thereon from MARK MATHEWS MANKIN to PETER TRONE was
proved by the Oaths of HANSON RENO, PETER HANSBROUGH and JOHN GIBSON and
ordered to be recorded   Test ROBERT GRAHAM, Cl Cur

pp.   THIS INDENTURE made the twenty sixth day of May in year Seventeen hundred
393-   and ninety four Between WILLIAM TACKETT and FANNY his Wife of County of
397   Prince William of one part and ALEXANDER HENDERSON of County aforesaid of
         other part; Witnesseth that WILLIAM TACKETT and FANNY his Wife in consider-
ation of the sum of Two hundred and thirty seven pounds current money of Virginia to
them in hand paid by ALEXANDER HENDERSON, by these presents WILLIAM TACKETT and
FANNY his Wife do bargain and sell unto ALEXANDERHENDERSON and to his heirs a certain tract of land in County of Prince William now in the actual possession of said
ALEXANDER HENDERSON laying on the South side of the Main Run of OCCOQUAN on a
Branch thereof called FRENCH BRANCH, and (agreeable to a Survey thereof made by
JOHN KINCHELOE on the 17th January last) bounded Begining on said Branch at a Maple
in place of an Elm, then South Fifty six degrees West forty eight poles to a Cherry tree
corner to JOHN HOOE, then with HOOEs line South thirteen degrees West one hundred
and thirty two poles to a large white Oak in said line, then North seventy six degrees
East twenty eight poles to a red Oak, corner to RANDOLPHs Heirs, thence with the line of
said Heirs South eighty six degrees East thirty six poles to a Poplar, then South sixty
three degrees East one hundred and thirty poles to a red Oak, corner to said Heirs and to
SAMUEL JACKSON, then with JACKSONs line North thirty two degrees East sixty poles to
several marked bushes, then North fifteen degrees thirty minutes East sixty seven poles
to a red Oak, corner to JOHN McMILLION, then with his line North eighty degrees West
forty six poles to a box Oak, then North thirty eight degrees West thirty poles to the
head of the aforesaid Branch, then down the Branch and binding therewith North
eighty five degrees West ten poles, South eighty two degrees West twenty poles, North
seventy nine degrees West thirty two poles, North fifty six degrees West fity poles,
North thirty degrees West two poles, then North six degrees East twenty eight poles to
the begining, containing One hundred and fifty eight acres; Together with all rights
members and appurtenances to the same belonging; which tract of land is part of a
tract granted by the Proprietor of the Northern Neck to a certain WILLIAM SPILLER by
Deed bearing date the eleventh day of April in the year seventeen hundred and twenty
three for three hundred and Fifty acres of land, the said SPILLER by his Deed of Gift
bearing date the ninth day of June in year Seventeen hundred and Forty eight did
cnfey to JOHN MAYSEY and MARY his Wife a part containing by estimation One hundred and fifty acres more or less agreeable to bounds in said Deed described; and the
residue descended to WILLIAM SPILLER JUNR.and heir to the orginal grant which said
residue is the part herein granted and conveyed, was by WILLIAM SPILLER the
Younger conveyed to WILLIAM TACKETT by Deeds recorded on the 23rd day of June 1760
and by WILLIAM TACKETT was conveyed to WILLIAM TACKETT JUNR. (party to these
presents) by Deed bearing date the 2nd of January 1782 and admitted to Record on the
3rd day of February in the present year; To have and to hold the aforesaid tract of land
containing One hundred and Fifty eight acres with appurtenances unto ALEXANDER
HENDERSON his heirs, free and exonerated from all incumbrances; And WILLIAM
TACKETT and FANNY his Wife the tract of land unto ALEXANDER HENDERSON his heirs
against the claim of all persons shall warrant and forever defend; In Witness whereof
said WILLIAM TACKETT and FANNY his Wife have hereunto set their hands and seals the
day and year first within written
Signed Sealed and Delivered in the presence of
     THOS: LEE JUNR.,   THOS: HARRISON,   WILLIAM TACKETT
     J: LAWSON, H: ROSS,   FANNEY TACKETT
     JAS: LORIMORE,   JOHN GIBSON
Received from ALEXANDER HENDERSON the sum of One hundred and thirty seven
pounds current money of Virginia being the consideration in the foregoing Deed paid

to me on perfection thereof, Witness my hand this 26th of May 1794
Witnesses H. ROSS, J. LAWSON,   WILLIAM TACKETT
        JAS: LORIMORE, JOHN GIBSON
   The Commonwealth of Virginia to the REVD. THOMAS HARRISON, THOMAS LEE SENR.
and WILLIAM GRANT, Gentlemen, Greeting, Whereas (the Commission for the privy Examination of FANNY, the Wife of WILLIAM TACKETT); Witness ROBERT GRAHAM Clerk of our said
Court the 28th day of May 1794 and in the 18th year of the Commonwealth
   Prince William County to wit; In Obedience to the within, we the Subscribers have
caused to come before us the within named FANNY TACKETT and have examined her
privately (the return of the execution of the privy examination of FANNY TACKETT); Given
under our hands and seals this 21st day of May 1794   THOS: LEE SR.
                                                        THOS: HARRISON
   At a Court held for Prince William County the 7th day of July 1794
This Deed with a receipt thereon from WILLIAM TACKETT and FANNY his Wife to
ALEXANDER HENDERSON (a Dedimus for the privy examination of the feme being
returned executed) were proved (the Deed) by the Oaths of HECTOR ROSS, JOHN GIBSON
THOMAS LEE SENR. and JOHN LAWSON, and the Receipt by JOHN LAWSON, H. ROSS and
JOHN GIBSON, and ordered to be recorded   Test ROBERT GRAHAM, Cl Cur

pp.   The Commonwealth of Virginia to ALEXANDER LITHGOW, CHARLES EWELL and
397-   MATHEW HARRISON, Gentlemen, Justices Greeting; Whereas EDWARD NORMAN
399   JANE his Wife and THOMAS NORMAN and ELIZABETH his Wife by their certain
        Deed of Bargain and Sale dated the fifth day of September 1791 have sold and
conveyed unto ROBERT LUBRELL the fee simple Estate of Two hundred and forty seven
and a quarter acres of land be the same more or less lying in County of Prince William
and Whereas the said ELIZABETH cannot conveniently travel to the County Court of
Prince William to make acknowledgement of the same, therefore power is hereby given
unto you to receive the acknowledgement which said ELIZABETH shall be willing to
make before you (the Commission for the privy Examination of ELIZABETH, the Wife of THOMAS
NORMAN); Witness ROBERT GRAHAM Clerk of our said Court the 4th day of June in the
16th year of the Commonwealth 1792
   Prince William County to wit; Pursuant to the within Dedimus we have apart from her
Husband examined the within named ELIZABETH NORMAN (the return of the execution of
ELIZABETH NORMAN); Given under our hands and seals this 4th day of June 1792
                                        ALEXR. LITHGOW
                                        M. HARRISON
   At a Court held for Prince William County the 7th day of July 1794
This Dedimus was returned to the Court and ordred to be recorded
                        Test ROBERT GRAHAM, Cl Cur

pp.   The Commonwealth of Virginia to JAMES EWELL, JOHN TYLER and BERNARD
399-   HOOE Gentlemen Greeting; Whereas LEONARD HART and CATHARINE his Wife
400   by their certain Deed of bargain and sale dated the Second day of May 1785 sold
        and conveyed unto MOORE HOFF the fee simple Estate of One hundred and Sixty
acres of land lying in County of Prince William and Parish of Dettingen, Whereas the
said CATHARINE cannot conveniently travel to our County Court of Prince William to
make acknowledgement of the same, therefore power is given unto you to receive the
acknowledgement said CATHARINE shall be willing to make before you (the Commission
for the privy Examination of CATHARINE, the Wife of LEONARD HART); Witness ROBERT
GRAHAM Clerk of our said Court the 10th day of March in the 12th year of the Commonwealth 1788   ROBERT GRAHAM

Prince William Sct. By order of the within Commission to us directed, we have taken the examination of CATHARINE the Wife of LEONARD HART privily (the return of the execution of the privy examination of CATHARINE HART); Certified under our hands and seals this 15th day of March 1788   JA: EWELL
                                                                JOHN TYLER
At a Court held for Prince William County the 7th day of July 1794
This Dedimus was returned to the Court and ordered to be recorded
                              Test ROBERT GRAHAM, Cl Cur

pp.   (On margin: Deds. recorded in Liber 1 folio 190)
400-   THIS INDENTURE made the twentieth day of November one thousand seven
403   hundred and ninety three Between WALTER GRAHAM of County of FAUQUIER
             and SALLEY his Wife of one part and JOHN OVERALL of Town of DUMFRIES County of Prince William of other part; Witnesseth that WALTER GRAHAM in consideration of the sum of Twenty four pounds current money of Virginia to him in hand paid by JOHN OVERALL, they the said WALTER GRAHAM and SALLY his Wife do bargain and sell unto JOHN OVERALL and his heirs a certain part of a lott of land in Town of DUMFRIES known by the number Sixty Seven, which is bounded, Begining at the most Easterly corner of the said lott number Sixty Seven on WATER STREET and thence runing with WATER STREET eighty feet thence at right angles with the said Street & parallel with PRINCES STREET to the line which divides Lott Sixty Seven from Sixty Six, thence with that dividing line eighty feet to PRINCES STREET, thence with PRINCES STREET to the begining; which lott number Sixty Seven was conveyed to WALTER GRAHAM by HENRY LEE Esqr., by Deed bearing date the 25th day of March 1791 and duly recorded in the County Court of Prince William aforesaid; Together with all houses gardens streets lanes alleys profits and appurtenances belonging; To have and to hold the lott of ground hereby conveyed with its appurtenances unto JOHN OVERALL his heirs; And WALTER GRAHAM and SALLY his Wife and their heirs shall warrant and for ever defend by these presents; In Witness whereof the said WALTER GRAHAM and SALLY his Wife have hereunto set their hands and seals the day month and year first within written
                              WALTER GRAHAM
                                        SALLY GRAHAM
Signed Sealed and Delivered in presence of
     SAML. TEBBS, NAT: TRIPLETT, GEORGE MURREN
Reacknowledged the 13th day of May 1794 before us
     JOHN HEDGES, DAVID W. SCOTT,   JOHN WILLIAMS,
     GEO: WILLIAMS, WM. SMITH
     Received the day and year first within written of JOHN OVERALL the sum of Twenty four pounds current money of Virginia the consideration within mentioend, Witness my hand   WALTER GRAHAM
Witnesses SAML. TEBBS, NAT. TRIPLETT, GEORGE MURREN
Reacknowledged the 13th day of May 1794 before us
     JOHN HEDGES, DAVID W. SCOTT, JOHN WILLIAMS,
     GEORGE WILLIAMS WM. SMITH
At a Court held for Prince William County the 7th day of July 1794
This Deed with the Receipt thereon from WALTER GRAHAM and SALLY his Wife to JOHN OVERALL were proved by the Oaths of WILLIAM SMITH, GEORGE WILLIAMS and JOHN WILLIAMS and ordered to be recorded   Test ROBERT GRAHAM, Cl Cur

pp.   (On margin: Examd. & delivered April the 27th 1797, J. WMS.)
404-   THIS INDENTURE made this Eighth day of July one thousand seven hundred and
405   ninety four Between JESSE EWELL JUNR. of County of Prince William of one part
           and GEORGE LANE of the aforesaid County of other part; Witnesseth that JESSE
EWELL JUNR. in consideration of the sum of One hundred and forty pounds current
money of Virginia to him in hand paid by GEORGE LANE, said JESSE EWELL JUNR. doth
bargain sell and confirm unto GEORGE LANE all that lott of land lying in Town of DUM-
FRIES and County aforesaid which said EWELL purchased of SAMUEL TEBBS the same
being part of the lott conveyed to FOUSHEE TEBBS Gt., deced., from him to WILLOUGHBY
TEBBS, from WILLOUGHBY TEBBS to NATHANIEL TRIPLETT, from NATHANIEL TRIPLETT to
JOHN POPE, from him the said POPE to the aforesaid SAMUEL, begining at the intersection of PRINCESS and FAIRFAX STREETs thence with PRINCESS STREET to that part of said
Lott conveyed by JOHN POPE to a certain WILLIAM TYLER, thence runing with TYLERs
line Eighty feet, thence at right angles with said TYLERs line and parrellel with PRIN-
CESS STREET to FAIRFAX STREET, then to the begining; the said lott being discribed by
the number Fifty Nine; To have and to hold to GEORGE LANE his heirs and the said
EWELL his heirs unto GEORGE LANE his heirs do by these presents forever warrant and
defend against the claims of all persons; In Witness whereof the said JESSE EWELL hath
hereunto set his hand and seal the 8th day of July 1794
Signed Sealed and Delivered in presence of
        WILLIAM TYLER, WILLOUGHBY TEBBS,   JESSE EWELL JUNR.
        JAMES JAMES, JAMES McDONALD,
        ADAM COOK, JOHN LEDLEE
   DUMFRIES 8th July 1794. Then received of Mr. GEORGE LANE the sum of One hundred
and forty pounds in full consideration of the within purchase money
Test JAMES JOHNSTON   JESSE EWELL JUNR.
        SAMUEL CORNWELL
   At a Court held for Prince William County the first day of September 1794
This Deed from JESSE EWELL JUNR. to GEORGE LANE was proved by the Oathes of JAMES
JAMES, JAMES McDONALD and ADAM COOK and the Receipt by JAMES JOHNSTON and
ordered to be recorded   Teste ROBERT GRAHAM, Cl Cur

pp.   THIS INDENTURE made this twenty third day of August one thousand seven
406-   hundred and ninety four Between JOSEPH FLORANCE of County of Prince William
407   of one part and GEORGE FLORANCE of County aforesaid of other part; Witnesseth
           that said JOSEPH in consideration of the natural love and affection which he
beareth to his Son, GEORGE FLORANCE, by these presents have granted unto GEORGE
FLORANCE his heirs one Negro man named Frank and a Negro Child named Dafney and
all the Estate right title and demand of said JOSEPH FLORANCE in the said Negroes Frank
and Dafney; To have and to hold the said Negro man and Child named Frank and Dafney
hereby given unto GEORGE FLORANCE his heirs said JOSEPH FLORANCE his heirs shall
warrant and forever defend by these presents; In Witness whereof the said JOSEPH
FLORANCE have hereunto set his hand and seal the same day and year above written
Signed Sealed and Delivered in the presence of
        HUGH ATTWELL,   JOSEPH his mark ─┼─ FLORANCE
        WILLIAM LEACHMAN, JOHN ⟋ MORDOCK,
        WILLIAM FLORANCE, WILLIAM BUTLER
   At a Court held for Prince William County the first day of September 1794
This Deed of Gift from JOSEPH FLORANCE to GEORGE FLORANCE was proved by the Oaths of
WILLIAM LEACHMAN and WILLIAM BUTLER and admitted to Record
                Teste ROBERT GRAHAM, Cl Cur

pp.
407-
408
TO ALL PEOPLE to whom these presents shall come, I JOSEPH FLORANCE of County of Prince William send Greeting; Know ye that I said JOSEPH FLORANCE in consideration of the love and affection which I have and bear unto my beloved Daughter, ELIZABETH BUTLER, and for divers other good causes and considerations me hereunto moving by these presents do give and deliver unto ELIZABETH BUTLER a certain Negroe woman slave named Winney, To have and to hold the said Negroe Winney unto ELIZABETH BUTLER her heirs, And I said JOSEPH FLORANCE the said Negroe Winney (and her increase) to said ELIZABETH BUTLER and her heirs against the claim of all persons will warrant and forever defend by the presents; In Witness whereof I have hereunto set my hand and seal this 18th day of August one thousand seven hundred and ninety four

Signed Sealed and Delivered in presence of us
NINIAN PINKNEY
SIMON DAVIS, WILLIAM HIXON,
WILLIAM FLORANCE, GEORGE FLORANCE

JOSEPH his mark —|— FLORANCE

At a Court held for Prince William County on the first day of September 1794
This Deed of Gift from JOSEPH FLORANCE to ELIZABETH BUTLER was proved by JOSEPH FLORANCE and admitted to Record   Teste ROBERT GRAHAM, Cl Cur

pp.
408-
409
KNOW ALL MEN by these presents that I JOHN CALVERT of County of Prince William have sold and conveyed to RICHARD SCOTT BLACKBURN and BURR PEYTON the following slaves, to wit, William, Fanny and her Child. Witness my hand this the 4th day of January 1794.
The Condition of the above obligation is such that if the above bound CALVERT shall relieve the said RICHARD SCOTT BLACKBURN and BURR PEYTON from a Bond for One hundred and Eleven pounds five in which they had this day been bound with said CALVERT to JOHN JACKSON and JAMES ROACH, then the above obligation to be void else to remain in full force power and virtue in Law

Signed Sealed and Delivered in the presence of
QUINTON RATCLIFFE,
JAMES TRIPLETT, ALEXANDER CUMPTON

JOHN his mark —|— CALVERT

At a Court held for Prince William County the first day of September 1794
This Bill of Sale from JOHN CALVERT to RICHARD S. BLACKBURN was proved by the Oah of ALEXANDER CUMPTON and ordered to be recorded
Teste ROBERT GRAHAM, Cl Cur

pp.
409-
410
KNOW ALL MEN by these presents that I FRANCIS JACKSON of County of Prince William by these presents do bargain sell and confirm utno ISRAEL LACEY of LOUDOUN County in consideration of the sum of Two hundred and fifty pounds Virginia currency to me in hand paid, one Lease for three lives of the Plantation whereon I now live, two Negroe fellows slaves for life, the one named Jacob, the other Ceasar, five feather beds and their furniture, one horse and two mares, ten head of cattle, twenty one head of hogs and all my household furniture and plantation utensils of every kind. I do for myself my heirs undertake to warrant and forever defend the title of and in the said Lease, Negroes, horses, mares, househould furniture (including five beds) hogs and cattle and plantation utensils of every kind to said ISRAEL LACEY his heirs against the claim of every person; In Witness whereof I have hereunto set my hand and affixed my seal this 7th day of April 1794.

Sealed and Delivered in the presence of
W. A. ROGERS,   CALEB his mark —|— BRADY   FRANCIS JACKSON

At a Court held for Prince William County the first day of September 1794
This Bill of Sale from FRANCIS JACKSON to ISRAEL LACEY was proved by the Oath of
WILLIAM A. ROGERS and admitted to Record
Teste R. GRAHAM, Cl Cur

pp.   THIS INDENTURE made the Second day of September in year of our Lord one
410-   thousand seven hundred and ninety four Between THOMAS THORNTON and JANE
414   his Wife of County of Prince William of one part and ISAAC FARROW of County of
Prince William of other part; Witnesseth that THOMAS THORNTON and JANE his
Wife in consideration of the sum of Five shillings current money of Virginia to them in
hand paid by ISAAC FARROW, by these presents doth bargain and sell unto ISAAC FAR-
ROW all that tract of land lying in County of Prince William containing One hundred
and ninety nine acres more or less that was conveyed to him by his father, THOMAS
THORNTON and taken up by WILLIAM MOORE, And all houses water courses profits and
appurtenances belonging; To have and to hold the lands hereby conveyed unto ISAAC
FARROW his heirs during the term of one whole year paying therefore the Rent of one
pepper corn on Lady Day next if demanded to intent that by virtue of these presents
and by force of the Statute for transferring uses into possession said ISAAC FARROW
may be in actual possession of the premises and be thereby enabled to accept the release of the reversion and inheritance thereof; In Witness whereof the said THOMAS
THORNTON and JANE his Wife hath hereunto set their hands and seals the day and year
first above written
Sealed and Delivered in the presence of
     JAMES MUSCHETT,   THOMAS THORNTON
     MUNGO HANCOCK,   JANE CARR THORNTON
     JOHN MUSCHETT, CHARLES TYLER JUNR.
At a Court held for Prince William County the first day of Septr. 1794
This Lease from THOS: THORNTON and JANE his Wife to ISAAC FARROW was proved by the
Oaths of MUNGO HANCOCK, JOHN MUSCHETT JUNR. and CHARLES TYLER JUNR. and
ordered to be recorded   Teste ROBERT GRAHAM, Cl Cur

        THIS INDENTURE made this first day of September in year of our Lord one thou-
sand seven hundred and ninety four Between THOMAS THORNTON and JANE his Wife of
County of Prince William of one part and ISAAC FARROW of County of Prince William of
other part; Witnesseth that in consideration of the sum of One hundred and Ninety
eight pounds current money of Virginia to THOMAS THORNTON and JANE his Wife in
hand paid by ISAAC FARROW, by these presents doth bargain sell release and confirm
unto ISAAC FARROW his heirs, in his actual possession now being by virtue of a bargain and sale to him thereof made and by force of the Statute for transferring uses into
possession, and his heirs all that tract of land lying in County of Prince William containing One hundred and Ninety nine acres more or less which was taken up by WILLIAM
MOORE and now the property of said THOMAS THORNTON bounded, Begining at A., a
Hickory corner to HENRY HOLLEY and PHILLEMON WATERS Survey, thence with sd.
WATERS line No. 28 Wt. 56 poles to B., a box Oak, thence So. ( ) Wt. 82 poles to C., a red Oak
and white Oak in TAQUETs line, thence with TAQUETs line No. 34 Et. 66 poles to D., a white
Oake then No. 44 Wt. 31 poles to E., a large white Oak SPILLERs Corner, thence with his
lines No. 44 Et. 113 poles to F., two white Oaks, thence No. 3 E. 100 poles to G., a white Oak
on a Branch side, thence No. 78 E. 32 poles to H. a red Oak in or near RICHARD WRIGHTs
line, thence with his lines So. 27 E. 57 poles to J, two red Oaks, thence So. 67 E. 93 poles to
K, a Hickory near ( ) line, thence So. 28 W. 93 poles to L., a red Oak, thence So. 33 ( )
poles to the begining: including 199 acres; And all houses orchards profits commodities

and appurtenances belonging; To have and to hold the lands hereby conveyed unto
ISAAC FARROW his heirs free and clear from all incumbrances whatsoever; the Quit-
rents hereafter to grow due and payable to his Lordship his heirs in respect to the premises only excepted and foreprized, And THOMAS THORNTON and JANE his Wife unto
ISSAC FARROW his heirs against them and their heirs shall warrant and forever defend
by these presents; In Witness whereof the said THOMAS THORNTON and JANE his Wife
hath hereunto set their hands and seals the day and year above written
Sealed and Delivered in the presence of
         JAMES MUSCHETT, MUNGO HANCOCK,   THOMAS THORNTON
         JOHN MUSCHETT, CHARLES TYLER JUNR.   JANE CARR THORNTON
   At a Court held for Prince William County the first day of Setpember 1794
This Release from THOMAS THORNTON and JANE his Wife to ISAAC FARROW was proved
by the Oaths of MUNGO HANCOCK, JOHN MUSCHETT and CHARLES TYLER JUNR. and
ordered to be recorded   Teste ROBERT GRAHAM, Cl Cur

pp.   (On margin: Exd. & Deld. Septr. 21st 1796; J. WMS. Cl. C.)
414-   KNOW ALL MEN by these presents that I ASA WARDEN of CHARLES County in
416   State of MARYLAND in consideration of the sum of One hundred and fifty pounds
        of good and lawful money of Virginia to me in hand paid by JAMES SMITH of
DUMFRIES State of Virginia; have bargained and sold JAMES SMITH his heirs all that
tract of land containing by estimation One hundred and Fifty acres of land with Eighteen acres of Marsh adjoining, be the same more or less, lying in County of Prince
William, Parish of Dittengen in Virginia on POTOMACK RIVER and South side of
POWELLS CREEK joining the land formerly of ISAAC DAVIS, JOHN BLAND and RICHARD
CRUPPER, Begining at the mouth of a Branch which divides this land from the lands
now of RICHARD GRAHAM upon POWELLS CREEK thence runing up said Creek including
the Marsh above mentioned to the line of the lands purchased by said SMITH from
JAMES HALLEY, then with his line to the back line aforesaid joining the lands of JOHN
BLA( ) now of the Heirs of SAVAGE, then with that line to the Branch aforesaid and
down the Branch the meanders thereof to the begining; being the same tract of land
purchased of DERBY GALLAHUE by RICHARD WARDEN, my Father, who by his Will
devised the same to me; And all houses profits commodities and appurtenances to said
land and Marsh belonging; To have and to hold the One hundred and Fifty acres and
Eighteen acres of Marsh with all the appurtenances unto JAMES SMITH his heirs free
and clear from all incumbrances; In Witness whereof the said ASA WARDEN hath to this
present Deed set his hand and seal at DUMFRIES this Twenty ( ) day of June in the year
of our Lord one thosuand seven hundred and ninety four
Signed Sealed and Delivered in presence of
         TIMOTHY BRUNDIGE, WM. BARNES,   ASA WORDEN
         JOHN KING, JOHN DAROCH
   At a Court continued and held for Prince William County the Second day of September
1794   This Deed from ASA WARDEN to JAMES SMITH was proved by the Oaths of JOHN
KING, JOHN DAROCH and WILLIAM BARNES and ordered to be recorded
                        Teste ROBERT GRAHAM, Cl Cur

p.   KNOW ALL MEN by these presents that I JAMES WALTER COLQUHOUN of Town of
417   DUMFRIES in consideration of Five pounds current money to me in hand paid by
        WILLIAM SCOTT of same Town, Joiner, do by these presents sell release and con-
firm unto WILLIAM SCOTT or assigns all my right in reversion to one Negro boy six
years old named Peter now in possession of said WILLIAM SCOTT and is a forth coming
promise, he the said Negro boy Peter having been taken by distress to satisfy the

Sheriff of Prince William County for Clerks Notes and Attendance of Witnesses due by ELIZABETH FALLIN of County of Prince William; To have and to hold all my right title and demand to the said Negro boy Peter to WILLIAM SCOTT and assigns against the claim of JAMES WALTER COLQUHOUN and all persons claiming under me. In Witness whereof I have hereunto set my hand and seal this Twenty fifth day of June 1794
Sealed and Delivered in the presence of

JOHN WATSON,   JAMES W. COLQUHOUN
JESSE TAYLOR

At a Court continued and held for Prince William County the second day of Septr: 1794 This Bill of Sale from JAMES W. COLQUHOUN to WILLIAM SCOTT was proved by the Oaths of JOHN WATSON and JESSE TAYLOR and ordered to be recorded
Teste ROBERT GRAHAM, Cl Cur

pp.   (On margin: Examd. & delivered Mr. ALEXR. HOWISON for Mr. ALLEN the
418-   24th Decr. 1801, JOHN WILLIAMS)
420   THIS INDENTURE made this Second day of September in year of our Lord one thousand seven hundred and ninety four Between CHARLES DIAL and SARAH DIAL his Wife, formerly SARAH CALVERT, Daughter of REUBEN CALVERT deceased, and THOMAS CALVERT, heir at Law of said REUBEN CALVERT deceased, and MARY EMBLY his Wife, all of the County of Prince William of one part and ZACHARIAH ALLEN of same County of other part; Witnesseth that said CHARLES DIAL and SARAH DIAL, THOMAS CALVERT and MARY EMBLY his Wife in consideration of Three hundred and Twenty three Dollars current money of the United States to them in hand paid by ZACHARIAH ALLEN, by these presents do bargain and sell unto ZACHARIAH ALLEN his heirs a certain tract of land lying in County of Prince William containing One hundred acres be the same more or less which is bounded, Begining at three white Oaks corner to AMOS FOX who purchased part of the tract of land originally granted, thence with said FOX's line So. 40 Wt. 70 poles to a white Oak, thence No. 75 West 30 poles to a white Oak, thence S: 73d. West 150 poles to a black Oak, thence North 66 1/2 West 88 poles to a Chesnut Oak, thence North 20d. East 96 poles to a marked teee another corner of said FOX, thence with that dividing line to the begining; which tract of land hereby conveyed is part of a tract of land granted to a certain BURDET HARRISON by the Proprietor of the Northern Neck of Virginia by Deed bearing date the Second day of March one thousand seven hundred and thirty for One hundred and eighty five acres and is the same tract of land which was conveyed to aforesaid REUBIN CALVERT by a certain PETER CORNWELL and SARAH his Wife by Deeds of Lease and Release dated the second and third days of December 1773 duly recorded in Prince William County Court; To have and to hold the tract of land hereby conveyed unto ZACHARIAH ALLEN his heirs, And CHARLES DIAL and SARAH DIAL and THOMAS CALVERT and MARY EMBLY his Wife for themselves their heirs the bargained premises unto ZACHARIAH ALLEN his heirs do by virtue of these presents for ever warrnt and defend against the claims of every person; In Witness whereof the said CHARLES DIAL and SARAH DIAL and THOMAS CALVERT and MARY EMBLY his Wife have hereunto set their hands and affixed their seals the day and year first within written
Sealed and Delivered in presence of

JOHN FRISTOE   CHARLES his mark X DYAL
THOS: HARRISON,   SARAH DOYAL
JOHN ATTWELL   THOMAS CALVERT
                               MARY EMBLY CALVERT

Received the day and year first within written of ZACHARIAH ALLEN the sum of Three hundred and Twenty three Dollars current money of the United State being the con-

sideration within mentioned to be paid by him to us
Witness JOHN ATTWELL,   CHARLES his mark ✗ DYAL
         DAVID JAMESON   THOMAS CALVERT
   At a Court continued and held for Prince William County the second day of September
1794   This Deed and Receipt from CHARLES DIAL and SARAH DIAL his Wife and THO-
MAS CALVERT and MARY EMBLY his Wife to ZACHARIAH ALLEN (the said femes being
privily examined and consenting thereto) were acknowledged by the said CHARLES and
THOMAS and the said said SARAH and MARY EMBLY and ordered to be recorded
                    Teste ROBERT GRAHAM, Cl Cur

pp.   (On margin: Exd. & Delivered Feby. 23d. 1795, J. WILLIAMS)
420-   THIS INDENTURE made this twenty second day of May in year of our Lord one
426   thousand seven hundred and ninety four Between JESSE EWELL SENR., Gentle-
        man, of Prince William County and CHARLOTTE his Wife of one part and PETER
FELIX MAUGER of the same County of other part; Whereas JESSE EWELL JUNR. and the
aforesaid JESSE EWELL SENR. by their certain Bond bearing equal date with these presents stand bound to PETER F. MAUGER in the Penal Sum of Three hundred and Forty
pounds, Thirteen shillings specie with a condition there under written for the payment
of One hundred and Seventy pounds, Six shillings and Six pence on the twenty fourth
day of September 1794; And also by one other bond bearing also equal date with these
presents in the Penal Sum of Three hundred and forty pounds, Thirteen shillings with
a condition thereunto written for the payment of One hundred and seventy pounds, Six
shillings and Six pence on the twenty fourth day of March 1795; And also by one other
bond of equal date in the sum of Three hundred and forty pounds thirteen shillings
with a condition for the payment of one hundred and seventy pounds six shilling and
six pence on the twenty fourth day of September 1795, And also one other bond of equal
date in the sum of Three hundred and forty pounds Thirteen shillings with a condition
thereunder written for the payment of One hundred and seventy pounds six shillings
and six pence on the twenty fourth day of March 1796; NOW THIS INDENTURE WITNES-
SETH that JESSE EWELL SENR. and CHARLOTTE his Wife in consideration of the aforesaid
Bond and for better securing the payment of the sums of money on the days on which
they respectively become payable, And also in consideration of the sum of Ten pounds
current money of Virginia in hand paid by said PETER F. MAUGER to JESSE EWELL SENR.
and CHARLOTTE his Wife, by these presents do bargain and sell unto PETER FELIX MAU-
GER his heirs all those several tracts of land which were purchased by CHARLES EWELL,
Father to the said JESSE EWELL SENR. out of the Land granted by Patent to JOHN WOOD
(except the Mansion Tract and also those several parcels of land which said CHARLES
EWELL purchased out of the Lands granted by Patents unto CORNELIOUS KEIFFE and
CHARLES TYLER, and also that tract of land which was granted to CHARLES EWELL by
Patent from the Proprietor of the Northern Neck, all which several tracts lie contigu-
ous to each other in the County of Prince William on NEABSCO RUN, including the said
JESSE EWELL SENR. Plantation and the Tenements of ELIJAH ATHEY, HENRY TURNBULL
and WILLIAM FOXWORTHY, and containing Twelve hundred and Forty eight acres more
or less which JESSE EWELL SENR. holds by desent; And all houses and appurtenances to
said parcels of land belonging; To have and to hold the hereby bargained and sold tracts
of land (except as before excepted) unto PETER F. MAUGER his heirs; PROVIDED Always
nevertheless that if JESSE EWELL SENR. his heirs shall pay unto PETER F. MAUGER or
assigns (the amounts and the dates of payment as before set forth are repeated) then these presents shall cease and be utterly null and void. This Indenture further witnesseth that
in case the aforesaid sums of money herein stipulated shall not be punctually paid on
the last day herein appointed that said JESSE EWELL SENR. do by these presents appoint

PETER F. MAUGER my true lawfull and irrevocable Attorney for me to sell and dispose of all or so much of the hereby bargained premises as will be sufficient to pay the sums of money that may be due at the time of such sale; In Witness whereof JESSE EWELL SENR. and CHARLOTTE his Wife have hereunto set their hands and affixed their seals the day and year first within written

Signed Sealed and Delivered (the several Easements by which that tract on POWELLS RUN whereon said JESSE EWELLs Mill stands and that tract in the occupation of WILLIAM CALVERT are excepted and by which the effect of the above Power of Attorney is put off untill the twenty fourth day of March 1796, being first made in the presence of

    JA: EWELL,   JESSE EWELL SENR.
    HENRY C. DADE,   GALVAN De BERNOUX

At a Court continued and held for Prince William County the second day of September 1794   This Deed from JESSE EWELL SENR. to PETER F. MAUGER was acknowledged by the said JESSE and admitted to Record   Teste ROBERT GRAHAM, Cl Cur

pp.   (On margin: Exd. & Delivered M. B. BURROUGHS Octr. 7th 1794; J. WILLIAMS)
426-   KNOW ALL MEN by these presents that I MARY BURRESS of FAUQUIER County
427   have this day bargained sold and delivered unto ROSSILL HILL and BENJAMIN
          BURRESS two Negro women, Vizt., Phillis and Mary, in consideration of the sum
of Two shillings to me in hand paid by ROSSILL HILL and BENJAMIN BURRESS, and I do
for my self my heirs warrant and defend the said Negroes Phillis and Mary to said
ROSSILL HILL and BENJAMIN BURRISS their heirs from every person; In Witness
whereof I have hereunto set my hand and seal this 18th day of August 1794
Sealed in presence of
    WILIA his mark X PIRSES,   MARY BURROUGHS
    MICKLE his mark ⤙ BURROUGHS

Memorandum; That whereas the Subscribers stand bound as securties to the within MARY BURROUGHS for a Judgment obtained against the said MARY BURRESS by JOHN HAMMITT in the County Court of Prince William that in case the said MARY BURRESS do satisfy the said Judgment and save us harmless, we hereby oblige ourselves to deliver up to the said MARY the said Negros, Phillis and Mary; Witness our hands this 18th day of August 1794   his mark ⤙ ROSEL HILL
                BENJ: BURROUGHS

At a Court continued and held for Prince William County the second day of September 1794 This Bill of Sale with the Memorandum thereon from MARY BURROUGHS to ROSSILL HILL and BENJAMIN BURROUGHS were acknowledged by the parties and admitted to Record   Teste ROBERT GRAHAM Cl Cur

pp.   KNOW ALL MEN by these presents that we WILLIAM LINTON and WM. TYLER
427-   are held and firmly bound unto HENRY LEE Esquire, Governor of Virginia or
428   his successors for the use of the Commonwealth in the sum of Four thousand
          Dollars to which payment well and truly to be made we bind ourselves our heirs
firmly by these presents; Sealed with our seals and dated this third day of September
1794   THE CONDITION of the above obligation is such that whereas the above bound
WILLIAM LINTON at a Court continued and held for the County of Prince William the 3d.
day of September was by the said Court recommended to be continued an INSPECTOR of
Tobo at QUANTICO WAREHOUSE; Now if said WILLIAM LINTON shall truly and faithfully
perform the duties of an Inspector at the aforesaid Warehouse agreeable to an Act of
Assembly intituled, "An Act for reducing into one the several Acts of Assembly for the
Inspection of Tobo." then the above obligation to be void or else to remain in full force
and virtue

Sealed and Deld. in presence of
The Court   WILLIAM LINTON
                                                   WILLIAM TYLER

At a Court continued and held for Prince William County the 3d. day of September 1794
This Bond from WILLIAM LINTON and WILLIAM TYLER to HENRY LEE Esqr., Governor of
Virginia, was acknowledged by the parties and admitted to Record
                    Teste ROBERT GRAHAM, Cl Cur

pp.   KNOW ALL MEN by these presents that we WILLIAM CARTER and ALEXANDER
428-   HENDERSON are held and firmly bound unto HENRY LEE Esquire, Governor of
429   Virginia and his successors for the use of the Commonwealth in the sum of Four
          thousand Dollars to which payment well and truly to be made we bind ourselves
our heirs firmly by these presents; Sealed with out seals and dated this Fourth day of
September 1794
THE CONDITION of the above obligation is such that whereas the above bound WILLIAM
CARTER at a Court continued and held for the County of Prince William the third day of
September was by the said Court recommended to be continued an INSPECTOR of Tobo: at
QUANTICO WAREHOUSE; Now if said WILLIAM CARTER shall truly and faithfully perform
the duties of an Inspector at the aforesaid Warehouse agreeable to an Act of Assembly
intituled, "An Act for reducing into one the several Acts of Assembly for the Inspection
of Tobacco," Then the above obligation to be void else to be and remain in full force and
virtue
Sealed and Delivered in the presence of
The Court   WILLIAM CARTER
                                                   ALEXR: HENDERSON

At a Court continued and held for Prince William County the 4th day of September 1794
This Bond from WILLIAM CARTER and ALEXANDER HENDERSON to HENRY LEE Esquire,
Governor of Virginia, was acknowledged by the parties and ordered to be recorded
                    Teste ROBERT GRAHAM, Cl Cur

pp.   A Return of the Situation of QUANTICO WAREHOUSES the Quantity of Tobacco
429-   taken the last Inspection & the Quantity they will contain at one time;
430   The Quantity of Tobo: taken the last Inspection   843 hhd.
          The Quantity they will contain at one time   1049 hhd.
The situation of the Warehouses Tolerable, the prises are all in bad order and wants
repairing.   LINTON & CARTER
At a Court held for Prince William County the 6th day of October 1794
This Return of the Situation of QUANTICO WAREHOUSES was presented to the Court and
admitted to Record   Teste ROBT. GRAHAM, Cl Cur

p.   KNOW ALL MEN by these presents that we JAMES WALTER COLQUHOUN of County
430   of Prince William in consideration of the sum of Ninety six pounds current
          money of Virginia to me in hand paid by WILLIAM SCOTT of the same County, do
by these presents bargain & sell unto WILLIAM SCOTT all my right title and demand in &
to four Negro slaves to wit, Ralph a man, Kate a woman and Dinah & Fanny, two young
girls, the two first mentioned being hired our in DUMFRIES by my Grand Mother,
ELIABETH FALLIN, the two girls in the possession of him the said WILLIAM SCOTT; To
have and to hold the said Negros & the increase of the females unto WILLIAM SCOTT &
assigns, And I JAMES WALTER COLQUHOUN the Negros aforesaid & their increase to said
WILLIAM SCOTT do by these presents warrant and defend against all persons, the right
of said ELIZABETH FALLIN for her life only excepted; In Witness whereof I hereunto set

my hand & seal this 20th day of September 1794
Sealed & Delivered in the presence of
        ROBERT GRAYSON,   JAMES W. COLQUHOUN
Witness CHARLES MOSER
    At a Court held for Prince William County the 6th day of October 1794
This Bill of Sale from JAMES WALTER COLQUHOUN to WILLIAM SCOTT was proved by the
Oaths of ROBERT GRAYSON & CHAS: MOSER and ordered to be recorded
                        Test ROBT. GRAHAM, Cl Cur

pp.   THIS INDENTURE made & entered into this 10th day of (March or May) one thou-
430-   sand seven hundred & ninety four Between SPILSBY STONE of one part of County
431   of Prince William & MARY HEDGES of County aforesaid of other part; Witnesseth
         that in consideration of a MARRIAGE to be held & solemnized between said
SPILSBY STONE and MARY HEDGES, it is agreed that all the property both real & personal
which said MARY HEDGES is now possessed of the said STONE shall have the use & profit
of so long as she shall live, Provided he should be the surviver then such property as
she now has togeather with its increase shall revert to her heirs and in case she should
be the surviver, then such property as she is possessed of before her Marrige she shall
take possession of on the death of the said STONE & the said MARY HEDGES doth agree
that said HEDGES shall renounce her Dower or what ever right or title she might claim
from the Laws of the Country at the time of said STONEs death to his Estate & doth hereby
acquit and release the Estate of said STONE from all claims and Dower which she might
have against the Estate of the said STONE in consequence of said Marriage In Witness
whereof the parties have hereunto affixed their hands & seals the day & year above
written
        JAMES GRIGSBY,   SPILSBY STONE
        BENJAMIN WELLS,   MARY her mark ʄ HEDGES
        GEORGE HOPKINS TOLSON
    At a Court held for Prince William County the 6th dy of October 1794
This Marriage Contract between SPILSBY STONE and MARY HEDGES was proved by the
Oaths of JAMES GRIGSBY and BEN: WELLS and ordered to be recorded
                        Test ROBT. GRAHAM, Cl Cur

pp.   THIS INDENTURE made this 7th day of March 1794 Between RHODHAM BLANCHET
431-   and JANE his Wife of County of Prince William of one part and HENRY PEAKE of
433   County of FAIRFAX of other part; Witnesseth that RHODHAM BLANCHET in con-
         sideration of the sum of One hundred pounds currt. money of Virginia to him in
hand paid by HENRY PEAKE, by these presents doth bargain sell & confirm unto HENRY
PEAKE his heirs all that tract of land that was granted to HUMPHREY PEAKE by Deed
from the Proprietors Office bearing date the 22d. day of December 1772, lying in Prince
William County on the Branches of OCCOQUAN in the possession of HENRY PEAKE whereon he had a quarter and bounded, Beginning at two white Oaks on the West side of
TUSSAKY BRANCH corner to THOMAS DAVIS & JOHN PEAKE, then S. 41 E. 160 po: to (blank)
on a barren Ridge, thence (   ) E. 78 po: & cross'd a Branch of the CROOKED BRANCH & at
118 poles the CROOKED BRANCH & in all 200 po: then leaving JOHN PEAKs line No. 23 E. 14
po: to said HUMPHREY PEAKEs Corner by a blazed Chesnut Oak, then along his line S. 85
W. at 60 poles crossing a Branch of the CROOKED BRANCH & the same course continued
in all 95 po:, then So. 20 E. 12 po: to (blank) near a blazed Spanish Oak and two Dogwoods
standing on North side of a Hill, then N. 15 W ( ) to (blank) on South side of a Hill, then
N. 85 E. crossing the CROOKED BRANCH 40 po: then No. 20 W. crossing said Branch 134 po:

then W. 34 po:, then N. 12 W. 38 po:, then N. 43 W: 32 po: then N. 18 W. 26 po: N. 1d. 30m.
W. 73 po. to an ancient marked Poplar in the line of another tract of said PEAKEs then
with that tract line to 2 red Oaks on a Ridge, then N. 62 W. 81 po. to said THOMAS DAVIS's
line & then with it up the TUSSAKY BRANCH W. 76 po: to the begining, containing by
estimation Three hundred & Twenty eight and one quarter acres be the same more or
less with every of its rights members and appurtenances belonging; To have and to
hold the said tract of land unto HENRY PEAKE his heirs against the claim of RHODHAM
BLANCHET his heirs & every other person claiming under him; In Witness whereof the
said RHODHAM BLANCHET hath hereunto set his hand & affixed his seal the day month &
year above written
Signed Sealed & Delivered in presence of us
    (no witnesses recorded)
                                RODHAM BLANCETT
                                JANE her mark ✝ BLANCETT

   March 7th 1794. Received of HENRY PEAKE One hundred pounds current money being
the consideration within mentioned as Witness my hand
                                RODHAM BLANCETT
   At a Court held for Prince William County the 6th day of Octr: 1794
This Deed with a Receipt thereon from RODHAM BLANCETT & JANE his Wife to HENRY
PEAKE (the feme being first privily Examined & consenting thereto) were acknow-
ledged by the said BLANCETT & Wife and ordered to be recorded
                  Test ROBT. GRAHAM, Cl Cur

p.   TO ALL PEOPLE to whom these presents shall come, I JOSEPH FLORENCE of Coun-
433   ty of Prince William send Greeting; Know Ye that I JOSEPH FLORENCE in con-
       sideration of the natural love & affection which I have and bear unto my be-
loved Son, WILLIAM FLORENCE, and for divers other good causes and consideration me
hereunto moving by these presents do give & deliver unto WILLIAM FLORENCE two certain Negroe boys slaves named George and Isac; To have and to hold the said Negroes
George & Isac unto WILLIAM FLORENCE & his heirs; And I JOSEPH FLORENCE the said
Negroes George & Isac to WILLIAM FLORENCE and his heirs against the claims of all
persons will forever warrant and defend the same by these presents; In Witness where-
of I have hereunto set my hand and seal this 18th day of August one thousand seven
hundred & ninety four
Signd. Seald. & Deliverd. in presence of
   NINIAN PINKNEY,
   SIMON DAVIS, WILLIAM HIXSON,   JOSEPH his mark ✕ FLORANCE
   WILLIAM BUTLER, GEORGE FLORANCE
   At a Court held for Prince William County the 6th day of October 1794
This Deed of Gift from JOSEPH FLORANCE to WILLIAM FLORANCE was proved by the Oath
of GEORGE FLORANCE and ordered to be recorded
                  Test ROBT. GRAHAM, Cl Cur

pp.   (On margin: Examd. & Deld. June 1st 1797, N. COX.)
434- THIS INDENTURE made the Seventh day of October one thousand seven hundred
435   and ninety four Between LEWIS RENO & ELIZABETH his Wife of County of Prince
       William of one part & JOHN KINCHELOE of County aforesd. of other part; Witnes-
seth that LEWIS RENO & ELIZABETH his Wife in consideration of the sum of One hundred
pounds specie to them in hand paid by JOHN KINCHELOE, do by these presents bargain
sell & confirm unto JOHN KINCHELOE his heirs all that tract of land containing One
hundred & forty two acres of land situate in County aforesd., and lying on lower side of
CEDER RUN & FELKINS's MILL BRANCH, it being land whereon MOSES JEFFRIS & RACHEL

his Wife now lives (who has a Lease of the said Land during their natural lives) and is bounded, Begining at a large Poplar standing on said FILKINS MILL BRANCH, thence N. 14d. E. 95 po: to a white Oak corner to ISAAC FARROW & JOHN WRIGHTs land, thence with a line of sd. WRIGHT No. 39 po: to the Main Road leading from RADFORD on CEDER RUN to DUMFRIES, then up the Road & binding therewith No. 61d. W. 26 po., then N. 55d. W: 56 po:, then N. 44d. W. 128 po: to CEDER RUN, then up said CEDER RUN & binding therewith S. 51d. W. 48 po: to the mouth of sd. FELKINS MILL BRANCH, then up sd. Branch and binding therewith S. 15d. W. 42 po: till up sd. Branch & binding therewith to the beginning; Also all houses profits and appurtenances to said tract of land in any wise appertaining; To have and to hold the tract of land with the appurtenances unto JOHN KINCHELOE his heirs; And LEWIS RENO & ELIZABETH his Wife for themselves & their heirs the tract of land against all persons to JOHN KINCHELOE & his heirs shall warrant and for ever defend by these presents; In Witness whereof said LEWIS RENO & ELIZABETH his Wife have hereunto set their hands and seals the date above written Signed Sealed and Delivered in presence of

(no witnesses recorded)   LEWIS RENO
                                                ELIZABETH RENO

Received this Seventh day of October one thousand seven hundred and ninety four from JOHN KINCHELOE the sum of One hundred pounds specie being the consideration mentioned for the within lands & premises & is in full for the same Recd. by me
                                                LEWIS RENO

At a Court held for Prince Wm. County the 6th day of October 1794
This Deed with a Receipt thereon from LEWIS RENO and ELIZABETH his Wife to JOHN KINCHELOE (the feme being first privily examined and consenting thereto) were acknowledged by the said RENO and Wife and ordered to be recorded
                         Test ROBT. GRAHAM, Cl Cur

pp.   THIS INDENTURE made this tenth day of April in year of our Lord one thousand
435-   seven hundred & Eighty four Between ROBERT HUTCHINSON of County of Prince
437   William of one part & THOMAS ATTWELL of County afsd. of other part; Witnesseth that ROBERT HUTCHINSON in consideration of the sum of One hundred & ninety pounds in hand paid by THOMAS ATTWELL, by these presents doth bargain & sell unto THOMAS ATTWELL his heirs all that tract of land containing One hundred & ninety acres be the same more or less lying in County of Prince William (the sd. Land is part of a Tract purchased by sd HUTCHINSON of THOMAS FALKNER deceased, and now sold to THOMAS ATTWELL by sd. HUTCHINSON) Begining at a large red Oak on a Branch of BROAD RUN corner to JAMES & WM. FOSTERs Land, then with WM. FOSTERs line S. 45 1/2 W. 69 po: to a fallen red Oak & small Hickory standing near the root thereof, then N. 84d. W. 38 po: to a Stake, then So. 1d. E. 122 po: to a white Oak on BROAD RUN near the mouth of sd Branch, a corner of sd. ATTWELLs then with said ATTWELLs lines No. 76 E. 54 po: to a white Oak on a small Branch, then So. 55 E. 24 po: to a white oak on the edge of an Old Field, then N. 69d. E. 111 po: to the Road in the line of the land RUTT JOHNSON purchased of BENJAMIN HUTCHINSON, then with sd. line & also with the line that divides the land sold to RUTT JOHNSON by said ROBERT HUTCHINSON N. 17 1/2 E. 162 po: to a three body'd red Oak in line of DANIEL MOORE, then with sd. MOOREs line & JAMES FOSTERs line N. 71 1/2 W. 150 po: to the beginning, together with all houses profitts comodities & advantages whatsoever to sd. One hundred & ninety acres of land belonging; To have and to hold the sd One hundred & ninety acres of land with appurtenancesunto THOMAS ATTWELL his heirs; free and clear from all incumbrances whatsoever; In Witness whereof the sd. ROBERT to this present Indenture of Bargain & Sale hath hereunto set his hand and seal the day month and year first above written

Signed Sealed and Delivered in presence of

JOHN KINCHELOE,	ROBERT HUTCHINSON
BENJAMIN COOPER, CHARLES ATTWELL	

April the Tenth one thousand seven hundred & Eighty four then Recd. of THOMAS ATTWELL one hundred and ninety pounds specie, it being the consideration for the within mentioned Land & premises, recd. by me,

Test JOHN KINCHELOE,	ROBERT HUTCHINSON
BENJAMIN COOPER, CHARLES ATTWELL	

At a Court held for Prince William County the 4th day of October 1784 This Deed with the Receipt thereon from ROBERT HUTCHINSON to THOMAS ATTWELL was proved by the Oath of CHARLES ATTWELL & ordered to be Certified; And at a Court held for said County the 6th day of October 1794, this same Deed and Receipt were fully proved by the Oaths of JOHN KINCHELOE & BENJAMIN COOPER and ordered to be recorded
Test ROBERT GRAHAM, Cl Cur

pp.
437-
438

THIS INDENTURE made this 10th day of June in year of our Lord one thousand seven hundred & ninety four Between RICHARD BARNES ALEXANDER of FAU-QUIER County of one part & FRANCES BROWN, Widow of ALEXANDER BROWN, late of Prince William County of other part; Witnesseth that RICHD: B: ALEXANDER in consideration of the love & affection for said FRANCES BROWN which is born towards her by said RICHD: ALEXANDER this day by these presents doth bargain & sell to FRAN-CES BROWN one Lease for Eight years yet to come now in the Occupation of sd. FRANCES & which was lately bought by sd. RICHARD ALEXANDER under an Exon: against the Estate of sd. ALEXANDER BROWN deced., as also another Lease belonging to the Estate of PETER BEVERLEY WHITING & now in the Occupation of said FRANCES BROWN in which there is a term of one year yet unexpired, which was also lately bought by sd. RICHD. ALEXANDER; as also three Negroes vizt. John, Michael & Beck, which were purchased by sd RICHD: ALEXANDER under the Exon. aforesaid as also three horses purchased at the same time; To have and to hold the sd. Leases with appurtenances together with the three slaves to her sd. FRANCES BROWN & her heirs; In Testimony whereof the sd. RICHD. BARNES ALEXANDER hath hereunto subscribed his name and affixed his Seal the day & year above mentioned
Signed Sealed and Delivered in the presence of

EDMD. BROOKE,	RICHARD B. ALEXANDER
M. WHITING, H. BROOKE	

At a Court held for Prince William County the 6th October 1794 This Deed from RICHARD B. ALEXANDER to FRANCES BROWN was proved by the Oath of EDMOND BROOKE & ordered to be recorded
Test ROBT. GRAHAM, Cl Cur

p.
438

(On margin: Examd. & delivered to WM. SMITH the 27th April 1797)
KNOW ALL MEN by these presents that I NATHL: HEDGMAN TRIPLETT of Prince William County in consideration of the sum of (   ) pounds specie to me in hand paid by JOHN WILLIAMS of the afsd. County, by these presents do bargain & sell unto JOHN WILLIAMS his heirs a Negroe Woman slave named Lettice & her future increase which said Lettice was mortgaged by lme to sd. JOHN WILLIAMS the 18th day of October 1793 for securing the payment of Twenty pounds with interest thereon from the 25th day of March 1792 as will more fully appear by reference to the said Mortgage which is duly recorded among the Records of County Court of Prince William; To have and to hold the Negroe woman slave Lettice together with her future increase unto JOHN WILLIAMS his heirs, And I NATHANIEL HEDGMAN TRIPLETT the said Negroe woman

slave Lettice unto JOHN WILLIAMS his heirs &c. against all persons do by these presents warrant and for ever defend; In Witness whereof I have hereunto set my hand & affixed my seal this Twenty second day of April Anno Dom: one thousand seven hundred & ninety four; Sealed & Delivd. in the presence of us & the said Negroe woman Lettice ws also delivered in presence of us
      ROBERT ALEXANDER,   N: TRIPLETT
      JOHN ATTWELL, COLIN CAMPBELL
   At a Court held for Prince William County the 6th day of October 1794
This Bill of Sale from NATHANIEL H. TRIPLETT to JOHN WILLIAMS was proved by the Oath of ROBERT ALEXANDER and ordered to be recorded
                   Test ROBT. GRAHAM, Cl Cur

p.   KNOW ALL MEN by these presents that I DANIEL RAILSBACK of CULPEPER
439   County in consideration of the sum of Forty five pounds current money to me in
       hand paid by DANIEL WILSON SCOTT of Town of DUMFRIES & County of Prince
William, by these presents do bargain & sell unto DAVID WILSON SCOTT his heirs one Negroe boy slave named Jeffry aged thirteen years and one month which said boy Jeffry I bought of THOMAS MINOR when of the age of five years; To have and to hold the said Negroe Jeffry unto DAVID WILSON SCOTT his heirs, And I DANIEL RAILSBACK the said Negroe boy Jeffry unto DAVID WILSON SCOTT his heirs against all persons do by these presents warrant & forever defend; In Witness whereof I have hereunto set my hand & affixed my Seal this Fifteenth day of August Seventeen hundred & Ninety four Signed Sealed & Delivd. in presence of
      JAMES E. MARSHALL,   DANIEL RAILSBACK
      JOHN WILLCOCKS
   At a Court continued and held for Prince William County the Seventh day of October 1794;   This Bill of Sale from DANIEL RAILSBACK to DAVID WILSON SCOTT was proved by the Oaths of JAMES E. MARSHALL and JOHN WILLCOCKS and ordered to be recorded
                   Test   ROBERT GRAHAM, Cl Cur

pp.   THIS INDENTURE made this 25th day of February in year of our Lord one thou-
439-   sand seven hundred & ninety four Between RODHAM BLANCETT & JANE his Wife
440   of County of Prince William of one part and WILLIAM FAIRFAX, Exor. of WIL-
       LIAM FAIRFAX deced. of County aforesd. of other part; Witnesseth that in con-
sideration of the sum of Four hundred and Fifty pounds specie to RODHAM BLANCETT in hand paid by WILLIAM FAIRFAX, Executor to sd. WILLIAM FAIRFAX deced., by these presents doth bargain sell & confirm unto sd. FAIRFAX, Exr. as aforesd., & his all all that tract of land sold by WM. VEALE to ISAAC DAVIS deced. containing 116 acres by Deed bearing date 1762 and conveyed to sd. BLANCETT by CORNELIUS DAVIS, Son to said ISAAC also another track taken up by sd. BLANCETT adjoining the South side of OCCOQUAN & the aforesd. tract containing 268 acres bearing date 1788, also another tract containing nine acres granted to sd. BLANCETT & adjoining the aforesd. tract & JAMES FOLEYs dated in 1788; also part of tract of 715 acres granted to sd. BLANCETT in 1788, also part of another tract of land granted to WM. VEALE in 1777 and conveyed to ALEXANDER HEN-DERSON in 1779 and from said HENDERSON to sd. BLANCETT in 1788, lying in County afsd. & bounded, Begining at a pile of Stone on South side of the Main Road, corner to BURDET ASHTON and VEALEs Patents, then No. 3d. W. 88 po: to a Poplar Stump in cleared land corner to VEALEs Old Patent, then No. 7d. W. 40 po. to a white Oak corner to ASHTON & VEALEs Old Patent, then with that line No. 2d. W. 260 po: to OCCOQUAN, then up sd. OCCO-QUAN and binding therewith S. 37 W. 28 po; then S. 55 W. 16 po; then S. 84 W. (   ), then N. 68d. W. 18 po: then N. 53 W. 22 po: then N. 66d. W. 26 po:, thence N. 45d. W. 78 po: to

JAMES FOLEYs corner on sd. OCCOQUAN, about three poles above the mouth of a Branch, then with FOLEYs lines S. 53 E. 130 poL, then N. 19d. W. 68 po: to WILLIAM DAVIS line, thence with his line S. 2d. E. 104 po: to DAVIS & REAVES's Corner, then S. 20d. E. 40 po: to VEALEs & BLANDs intersection, then So. 84 po. to an Oak on another Corner to VEALEs Old Plantation, then S. 13d. 30m. E. 18 po. to an Oak to HENRY PEAKE, then with sd.
PEAKEs line So. 26d. 30m. E. 115 po. to a white Oak and dead red Oak another corner of PEAKE, then with his line No. 71d. 30m. W. 102 to a dead box Oak then So. 50d. W. 8 po: to a Poplar by a Branch, the begining corner of HENRY PEAKs Old Patent, then with sd. PEAKs lines So. 63d. E. d146 po: to a white Oak by a Branch, then N. ( ) E. 30 po: to a dead white Oak by a small Branch, then S. 20d. E. 200 po: to a Chesnut Oak on South side of COCKRILLS MOUNTAIN, then with the lines of HENRY PEAKEs Younger Patent S. 22d. W. 14 po:, then South 65d. W. 200 po: to a Barron Ridge, then with the Heirs of JOHN PEAKs line N. 38d. E. 75 po: to a Branch, then S. 83d. E. 85 po: to a Poplar in a Branch, then N. 63d. E. 195 po: to a corner of sd. BLANCETTs, then with his lines No. ( ) W: 121 po: then to the first station including One thousand & four acres & the four acres is excepted so as to include the MEETING HOUSE & MEETING HOUSE SPRING and all houses orchards profits and appurtenances bleonging; To have and to hold the said One thousand & four acres except as before excepted unto WILLIAM FAIRFAX, Exr. as aforesd., his heirs free and clear from all incumbrances whatsoever; and RODHAM BLANCETT & JANE his Wife & their heirs shall warrant & forever defend by these presents; In Witness whereof the sd. RODHAM BLANCETT & JANE his Wife hath hereunto set their hands & seals the day & year first above written
Sealed & Delivered in presence of

JAMES FOLEY, STEPHEN HOWISON,   RODHAM BLANCETT
SARAH FAIRFAX   JANE BLANCETT

Received from WILLIAM FAIRFAX, Exr. as aforesaid, the sum of Four hundred & fifty pounds being the consideration lmentioned in the above Deed 25 February 1794
RODHAM BLANCETT

At a Court continued and held for Prince William County the seventh day of October 1794 This Deed & the Receipt thereon from RODHAM BLANCETT & JANE his Wife to WILLIAM FAIRFAX, Executor of WILLIAM FAIRFAX deced., were acknowledged by the said RODHAM BLANCETT & ordered to be recorded
Test ROBERT GRAHAM, Cl Cur

pp.   (On margin: Examined & delivered to Mr. FAIRFAX 16th Decr. 1794)
442-   THIS INDENTURE made this seventh day of October in year of our Lord 1794 Be-
444   tween RODHAM BLANCETT & JANE his Wife of one part & HEZEKIAH FAIRFAX,
         WILLIAM FAIRFAX, JOHN FAIRFAX, Sons & Devisees of WILLIAM FAIRFAX deced.,
of the other part; Whereas WILLIAM FAIRFAX deced., did in his life time purchased of sd. RODHAM one thousand acres of land for which the RODHAM never made sd. WIL-LIAM deced. in his life time Deeds but gave him a Bond obligating himself & his heirs to make Deeds in fee simple for sd. WILLIAM deced. & his heirs for afsd. land & Whereas the said WILLIAM deced., did by his Will bearing date on the 4th day of October 1793 and recorded in the Office of the County Court of Prince William devise unto his Son, HEZE-KIAH four hundred & fifty acres of land, also four hundred acres thereof to his Son, WILLIAM, & the other hundred & fifty acres to his Son, JOHN, And whereas sd RODHAM meaning to fullfill his Bond and comply with the Will of said WILLIAM deced., did by Deed bearing date February 25th 1794 convey the whole of the One thousand acres of land unto WILLIAM FAIRFAX the Son as Exr. of WILLIAM FAIRFAX deced., thinking that by such conveyance he would be seized of the land to the use of the Will and that Divi-sion would consequently take place among the Sons of sd. WILLIAM deced., agreeable &

according to sd. Will, & Whereas the parties to this Deed are now advised that the sd. Deed afsd. made by sd RODHAM to said WILLIAM will not have the desired effect & operation but that the said conveyance conveying the fee simple estate of the whole thousand acres unto WILLIAM the Executor who wishes only the part of the same bequeathed to him by said Will, reference to sd. Will the portion of ech of the devisees will particularly appear; Now to the end that each of the grantees Sons & devisees of sd. WILLIAM deced. may have conveyed to each of them & their several heirs the particular portion allowed and bequeath them by sd. Will this Deed Witnesseth that the sd. RODHAM & JANE his Wife in consideration of the premises and the further sum of Five shillings in lhand paid to sd. RODHAM & JANE by the sd. Grantees Sons & Devisees of sd. WILLIAM deced., do by these presents bargain & sell unto the said HEZEKIAH, WILLIAM JUNR. & JOHN, Sons as afsd. the thousand acres of land together with all appurtenances to be divided & allotted among them according to the division thereo made in sd. Will of sd. WILLIAM deced., To have and to hold the afsd. land unto HEZEKIAH, WILLIAM JUNR. and JOHN & their several heirs agreeable to the Will of sd. WILLIAM deced., In Testimony whereof the parties hereunto set their hands & affixed their seals the day & year In presence of

(no witnesses recorded)   RODHAM BLANCETT
                                 JANE BLANCETT

At a Court continued & held for Prince William County the seventh day of October 1794 This Deed from RODHAM BLANCETT & JANE his Wife to WILLIAM FAIRFAX & JOHN FAIRFAX, Sons & Devisees of WILLIAM FAIRFAX deceased was acknowledged by the said RODHAM and ordered to be recorded   Test ROBERT GRAHAM, Cl Cur

pp. 444-445   KNOW ALL MEN by these presents that we THOS: HARRISON, JOHN McWILLIAMS, MATTHEW HARRISON JUNR. WILLIAM BARNES, GEORGE LANE, JAMES WIGINTON are held and firmly bound unto HENRY LEE Esquire, Governor of Virginia, & his Successors for the use of the Commonwealth in the sum of Thirty thousand Dollars current money to which payment well and truly to be made we bind ourselves our heirs firmly by these presents; Sealed with our seals & dated this 3d. day of Novr. 1794
THE CONDITION of the above obligation is such that whereas the above bound THOMAS HARRISON is appointed SHERIFF & COLLECTOR of the Taxes due in Prince William County, Now if the said THOMAS HARRISON shall truly collect & pay into the Treasury the taxes that are or shall be due & payable within the term of time of his said Office at the times and termes the same shall be payable by, Then the above obligation to be void else to remain in full force & virtue

Sealed & Delivd. in presence of   THOMAS HARRISON   JOHN McMILLIAN
The Court   M. HARRISON JUNR. WM. BARNES
                                   GEORGE LANE,   JAMES WIGGINTON

At a Court held for Prince William County the third day of November 1794 This Bond from THOMAS HARRISON, JOHN McMILLIAN, M. HARRISON JUNR., WILLIAM BARNES, GEORGE LANE and JAMES WIGGINTON to HENRY LEE Esqr., was acknowledged & ordered to be recorded   Test ROBT. GRAHAM, Cl Cur

p. 445   KNOW ALL MEN by these presents that I THOMAS HARRISON, JOHN McMILLIAN, MATTHEW HARRISON JUNR., WILLIAM BARNES, GEORGE LANE & JAMES WIGGINTON are held & firmly bound unto his Excellency, HENRY LEE Esqr. Governor of Virginia & his successors for the use of the Commonwealth in the sum of Twenty thousand Dollars to which payment well and truly to be made we bind ourselves our heirs firmly by these presents; Sealed with our seals & dated this 3d day of November 1794
THE CONDITION of the above obligation is such that whereas the above bound THOMAS

HARRISON, Clerk, is appointed Sheriff of County of Prince William by a Commission from the Lieutenant Governor under the Seal of the Commonwealth dated the 15th day of October last past; If therefore the said THOMAS HARRISON, Clerk, shall well & truly collect all levies & account for & pay the same in such manner as is by Law directed, Also all fines forfeitures & amercements becoming due to the Commonwealth and shall in all things truly execute the said Office of Sheriff during his continuance therein, Then the above obligation to be void otherwise to remain in full force & virtue

Sealed & Delvd. in presence of   THOS: HARRISON JOHN McMILLIAN
  The Court   M. HARRISON JUNR. JAMES WIGGINTON
            GEORGE LANE

 At a Court held for Prince William County the 3d day of November 1794
This Bond acknowledged & ordered to be recorded
      Test ROBT. GRAHAM, Cl Cur

p. KNOW ALL MEN by these presents (another Bond by the persons named in the
446 preceding two bonds for the Sheriff to truly execute & due return make of all process &
   precepts to him directed) Then the above obligation to be void otherwise to remain
in full force & virtue

Sealed & Delivered in presence of THOMAS HARRISON JOHN McMILLIAN
  The Court   WM. BARNES   M. HARRISON JUNR.
          JAMES WIGGINTON GEO: LANE

 At a Court held for Prince William County the 3d. day of November 1794
This Bond was acknowledged & ordered to be recorded
      Test ROBT. GRAHAM, Cl Cur

pp. THIS INDENTURE made this Sixteenth day of October in year of our Lord one
447- thousand seven hundred and ninety four Between HUGH DAVIS of County of
448 Prince William and JANE his Wife of one part and WILLIAM SMITH of the same
   County of other part; Whereas HUGH DAVIS by his certain Bond bearing equal
date with these presents stands firmly bound unto WILLIAM SMITH in the penal sum of
Two hundred & ten pounds current money of Virginia with a condition thereunder
written for the payment of One hundred & five pounds like month with Interest
thereon after the rate of five per centum per annum to be computed from the date
hereof on the Twenty fifth day of December one thousand seven hundred & ninety five;
THIS INDENTURE Witnesseth that HUGH DAVIS & JANE his Wife for the better securing
the payment of the aforesaid sum and in consideration of Ten dollars in hand paid by
WILLIAM SMITH, by these presents doth bargain and sell unto WILLIAM SMITH and his
heirs all those two tracts of land situate in County of Prince William and which were
this day conveyed to HUGH DAVIS by WILLIAM SMITH & ANN his Wife; And all houses
and appurtenances belonging; To have and to hold the land unto WILLIAM SMITH his
heirs; Provided always that if HUGH DAVIS his heirs shall pay WILLIAM SMITH his
heirs the aforementioned sum with legal interest thereon at or upon the Twenty fifth
day of December 1795, then these presents shall cease and be utterly null & void; In
Witness whereof the said HUGH DAVIS & JANE his Wife have hereunto set their hands
and affixed their seals the day and year first within written
Sealed & Delivered in presence of
  PHILIP DAWE, JOSEPH GILBERT, HUGH DAVIS
  JAMES E. MARSHALL, JOHN WILLIAMS JANE DAVIS
  JAMES GRIGSBY
 At a Court held for Prince William County the first day of December 1794
This Deed of Mortgage from HUGH DAVIS & JANE his Wife to WILLIAM SMITH was proved

by the Oaths of PHILIP DAWE, JOSEPH GILBERT & JOHN WILLIAMS & ordered to be
recorded   Test ROBT. GRAHAM, Cl Cur

pp.   Whereas ELEANOR BRENT, DANIEL CARROLL BRENT & RICHARD BRENT, Execu-
449-   trix & Executors of WILLIAM BRENT, late of STAFFORD County deceased, did by
450   their Deed of Bargain & Sale bearing date the twenty second day of July in the
         year 1786, convey unto JOHN THORNTON FITZHUGH Esqr. a certain tract of land
situated in BRENTON in Prince William County & Whereas the boundaries of said tract of
land as described in the said Deed are found to interfere with the boundaries now con-
tended for by a certain WILLIAM ALEXANDER so that controversy is like to arise respecting the same and DANIEL CARROLL BRENT having previous to said Deed of Bargain
& Sale by him made to said FITZHUGH engaged to lay off the boundaries of said parcel of
land so as to be free of any controversy and WILLIAM ALEXANDER having lately set up
a claim to a straight line from a Stone on CEDAR RUN up to a white Oak, corner to BRENT
& FOOTE in the back line of BRENTON and said DANIEL CARROLL BRENT being unwilling
that said FITZHUGH should be involved in any controversy on account of any dispute
respecting the said boundaries; NOW THIS INDENTURE that DANIEL CARROLL BRENT of
one part & JOHN THORNTON FITZHUGH of other part Witnesseth that JOHN THORNTON
FITZHUGH with an intent to avoid all legal controversy and for the sum of Twenty
pounds current money to him in hand paid by DANEIL C. BRENT, by these presents doth
bargain and sell unto DANIEL CARROLL BRENT and his heirs so much of the parcel of
land situated in BRENTON and formerly by Deed bearing date the 22nd day of July in the
year 1786 conveyed by said ELEANOR, DANIEL C. & RICHARD BRENT to the said FITZHUGH
as is situated on South side of a straight line to be run from a Stone on CEDAR RUN,
claimed by the said WILLIAM ALEXANDER as his corner up to a white Oak in the back
line of BRENTON, corner to FOOTE & BRENT; To have and to hold to said DANIEL CARROLL
BRENT and his heirs; In Witness whereof I have hereunto set my hand & affixed my
seal this 17th day of May in the year 1794
Signed Sealed and Delivered in the presence of
         JAS: LORIMER, JAMES HAYES JR.   JOHN T. FITZHUGH
         GEO: GRAHAM, RD. FOOTE, DANL. BRENT,
         EZEKIEL DONNELL, WM. BARNES
    At a Court held for Prince William County the first day of December 1794
This Deed from JOHN THORNTON FITZHUGH to DANIEL CARROLL BRENT was proved by the
Oaths of GEORGE GRAHAM, RICHARD FOOTE & JAMES HAYES and ordered to be recorded
                         Test R. GRAHAM, Cl Cur

pp.   THIS INDENTURE made this 19th dy of November one thousand seven hundred
450-   and ninety three Between CLARY BYRN, Wife of SAMUEL BYRN deced., and her
452   Son, PEYTON BYRN, Executors, of Prince William County of one part & WILLIAM
         HIXSON of County aforesaid of other part; Witnesseth that CLARY BYRN & PEY-
TON BYRN in consideration of the sum of Seventy five pounds current money of Virginia to them in hand paid by WILLIAM HIXSON, by these presents doth bargain sell and
confirm unto WILLIAM HIXSON his heirs all that tract of land lying in Prince William
County adjoining the land of ASA REEVES in the Fork between BULL RUN & OCCOQUAN
and bounded; Beginning at two white Oaks on North side of REEVES MILL BRANCH corner trees to the sd. ASA REEVES, and also corner to BLAND, thence along REEVES line
North eighty seven degrees West one hundred & seventy poles to a white Oak, thence
along another of REEVES lines South fifty nine degrees & thirty minutes West thirty
two poles to the line of MAJOR JEREMIAH MURDOCK, thence along sd. MURDOCKs line
revers'd South eighty five degrees thirty minutes East sixty one poles, South twelve de-

grees & thirty minutes East fifty six poles, South thirty eight degrees & thirty minutes
East fifty six poles, South twenty nine degrees & thirty minutes East twenty four poles,
South eight degrees & thirty minutes East one hundred & twenty poles to a fallen white
Oak near a marked red Oak & Hickory, being corner to said MURDOCK and JOHN REEVES,
thence along REEVES line North twelve degrees East Two hundred & fifty eight poles to
the beginning, containing and laid out for One hundred acres of land more or less together with all rights profits benefits and priviledges thereunto belonging; To have
and to hold the said premises unto WILLIAM HIXSON his heirs, And CLARY BYRN &
PEYTON BYRN doth for themselves & their heirs the sd. land against all persons unto
WILLIAM HIXSON shall warrant & forever defend by these presents; In Witness whereof the parties first to these presents hath put their hands and affixed their seals the day
& year first above written
Signed Sealed & Delivered in the presence of

ROWLD. GAINES, RUT JOHNSON SENR.	CLARY BYRN
JOHN his mark X MORDOCK,	PEYTON BYRN
NOAH his mark X MILSTEAD	
JOHN BEAVER	

November 19th 1793. Then received of Mr. WILLIAM HIXSON the sum of seventy five
pounds in full

ROWLD. GAINS, JOHN BEAVER,	PEYTON BYRN, Exr. of
RUT JOHNSON SENR.	SAML. BYRN deced.

At a Court held for Prince William County the seventh day of April 1794
This Deed with the Receipt thereon from CLARY BYRN and PEYTON BYRN, Exrs. of
SAMUEL BYRN deced. to WILLIAM HIXSON was proved by the Oaths of RUT JOHNSON and
ordered to be Certified; And at a Court held for said County the first day of December
1794, the said Deed & Rect. were fully proved by the oaths of ROWLAND GAINES and JOHN
BEAVERS and ordered to be recorded   Test ROBT. GRAHAM, Cl Cur

pp.   THIS INDENTURE made this first day of September one thousand seven hundred
452-   & ninety four Between JOHN POPE of County of Prince William and MARGARET
454   his Wife of one part and JAMES MITCHELL of County of STAFFORD of other part;
            Witnesseth that JOHN POPE & MARGARET his Wife in consideration of the sum of
Three hundred Dollars current money of the United States to them in hand paid by said
JAMES MITCHELL, do by these presents bargain & sell unto JAMES MITCHELL and his
heirs all that remaining part of a Lott of Land lying in TOWN of DUMFRIES and described by the number Fifty Nine which said part of a lott hereby conveyed is bounded,
Begining at the most Northern corner of that part of said Lott which was conveyed by
said JOHN POPE & MARGARET his Wife to a certain WILLIAM TYLER on the tenth day of
October one thousand seven hundred and eighty nine and which now is the property of
said JAMES MITCHELL and runing with the dividing line of said lott & Lott No. Forty
Eight on which the COURTHOUSE is erected to the corner of said Lott on the Street caled
FAIRFAX, thence runing with said Street to the most Northerly corner of that part of
the said Lott No. 59 which was conveyed by said JOHN POPE and MARGARET his Wife to a
certain SAMUEL TEBBS on the second day of May one thousand seven hundred and
ninety one, thence with the line of said TEBBS to the part of said lott conveyed to WIL-
LIAM TYLER as aforesaid, thence with said TYLERs line to the begining; To have and to
hold the said part of the lott hereby conveyed unto JAMES MITCHELL his heirs and JOHN
POPE and MARGARET his Wife for themselves their heirs the bargained premises unto
JOHN MITCHELL his heirs do by virtue of these presents warrant and defend against the
claim of every person; In Witness whereof the said JOHN POPE and MARGARET his Wife
have hereunto set their hands and affixed their seals the day and year first written

Sealed and Delivered in presence of
WM. SMITH,   PHILIP DAWE,   JOHN POPE
ROBERT ALEXANDER, JOHN WILLIAMS   MARGARET POPE
JOHN ATTWELL,   JOHN LAWSON
ALEXR. LITHGOW

Received the day and year within written from JAMES MITCHELL the sum of Three
hundred Dollars current money of the United States being the consideration within
mentioned to be paid by him to me
            (same witnesses)   JOHN POPE
The Commonwealth of Virginia to ALEXANDER LITHGOW, WILLIAM BARNES & JOHN
LAWSON Gentlemen, Greeting; Whereas (the Commission for the privy Examination of MAR-
GARET, the Wife of JOHN POPE); Witness ROBERT GRAHAM Clerk of the said Court the 12th
day of Septr: 1794 and in the 19th year of the Commonweath
    (The return of the Execution of the privy Examination of MARGARET POPE is not recorded.)
    At a Court held for Prince William County the first day of December 1794
This Deed with a Receipt thereon from JOHN POPE and MARGARET his Wife to JAMES
MITCHELL were proved by the Oaths of WILLIAM SMITH, PHILIP DAW & JOHN
WILLIAMS and with a Dedimus for the privy examination of the feme returned executed
ordered to be recorded   Test ROBT. GRAHAM, Cl Cur

p.   TO ALL TO WHOM these presents shall come, WILLIAM DAVIS of County of
455   Prince William sendeth Greeting. Whereas said WILLIAM DAVIS now at the time
         of sealing and delivery of these presents is and stands justly indebted to CUM-
BERLAND WILSON of said County & Town of DUMFRIES, Merchant, about the sum of
Three hundred pounds Virginia Currency. Now Know ye that WILLIAM DAVIS for the
better securing the payment of the sum of money & for sum of Five shillings to me in
hand paid by CUMBERLAND WILSON by these presents do bargain sell & set over unto
CUMBERLAND WILSON all the several Negroes hereafter mentioned, to wit; Bob, Dick,
Lid, Diana, Clara, Innis & Sall, To have and to hold the said Negroes unto CUMBERLAND
WILSON his heirs according to the amount of his Debt and no other intent; In Witness
whereof I the said WILLIAM DAVIS have hereunto set my hand & seal this Eighteenth
day of November one thousand seven hundred & ninety four
Sealed & Delivered in presence of
JESSE TAYLOR,   WM. DAVIS
WILLIAM SCOTT
    At a Court continued and held for Prince William County the 2nd day of December 1794
This Deed for Slaves from WILLIAM DAVIS to CUMBERLAND WILSON was proved by the
Oaths of JESSE TAYLOR & WILLIAM SCOTT and ordered to be recorded
                        Test ROBERT GRAHAM, Cl Cur

pp.   THIS INDENTURE made this Sixteenth day of October in year of our Lord one
455-   thousand seven hundred and ninety four Between WILLIAM SMITH and ANN his
457   Wife of County of Prince William of one part and HUGH DAVIS of same County of
         other part; Witnesseth that WILLIAM SMITH and ANN his Wife in consideration
of the sum of Two hundred and five pounds current money to them in hand paid by
HUGH DAVIS, do by these presents bargain & sell unto HUGH DAVIS and his heirs all
those tracts of land lying in County of Prince William containing Two hundred & thirty
acres which said tracts of land were conveyed to WILLIAM SMITH by a certain RODHAM
BLANCETT & JANE his Wife as will more fully appear by reference to two certain Deeds
duly recorded in the aforesaid County, the one bearing date the 9th day of November
1792, and the other the 30th day of June in the present year; one of said tracts contains

One hundred and thirty three acres more or less and is bounded Begining at a Poplar standing on South side of BULL RUN corner to ROBERT SPITTLE and runing with his line So. 68 Wt. 125 poles to a red Oak, another corner to SPITTLE, thence So. 35 3/4 Et. 180 poles to a white Oak, corner to the Original Patent, thence with the line of the Old Patent So. 72 1/2 Et. ( ) poles to a small Hicory on the bank of BULL RUN, thence up said Run according to the several meanders thereto to the begining; the other tract is bounded Beginning at the mouth of the North Run of OCCOQUAN RIVER and running up the same No. 150 poles to a marked Hickory on upper side of said Run, thence No. 75 Wt. 100 to a marked Maple standing at the upper end of a piece of low ground on the River side, thence down the River the several meanders thereof to the beginning; And all houses orchards profits and appurtenances to the same appurtaining; To have and to hold the aforesaid tracts of land unto HUGH DAVIS his heirs; And WILLIAM SMITH and ANN his Wife for themselves their heirs do by these presents forever warrant & defend the said tracts of land to HUGH DAVIS against the claim of all persons; In Witness whereof the said WILLIAM SMITH and ANN his Wife have hereunto set their hands & affixed their seals the day and year first within written

Sealed and Delivered in presence of

PHILIP DAWE;   JOSEPH GILBERT,   WILLIAM SMITH
JAMES E. MARSHALL,   ANN SMITH
JOHN WILLIAMS,   JAMES GRIGSBY

At a Court continued and held for Prince William County the second day of December 1794   This Deed from WILLIAM SMITH and ANN his Wife to HUGH DAVIS was acknowledged by the said WILLIAM SMITH and ordered to be recorded
Test ROBERT GRAHAM, Cl Cur

pp.   THIS INDENTURE made the 20th dy of October Seventeen hundred & ninety four
457-   Between SAMUEL STONE of FAIRFAX County and ANN his Wife of one part and
460   JOHN DYE of County of Prince William of other part. Whereas FRANCIS STONE of
           Parish of Overwharton in County of STAFFORD by his Deeds of Lease & Release
dated the 20th & 21st days of April 1721 did convey unto JOHN PEAKE of the same Parish and County the fee simple Estate of and in one hundred & twenty acres of land more or less lying then in Parish of Overwharton and County of STAFFORD but in the County of Prince William on both sides of the Main Run of OCCOQUAN RIVER at the present time, And Whereas JOHN PEAKE on the 2nd day of August 1728 by his Deed did give and grant unto his Son in Law, SAMUEL STONE, part of the above described lands in consequence of which last conveyance the said SAMUEL STONE dyed seised of the said lands therein contained, and which descended to SAMUEL STONE his Eldest Son & heir at Law;
   NOW THIS INDENTURE Witnesseth that the last mentioned SAMUEL STONE, party to these presents, in consideration of the sum of Ninety one pounds Two shillings & six pence current money of Virginia to him in hand paid by JOHN DYE, by these presents do bargain sell and confirm unto JOHN DYE and to his heirs all that land contained in JOHN PEAKEs Deed to SAMUEL STONE the Elder that lies on the uper or North side of the Main Run of OCCOQUAN RIVER which is found by an accurate survey made by JOHN COFFER to be One hundred & Twenty two acres, excepting and always reserving one half acre for a BURYING GROUND where this heretofore has been occupied for that purpose; And all houses orchards profits and appurtenances; To have and to hold the said One hundred & Twenty one and half acres of land unto JOHN DYE & his heirs free and clear from the claims of all persons; In Witness whereof SAMUEL STONE & ANN his Wife have hereunto set their hands & seals the day month & year first within written

Sealed and Delivered in presence of
> JAMES MUSCHETT,   SAMUEL STONE
> MUNGO HANCOCK, JOHN MUSCHETT   ANN her mark X STONE

The Commonwealth of Virginia to RICHARD CHICHESTER and THOMPSON MASON Gentlemen, Greeting; Whereas (the Commission for the privy Examination of ANN, the Wife of SAMUEL
STONE); Witness ROBERT GRAHAM Clerk of our said Court the 25th day of October 1794
and in the 19th year of the Commonwealth   ROBT. GRAHAM

In Obedience to the within, we the Subscribers have caused to come before us the
within named ANN and have examined her privately (the return of the execution of the
privy Examination of ANN STONE); Given under our hands and seals this 25th day of
October 1794   RICHARD CHICHESTER
                                          THOMSON MASON

At a Court held for Prince William County the first day of December 1794
This Deed from SAMUEL STONE & ANN his Wife to JOHN DYE was proved by the Oaths of
JAMES MUSCHETT & MUNGO HANCOCK and ordered to be Certified; And at a Court continued and held for the said County the second day of December 1794, This Deed was
fully proved by the Oath of JOHN MUSCHETT and with the Dedimus for the privy examination of the feme returned executed, ordered to be recorded
                         Test ROBERT GRAHAM, Cl Cur

pp.   (On margin: Examd. & Deld. Apl. 27. 1797, N. COX)
460-   THIS INDENTURE made this third day of July in year of our Lord one thousand
461   seven hundred & ninety four Between WILLOUGHBY TEBBS and BETSEY his Wife
        of County of Prince William of one part and DAVID WILSON SCOTT of same County
of other part; Witnesseth that WILLOUGHBY TEBBS and BETSEY his Wife in consideration of the sum of Sixty pounds current money of Virginia to said WILLOUGHBY TEBBS
in hand paid by DAVID WILSON SCOTT, by these presents do bargain & sell unto DAVID
W. SCOTT & his heirs a certain tract of Marsh Land lying on QUANTICO CREEK in County
afsd., purchased by WILLOUGHBY TEBBS of a certain WILLIAM BRENT on the 28th day of
March ( ) who purchased the same from a certain WILLIAM TEBBS which tract of
Marsh Land is bounded; Begining at A., two Locust posts the lowermost corner of MAC-
RAE's Marsh on the Creek and runing with his line North 80d. East thirty four poles to
B., a corner of his Marsh, thence with his other lines No. 30 W. 80 poles to C., the great
gut, thence with said Gut No. 60d. East 20 poles to D., the mouth of said Gut, thence along
the Creek side to E., the mouth of the narrows of the Creek, thence No. 38d. Wt. up the
said Creek to the begining, containing Eight acres & one tenth of an acre be the same
more or less by a Survey thereof made by THOMAS TEBBS the Sixteenth day of May 1778,
together with all the appurtenances to said parcel of Marsh belonging; To have and to
hold the said tract of Marsh and all its appurtenances unto DAVID WILSON SCOTT his
heirs and WILLOUGHBY TEBBS & BETSY his Wife for themselves & their heirs do covenant with DAVID WILSON SCOTT his heirs the Eight acres & one tenth of an acre of
Marsh Land to warrant and forever defend against all persons; In Witness whereof the
said WILLOUGHBY TEBB & BETSY his Wife have hereunto set their hands and seals the
day and year first within written
Sealed & Delivered in presence of
> ANTHONY McDONNELL,   WILLOUGHBY TEBBS
> GALVAN De BERNOUX, JOHN O"CONNER   BETSY TEBBS

At a Court held for Prince William County the 5th day of January 1795
This Deed from WILLOUGHBY TEBBS & BETSY his Wife to DAVID WILSON SCOTT was acknowledged and ordered to be recorded   Teste ROBT. GRAHAM, Cl Cur

pp.   THIS INDENTURE made this twenty first day of June in year of our Lord one
461-   thousand seven hundred and ninety four Between JOHN CANNON of County of
462   Prince William of one part & JOHN McMILLIAN of County afsd. of other part;
Witnesseth that JOHN CANNON in consideration of the sum of Six hundred &
Eighty four pounds current money of Virginia to him in hand paid by JOHN McMIL-
LIAN by these presents doth bargain & sell unto JOHN McMILLIAN the following slaves
household. furniture stock & plantation utensils, to wit, Dublin, Jenny, Lett, Ann,
Harry, James, DAniel, Henson, Lenny, Nell, Charles, Zachary, Kate, Nan, Molly,
Gerrard, Phillis, Mary and Sall. three feather beds & furniture, one old Desk, three
tables, fifteen chairs, two looking glasses, five pictures, one leather trunk, one case &
bottles, three iron pots, one Dutch oven, one nest of wooden ware, 2 Stills & Still house
utensils, twenty five head od dry cattle, nine cows & calves, seven horses, twenty to
head of sheep, two carts, seven plows & gear, six grubing hoes, nine old weeding & hil-
ling hoes, five Sithes & cradles, & two grass sithes, & fifty head of Hogs, To have and to
hold the said slaves household furniture stock & plantation utensils unto JOHN McMIL-
LIAM his hiers, And JOHN CANNON for himself his heirs against all persons to said JOHN
McMILLIAN his heirs will warrant and for ever defend by these presents; In Witness
whereof the said JOHN CANNON hath hereunto set his hand and seal the day and year
above written
Signed Sealed & Delivered in the presence of
    MUNGO HANCOCK,   JOHN CANNON
    CHARLES TYLER JUNR. JOHN MUSCHETT
At a Court continued & held for Prince William County the sixth day of January 1795
This Bill of Sale from JOHN CANNON to JOHN McMILLIAN was acknowledged & ordered to
be recorded   Teste ROBT. GRAHAM, Cl Cur

pp.   THIS INDENTURE made this twenty first day of June in year of our Lord one
462-   thousand seven hundred & ninety four Between JOHN CANNON of County of
463   Prince William of one part and JOHN McMILLIAN of said County of other part;
Witnesseth that JOHN CANNON in consideration hereafter to be mentioned by
these presents doth demise set & to farm lett unto JOHN McMILLIAN his heirs all that
tenement of Land situated on POWELLS RUN in County aforesaid, which JOHN CANNON
purchased of FITZHUGH & TAYLOE containing by estimation Three hundred acres more
or less; To have and to hold lthe said tract of land together with all its rights members
and appurtenances thereunto belonging from the date hereof during the term of Six
years & six month reserving only unto JOHN CANNON his heirs out of said tract the
Mansion House, fifteen acres of land round about the said House with the appurtenances belonging; paying upon the tenth day of January the rent of Ten pounds Virginia currency unto JOHN CANNON his heirs which rent will first become due in the
year one thousand seven hundred and ninety five; In Witness whereof the said JOHN
CANNON hath hereunto set his hand and seal the day and year first above written
Signed Sealed and Delivered in the presence of
    CHARLES TYLER JUNR.   JOHN CANNON
    MUNGO HANCOCK, JOHN MUSCHETT
At a Court continued and held for Prince William County the sixth day of January 1795
This Lease from JOHN CANNON to JOHN McMILLIAN was acknowledged and ordered to be
recorded   Teste ROBT. GRAHAM; Cl Cur

pp.   THIS INDENTURE made this twenty first day of June in year of our Lord one
463-   thousand seven hundred & ninety four Between JOHN CANNON & SARAH his Wife
464   of Prince William County of one part & JOHN McMILLIAN of said County of other

part; Witnesseth that JOHN CANNON & SARAH HARRISON CANNON his Wife for the consideration hereafter to be mentioned by these presents doth demise set and to farm let unto JOHN McMILLIAN his heirs all that tenement of Land situate on the Waters emptying into BROAD RUN in County aforesaid which said CANNON purchased of JOHN FOUSHEE containing by survey Two hundred thirty two and a half acres of land; To have and to hold the tract of land together with all rights members & appurtenances thereunto belonging unto JOHN McMILLIAN his heirs from the date hereof during the term of Six years & six months paying yearly upon the Tenth day of January unto JOHN CANNON his heirs the sum of Fifteen pounds Virginia currency which rent will first become due in the year one thousand seven hundred and ninety five; In Witness whereof said parties to these presents have hereunto set their hands & seals the day & year first above written

Signed Sealed and Delivered in the presence of
    MUNGO HANCOCK,   JOHN CANNON
    CHARLES TYLER JUNR., JOHN MUSCHETT

At a Court continued & held for Prince William County the 6th day of January 1795 This Lease from JOHN CANNON to JOHN McMILLIAN was acknowledged by the said CANNON and ordered to be recorded   Teste ROBT. GRAHAM, Cl Cur

p.   KNOW ALL MEN by these presents that I COLIN CAMPBELL of Prince William
465   County in consideration of the sum of Forty five pounds current money of Virginia to me in hand paid by WILLIAM BARNES of the same County, by these presents do bargain sell and confirm unto WILLIAM BARNES one Negro woman named Mary; To have and to hold the said Negro Mary unto WILLIAM BARNES his heirs and COLIN CAMPBELL the said Negro Mary unto WILLIAM BARNES his heirs against all persons will warrant and forever defend by these presents; of which Negro Mary said COLIN CAMPBELL hath put said WILLIAM BARNES in full possession; In Witness hereof I have hereunto set my hand and affixed my seal this (blank) day of December 1794

Signed Sealed & Delivered in presence of us
    GEORGE JOHNSTON,   COLIN CAMPBELL
    DAVID RICKETTS

At a Court continued and held for Prince William County the sixth day of January 1795 This Bill of Sale from COLIN CAMPBELL to WILLIAM BARNES was acknowledged by the said CAMPBELL and ordered to be recorded Teste ROBT. GRAHAM, Cl Cur

pp.   KNOW ALL MEN by these presents that I GEORGE PERRY of MONTGOMERY
465-   County in Commonwealth of Virginia in consideration of the sum of Fifty four
466   pounds current money of Virginia to me in hand paid by WILLIAM BARNES of Town of DUMFRIES in County of Prince William by these presents do bargain sell and confirm unto WILLIAM BARNES one Negro woman named Esther, formerly the property of COLIN CAMPBELL; To have and to hold the said Negro woman unto WILLIAM BARNES, And I said GEORGE PERRY the said Negro Esther unto said BARNES against every person will warrant and forever defend by these presents of which Negro woman I said GEORGE PERRY have put said WILLIAM BARNES in full possession; In Witness whereof I have hereunto set my hand and affixed my seal this 2nd day of December 1794

Signed Sealed and Delivered in presence of us
    WM. BEALE JR.,   G: PEERY
    WM. CARR, L. CANNON

At a Court continued & held for Prince William County the sixth day of January 1795 This Bill of Sale from GEORGE PEERY to WILLIAM BARNES was proved by the Oath of

WILLIAM CARR and ordered to be recorded Teste ROBT. GRAHAM, Cl Cur

pp.   THIS INDENTURE made this thirteenth day of November one thousand seven
466-   hundred and ninety four Between GWYN PAGE of County of Prince William of
468   one part and LEONARD BRASFIELD of County aforesaid of other part; Witnesseth
         that GWYN PAGE in consideration of the sum of Two hundred & Thirty two
pounds, Ten shillings specie to sd. GWYN PAGE in hand paid by LEONARD BRASFIELD, by
these presents doth bargain sell and confirm unto LEONARD BRASFIELD & his heirs, a
tract of land lying in County aforesaid on North side of South Fork of BULL LRUN being
part of a tract given to GWYN PAGE by his Brother, MANN PAGE, & recorded in the
District Court held at DUMFRIES & bounded, Beginning at two white Oaks in the line of
THOMAS NEWMAN (and corner to MATTHEW PAGE his Brother), then with line of sd.
MATTHEW PAGE S. 260 po. on South Fork of BULL RUN, then up sd. Run & binding
therewith S. 73d. W. 7 po. to a Poplar, then N. 62d. W. 366 po: to a black Oak & post Oak in
the out line, then with sd. line & binding on the lines of WHITING & THOMAS NEWMAN S.
74d. W. 332 po: to the begining, containing Two hundred & sixty seven acres with all
houses and advantages belonging; To have and to hold the tract of land unto LEONARD
BRASFIELD his heirs freed and discharged from all incumbrances, the taxes hereafter
become due excepted; And GWYN PAGE and his heirs the land unto LEONARD BRASFIELD
his heirs from the claim of all persons shall warrant and forever defend by these presents; In Witness whereof the sd. GWYN PAGE hath hereunto set his hand and affixed
his seal the day and year first above written
Signed Sealed & Delivered in presents of
         JNO: KINCHELOE, THOS: NEWMAN,   GWYN PAGE
         JACOB BRASFIELD
   At a Court held for Prince William County the first day of December 1794
This Deed with the Receipt thereon from GWYN PAGE to LEONARD BRASFIELD, the Deed
was proved by the Oaths of JOHN KINCHELOE and JACOB BRASFIELD (and the Receipt
proved by the Oath of JOHN KINCHELOE) and ordered to be Certified; And at a Court held
for the said County the fifth day of January 1795; This Deed & Receipt were fully proved
by the Oath of THOMAS NEWMAN and ordered to be recorded
                         Teste ROBT. GRAHAM, Cl Cur

pp.   (On margin: Examd. & delivered May 16th 1796, J. WILLIAMS)
468-   The Commonwealth of Virginia to RICHARD GRAHAM, ALEXANDER LITHGOW &
469   WILLIAM BARNES Gentlemen Greeting, Whereas THOMAS BLACKBURN &
         CHRISTIAN his Wife by their certain Deed of Bargain and Sale dated the 6th day
of January 1794 have sold & conveyed unto WILLIAM LINTON the fee simple Estate in
Eight hundred & eighty acres of land more or less situate in Prince William County &
whereas the sd. CHRISTIAN cannot conveniently travel to our County Court of Prince
William to make acknowledgement of the same, therefore power is given you to receive
the acknowledgement which sd. CHRISTIAN shall be willing to make before you (the
Commission for the privy Examination of CHRISTIAN, the Wife of THOMAS BLACKBURN); Witness
ROBERT GRAHAM Clerk of the said Court this 3d day of December 1794 and in the 19th
year of the Commonwealth   . ROBERT GRAHAM
   Prince William County, to wit; In Obedience to the within, we the subscribers have
caused to come before us the within named CHRISTIAN BLACKBURN and have examined
her privately (the return of the execution of the privy Examination of CHRISTIAN BLACKBURN);
Given under our hands & seals this 3d. day of December 1794
                         ALEXANDER LITHGOW
                         WILLIAM BARNES

At a Court held for Prince William County the 2nd day of February 1795
This Dedimus was returned into Court & ordered to be recorded
Teste ROBT. GRAHAM, Cl Cur

pp.
469-
471

THIS INDENTURE made the Twenty third day of December one thousand seven hundred & ninety four Between WILLIAM ROBINSON & JANE his Wife of Prince William County of one part & JAMES BURK of the County aforesd. of other part; Witnesseth that WM: ROBINSON & JANE his Wife in consideration of One hundred & sixty nine pounds specie to sd. WM. ROBINSON & JANE his Wife in hand paid by JAMES BURK, by these presents doth bargain & sell unto JAMES BURK his heirs all that tenement of Land lying in County aforesd. containing One hundred & Fifty eight acres & three Rood, the three Rood being reserved for a BURYING GROUND, the sd. Land lying on a small Branch of OCCOQUAN; given to ASA REEVE by his Fathers Last will and Testament who sold the same to sd. WM. ROBINSON in 1789, begining at a corner of JOHN HAMMITTs in the line of JOHN KINCHELOE former BERRYMAN, then S. 80d. W. 37 po: to a white Oak corner to sd. KINCHELOE & HOWSON HOOE, still continuing the course S. 80d. W. 164 po: with said HOOE's line to a white Oak, corner to BRAWNER in sd. line by the Main Road leading to DUMFRIES, then down said Road S. 9d. 30m. E. 132 po. to an Oak in a Fork of sd. Road, then (   ) 30m., E. 66 po: to a Stake, then E. 148 po: to a white Oak on the East side of a Branch, then up the Branch & binding therewith N. 23 poles, N. 81d: 30m. W. 20 po; then No. 54d. W. 16 po: to a Fork of sd. Branch, then up the North East Fork & bindg: therewith No. 12 E. 26 po; then No. 10d. E. 92 po: to the begining; Also all houses trees profits commodities and appurtenances belonging; To have and to hold the tenement with the appurtenances unto JAMES BURK his heirs; and WILLIAM ROBINSON and JANE his Wife for himself & their heirs against all persons to JAMES BURK his heirs shall warrant & forever defend by these presents; In Witness whereof the sd. WILLIAM ROBINSON & JANE his Wife hath hereunto set their hands & seals the day & year first above written
Signed Sealed and Delivered in presents off

ALEXR: LITHGOW, WM. BARNES,   WM. ROBERTSON
HECTOR ALEXANDER   JANE her mark X ROBERTSON

The Commonwealth of Virginia to ALEXANDER LITHGOW, CHARLES EWELL and WILLIAM BARNES Gentlemen, Greeting, Whereas (the Commission for the privy Examination of JANE, the Wife of WILLIAM ROBERTSON); Witness ROBERT GRAHAM Clerk of the said Court the 8th day of January 1795 and in the 19th year of the Commonwealth

Prince William County, to wit; In Obedience to the within, we the Subscribers have caused to come before us the within named JANE ROBERTSON & have examined her privately (the return of the execution of the privy examination of JANE ROBERTSON); Given under our hands & seals this 8th day of January 1795   ALEXANDER LITHGOW
     WILLIAM BARNES

At a Court held for Prince William County the 2nd day of Feby: 1795
This Deed & the Receipt thereon from WILLIAM ROBERTSON & JANE his Wife to JAMES BURK (a Dedimus for the privy examination of the feme being returned executed) were acknowledged by the said ROBERTSON and ordered to be recorded
Teste ROBT. GRAHAM, Cl Cur

pp.
472-
474

(On margin: Exd. & delivd. July 20th 1797, J. WMS:)
THIS INDENTURE made this 18th day of August in year of our Lord one thousand seven hundred & Eighty Eight Between ROBERT CATLETT & MARY CATLETT his Wife of County of FREDERICK in Colony of Virginia of one part & BENJAMIN PRITCHARD of STAFFORD County of other part; Witnesseth that ROBERT CATLETT &

MARY his Wife in consideration of the sum of Eighty five pounds current money of
Virginia to them in hand paid by BENJAMIN PRITCHARD, by these presents do bargain
sell & confirm unto BENJAMIN PRITCHETT his heirs one certain tract of land lying in
Parish of Dittingen in County of Prince William & containing One hundred acres of
land be the same more or less which is all the Land now held by ROBERT CATLETT &
MARY his Wife in County of Prince William, lying on South West side of GOOSE RUN &
East side of a Branch that runs through the Old Fields that formerly belong'd to Capt.
CUTHBERT HARRISON: To have and to hold the One hundred acres of land to BENJAMIN
PRITCHETT his heirs; And ROBERT CATLETT & MARY his Wife docovenant with BENJAMIN
PRITCHETT his heirs that they will warrant & defend the Land against all persons
claiming under them; In Witness whereof the said ROBERT CATLETT and MARY his Wife
to these presents hath hereunto set their hands and affixed their seals the day month &
year first above written
Sign'd Seal'd & Delivered in the presence of
    JOHN FRISTOE, WM. FRISTOE,   ROBERT CATLETT
    JOHN EDRINGTON, JOHN FRISTOE JUNR. MARY CATLETT
  The Commonwealth of Virginia to THOMAS THROCKMORTON, RICHARD MEAD, JOHN S.
WOODCOCK & JOHN THRUSTON, Gentlemen Greeting, Whereas (the Commission for the privy
examination of MARY, the Wife of ROBERT CATLETT); Witness ROBERT GRAHAM Clerk of the
said Court the 8th day of August in the 13th year of the Commonwealth 1788
  FREDERICK County to wit: Pursuant to the within Commission to us directed, we have
examined the sd. MARY CATLETT privily (the return of the execution of the privy examination
of MARY CATLETT); Given under our hands and seals the 18th day of August 1788
                    THOS: THROCKMORTON
                    JOHN S. WOODCOCK
  At a Court held for Prince William County the first day of Septr. 1788
This Deed & the Receipt thereon from ROBERT CATLETT & MARY his Wife to BENJAMIN
PRITCHARD (a Dedimus for the privy examination of the feme being returned executed)
were proved by the Oaths of JOHN FRISTOE and WILLIAM FRISTOE and ordered to be Certified; And at a Court held for the aforesaid County on the first day of October 1792, the
sd. Deed & Receipt were further proved by the Oath of JOHN EDRINGTON & ordered to be
further certified; And at a Court held for the sd. County the second day of February 1795
the said Deed & Receipt were fully proved by the Oath of WM. FRISTOE & together with
the aforesaid Dedimus ordered to be recorded
                Teste ROBT. GRAHAM, Cl Cur

pp.   THIS INDENTURE made this 24th day of June in the year of our Lord one thou-
474- sand seven hundred and ninety four Between HENRY LEE of County of WEST-
477   MORELAND and ANN his Wife of one part & HENRY SELECTMAN of the other part;
     Witnesseth that HENRY LEE in consideration of the sum of Five shillings current
money of Virginia to him in hand paid by HENRY SELECTMAN, by these presents doth
bargain & sell unto HENRY SELECTMAN his heirs that tract of land lying on South side
of OCCOQUAN RIVER in County of Prince William & bounded; Beginning on the side
WHORES CREEK in KIRKBRIDE line, then up the meanders of said Creek & binding therewith South sixty six & one fourt degrees West forty one poles, South thirty three degrees
West eighteen poles, North eighty nine West thirty two poles, South thirty two West
eighteen poles, South twenty six & one fourth EAst twelve poles, South forty one & an
half East thirty four poles, South fifty & one fourth West thirty four poles, South nine
East twenty poles, South forty three degrees & one half West five poles to the mouth of a
Branch corner to a tract of land sold by said LEE to DANIEL DAUGHERTY, thence still
continuing up the Creek South eighty nine West fourteen poles, South fifty West nine

poles, North sixty five West six poles, North fourteen West twenty seven poles, South eighty nine West seven poles, South seventy three West twenty eight poles, South thirty West twenty poles, South twelve poles, South seventy eight East thirty three poles, South four West fifty eight poles, South fifty two West fourteen poles, South nine East thirteen poles, South four & an half East thirteen poles, North eighty eight West six poles to a large pile of Rocks marked H. S., thence North sixty five East two hundred & eighteen poles to the intersection of KIRKBRIDEs line, thence along his line North twenty three West one hundred & fifty seven poles to the beginning, containing One hundred & Fifty seven & one half acres; Together with all water courses profits commodities & appurtenances belonging; To have and to hold the tract of land unto HENRY SELECTMAN his heirs, And HENRY LEE & his heirs will forever warrant & defend by these presents; In Witness whereof the parties to these presents have hereunto set their hands & seals the day & year first above written
Signed Sealed & Delivered in presence of
        CHAS: LEE,   GEO: BEARD,   HENY: LEE
        WM. ERWIN,   JOHN POTTS,   ANNE LEE
        JOHN FISHER,   DANL. DOUGHERTY
   The Commonwealth of Virginia to ROBERT MITCHELL, ANDREW DUNSCOMB & JOHN GREENHOW Gentlemen Greeting, Whereas (the Commission for the privy Examination of ANN the Wife of HENRY LEE); Witness ROBERT GRAHAM Clerk of our said Court the 12th day of July 1704 & in the 19th year of the Commonwealth   ROBERT GRAHAM
   CITY of RICHMOND to wit; In Obedience to the within, we the Subscribers have caused to come before us the within named ANNE LEE & examined the sd. ANNE privily (the return of the execution of the privy Examination of ANNE LEE); Given under our hands & seals the 15th day of Septr: 1794   ANDREW DUNSCOMB
                                              JOHN GREENHOW

   At a Court held for Prince William County the sixth day of October 1794
This Deed from HENRY LEE & ANNE his Wife to HENRY SELECTMAN (a Dedimus for the privy examination of the feme being returned executed) was proved by the Oathes of DANIEL DAUGHERTY & JOHN FISHER and ordered to be certified; And at a Court held for the aforesaid County the second day of February 1795, the said Deed was fully proved by the Oath of GEORGE BEARD and (together with the aforesaid Dedimus) were ordered to be recorded   Teste ROBT. GRAHAM, Cl Cur

pp.   THIS INDENTURE made this 24th day of June in year of our Lord one thousand
477-   seven hundred and ninety four Between HENRY LEE of County of WESTMORE-
480   LAND and ANN his Wife of one part & DANIEL DAUGHERTY of the other part;
           Witnesseth that HENRY LEE in consideration of the sum of Five shillings current money of Virginia to him in hand paid by DANIEL DAUGHERTY by these presents doth bargain sell & confirm unto DANIEL DAUGHERTY & his heirs the following tract of land lying on South side of OCCOQUAN RIVER in County of Prince William, Begining at two Sycamore on the South side of sd. River corner to the land sold to JOSEPH KIRKBRIDE, thence up the several courses & meanders of sd. River & binding therewith South 88 W. 50 po; N. 51d. W. 22 po;, N. 79d. W. 20 po;, N. 50d. W. 31 1/2 po., N. 52 1/2 W. 14 po., N. 45 W. 52 po., No. 61d. W. 12 po., N. 67d. W. 24 po. N. 84 W. 16 po. to the mouth of a Branch emptying into the River below a Chesnut Oak & a Poplar, thence South twenty five degrees West eighty six poles to a Pine on South side of the MILL or River side, thence South forty five degrees, East two hundred & twenty five poles to WHORES CREEK opposite the mouth of a Branch, thence down the several courses & meanders of sd. Creek & binding therewith No. forty three & half degrees East five poles, North nine West twenty poles North sixty six & one fourth East forty one poles to the Intersection with

KIRKBRIDEs line thence with his line North twenty three degrees West sixteen poles to the begining; including One hundred & Fifty six acres together with all water courses profits commodities thereunto belonging; To have and to hold the tract of land to sd. DANIEL DAUGHERTY his heirs free and clear from all incumbrances, And HENRY LEE & his heirs will warrant & defend by these presents; In Witness whereof the parties to these presents have hereunto set their hands and seals the day & year above written Signed Sealed & Delivered in presence of us

CHARLES LEE, GEO: BEARD,	HENRY LEE
WILLIAM ERVIN, JOHN POTTS	ANNE LEE
JOHN FISHER, HENRY SELECTMAN	

The Commonwealth of Virginia to ROBERT MITCHELL, ANDREW DUNSCOMB & JOHN GREENHOW, Gentlemen, Greeting, Whereas (the Commission for the privy Examination of ANNE, Wife of HENRY LEE); Witness ROBERT GRAHAM Clerk of our said Court the 12th day of July 1794 and in the 19th year of the Commonwealth   ROBERT GRAHAM

CITY of RICHMOND Sct. In Obedience to the within, we the Subscribers have caused to come before us the within named ANNE LEE & have examined her privily (the return of the execution of the privy examination of ANNE LEE); Given under our hands & seals this 15th day of Septr. An: Dom: 1794   AND. DUNSCOMB
    JNO: GREENHOW

At a Court held for Prince William County the Sixth day of October 1794 This Deed from HENRY LEE and ANNE his Wife to DANL: DAUGHERTY (a Dedimus for the privy examination of the feme being returned executed) was proved by the oathes of JOHN FISHER & HENRY SELECTMAN and ordered to be certified; And at a Court held for the said County the second day of February 1795, the said Deed was fully proved by the Oath of GEORGE BEARD & together with the afsd. Dedimus were ordered to be recorded
            Teste ROBT. GRAHAM, Cl Cur

pp.   (On margin: Examd. & delivered 11th May 1797, N. COX.)
480-   THIS INDENTURE made this 31st day of December in year of our Lord one thou-
481   sand seven hundred & ninety four Between CHARLES BENSON and ANNE his Wife
         of County of Prince William of one part and WILLIAM MERCHANT of County
aforesaid of other part; Witnesseth that CHARLES BENSON & ANN his Wife in consideration of the sum of Six pounds, Ten shillings current money to them in hand paid by
WILLIAM MERCHANT by these presents & agreable to the Act of Assembly in that case
made and provided, they said CHARLES BENSON & ANNE his Wife doth bargain sell & confirm unto WILLIAM MERCHANT, his heirs the following lott in Town of NEWPORT, that is
to say Lott Number Fifty five bounded by WATER STREET, SEVENTH STREET, QUANTICO
CREEK & Lott number Fifty three as by a Survey of said Town made by SAMUEL BYRN &
recorded in Court of County of Prince William, And all houses to same belonging; To
have and to hold the said lott unto WILLIAM MERCHANT his heirs and CHARLES BENSON
& ANNE his Wife their heirs against all persons shall warrnt & for ever defend by these
presents; In Witness whereof said CHARLES BENSON & ANNE his Wife hath hereunto set
their hands & seals the day month & year first before written
Signed Sealed & Delivered in presence of

| WILLIAM COCKE, JOHN GALLOWAY | CHARLES his mark 4 BENSON |
| JOHN DAROCH | ANN BENSON · |

At a Court held for Prince William County the Second day of February 1795 This Deed from CHARLES BENSON & ANN his Wife to WILLIAM MERCHANT (the feme being first privily examined and consenting thereto) was acknowledged & ordered to be recorded   Teste ROBT. GRAHAM, Cl Cur

pp.   THIS INDENTURE made this sixth day of January one thousand seven hundred &
482-   ninety five Between ALEXANDER KEITH & MARY his Wife of FAUQUIRE County of
484   one part and WILLIAM TEBBS of County of Prince William of other part; Witnes-
           seth that ALEXANDER KEITH & MARY his Wife in consideration of the sum of
Twenty seven pounds, Fifteen shillings current money of Virginia to them in hand paid
by WILLIAM TEBBS, by these presents do bargain & sell unto WILLIAM TEBBS his heirs
during the natural life of the above named MARY KEITH, formerly MARY THORNTON, a
certain parcel of land it being the Dower of the above named MARY KEITH by the
decease of her former Husband, CHARLES THORNTON, containing Thirty seven acres be
the same more or less situate in County of Prince William bounded, Begining at a white
& box Oak now TEBBS corner, formerly HOLSCLAW, thence North 5 E. 74 po: to a Stump in
cleared Land & thence N. 60 E. 60 po: to STONEs line, thence No. ( ) W: 22 po: along said
line, thence S. 77 W. along with the said STONEs line so far as to ascertain the Thirty
seven acres before mentioned & then to the begining; And all houses orchards profits
and appurtenances to the said Thirty seven acres appurtaining; To have and tohold the
said Thirty seven acres of land unto WILLIAM TEBBS his heirs and ALEXANDER KEITH &
MARY his Wife, & their heirs the premises unto said TEBBS his heirs against all persons
will warrant & defend by these presents; In Witness whereof the parties to these presents have hereunto set their hands & seals the day month & year first within written
Sealed & Delivered in presence of
        MUNGO HANCOCK,   ALEXANDER KEITH
        RICHARD DOWNTON,   GEORGE LANE,   MARY KEITH
        JESSE EVANS,   JOHN DAROCH,
        JOHN LAWSON,   JOHN WILLIAMS
 The Commonwealth of Virginia to JESSE EWELL, CHARLES EWELL & WILLIAM BARNES
Gentlemen, Greeting, Whereas (the Commission for the privy examination of MARY, the Wife of
ALEXANDER KEITH); Witness ROBERT GRAHAM Clerk of the said Court the sixth day of
January 1796 & in the 19th year of the Commonwealth   ROBERT GRAHAM
 Prince William County to wit; In Obedience to the within, we the subscribers have
causes to come before us the within named MARY KEITH and have examined her pri-
vately (the return of the execution of the privy examination of MARY KEITH); Given under our
hands & seals this 6th day of January 1795   JESSE EWELL
                                                WM. BARNES
 At a Court held for Prince William County the second day of February 1795
This Deed from ALEXANDER KEITH & MARY his Wife to WM. TEBBS (a Dedimus for the
privy Examination of the feme being returned executed) was proved by the oaths of
GEORGE LANE,   JOHN LAWSON & JOHN WILLIAMS and ordered to be recorded
                    Teste ROBT. GRAHAM, Cl Cur

pp.   THIS INDENTURE made the Twenty ninth day of September in year of our Lord
485-   one thousand seven hundred and ninety four Between JOHN TAYLOE and ANNE
487   his Wife of County of RICHMOND of one part and JOHN SOWDEN of County of
           Prince William of other part; Witnesseth taht JOHN TAYLOE and ANN his Wife in
consideration of the sum of Two hundred and Fifty five pounds, Thirteen shillings and
three half pence current money of Virginia to them in hand paid by JOHN SOWDEN, by
these presents do bargain & sell unto JOHN SOWDEN his heirs a certain tract of land
lying in County of Prince William on North Fork of QUANTICO RUN bounded, Beginning
at a marked red Oak Sapling on South side of North Fork of QUANTICO RUN, extending
thence across the said Run No. 55d. E. 6 poles crossing KEYSes ROAD to a Heap of Stones
near two marked Hickories, thence No. 6 Wt. 39 and six tenth poles to two marked red

Oaks on said Road side, thence No. 25d. 30m. Wt. 276 poles to a Stone on side of the same
Road and the out line of the Patent, thence with that line So. 64d. 30m.Wt. 162 poles to a
marked Poplar and Beach on South side of aforesaid Run, thence down the Run and
binding therewith to the first station, including by late survey two hundred and twenty
seven acres and forty poles; the same being part of a tract of land granted by WILLIAM
BERKLEY, Governor, to WILLIAM BEACH and RICHARD HALOST by Deed bearing date 22d
March 1665/6 for Two thousand two hundred acres and (the said HALOST having
assigned his Right by Deed bearing date the 16 of February 1666 to RICHARD NORMAN-
SEL), by said RICHARD NORMANSEL & WILLIAM BEACH conveyed to a certain ABRAHAM
JEWSON by Deed bearing date the 27th May 166(blank) all which conveyances are
recorded in the County Court of STAFFORD and the said Tract by said ABRAHAM JEWSON
conveyed to the Revd. EMANUEL JONES and by said JONES to JOHN TAYLOE, deced., from
whom the said JOHN TAYLOE, party to these presents, inherited the same; And also all
profits commodities & appurtenances belonging; To have and to hold the tenement
unto JOHN SOWDEN his heirs; And JOHN TAYLOE and ANN his Wife for themselves and
their heirs the tenement against all persons to JOHN SOWDEN his heirs shall warrant
and forever defend by these presents; In Witness whereof the said JOHN TAYLOE and
ANN his Wife have hereunto set their hands and seals the day and year above written
Signed Sealed and Delivered in presence of

| WM. BEALE, JR., | JOHN TAYLOE |
| WILLIAM GORDON, NATHANAIEL HIILLYARD | ANN TAYLOE |

The Commonwealth of Virginia to ROBERT CARTER, VINCENT REDMAN and ROBERT
MITCHELL, Gentlemen Greeting, Whereas (the Commission for the privy Examination of ANN,
the Wife of JOHN TAYLOE); Witness ROBERT GRAHAM Clerk of our said Court the 16th day of
February 1795 and in the 19th year of the Commonwealth

RICHMOND County, to wit. In Obedience to the within, we the Subscribers have caused
to come before us the within named ANN TAYLOE and have examined her privately; (the
return of the execution of the privy examination of ANN TAYLOE); Given under our hands and
seals this 4th day of May 1795   RO: WORMELEY CARTER
                                                   VINCENT REDMAN

At a Court continued and held for Prince William County the 2d. day of December 1794
This Deed from JOHN TAYLOE and ANN his Wife to JOHN SOWDEN was proved by the Oaths
of WILLIAM BEALE JUNR. and WILLIAM GORDON and ordered to be Certified; And at a
Court held for the said County the second day of February 1795, the Deed was fully
proved by the Oath of NATHANL: HILLYARD and with the Commission thereto annexed
were ordered to be recorded   Teste ROBT. GRAHAM, Cl Cur

pp.   THIS INDENTURE made the 15th day of August in year of our Lord MDCCXCIII
488-   Between HENRY TYLER of Dittingen Parish in County of Prince William of one
489   part and JAMES GRIGSBY of said Parish and County of other part; Witnesseth
           that HENRY TYLER in consideration of the rents and covenants herein after
reserved on part of JAMES GRIGSBY to be paid and performed hath demised and to farm
let unto said JAMES a parcel of that tract of land whereon the said HENRY now lives as
also the said JAMES is now seated in the Northerly part thereof, and to be included in
the out lines of said HENRY's Tract, and seperated by the Road at present running across
the same from the part retained by said HENRY supposed to contain Fifty acres be the
same more or less; To have and to hold to the said JAMES GRIGSBY and his heirs during
the life of said HENRY TYLER paying annually on or before the twenty first day of
December in each year the rent of Five pounds current money Gold or Silver at its
passing value; And said JAMES to build a house fifteen feet by twenty two; In Testimony
and Confirmation of the premises, the parties affix their hands and seals the day and

year first above written
In presence of us JOHN HEDGES.
                BENJA: WELLS, JOHN his mark X MILLION   HENRY TYLER
                                                             JAMES GRIGSBY
        At a Court held for Prince William County the 2d. day of Febry: 1795
This Lease from HENRY TYLER to JAMES GRIGSBY was acknowledged by the said parties
to be their act and deed and ordered to be recorded
                        Teste ROBERT GRAHAM, Cl Cur

pp.   THIS INDENTURE made this (blank) day of February in year of our Lord one
489-   thousand seven hundred and ninety five Between JOHN FOSTER and CHLOE his
491   Wife of County of FAUQUIRE of one part and JOHN THOMAS of County of Prince
            William of other part; Witnesseth that JOHN FOSTER and CHLOE his Wife in con-
sideration of the sum of One hundred and twenty eight pounds, Seventeen shillings and
six pence specie, in hand paid by JOHN THOMAS, by these presents have bargained and
sold unto JOHN THOMAS his heirs part of a tract of land given to said JOHN FOSTER by his
Grand Fathers Last Will and Testament, lying in County of Prince William, Begining at a
white Oak in the line of HENRY WASHINGTON Gent., a Dividing Corner between JAMES
FOSTER and JOHN FOSTER, as agreed by the parties, then with said WASHINGTONs lines
No. 73d. 30m. Wt. 83 1/2 poles, thence No. 52d. W: 107 poles to a Hickory by a Branch,
then down said Branch and binding therewith W. 36 po:, then So: 42d. Wt. 24 poles, then
So: 35d. Wt. 24 po: to a white Oak, corner to BERNARD HOOE Gent., also a Dividing Corner
between MOORE HOFF and the aforesaid JOHN THOMAS, then with a Dividing Line between said HOFF and THOMAS So. 50d. Wt. 90 poles to a large Cherry Tree, then So. 45d.
30m. Wt. 45 po: to a Maple in a Branch, corner to MOORE HOFF and said THOMAS's other
land, thence with the said Branch and binding with THOMAS's lines So. 30d. Et. 46 po.,
then So. 26d. Et. 66 po: and 20 links to an Ash and Willow Oak, a corner agreed to by the
parties; and the aforesaid JAMES FOSTER, then with JAMES FOSTERs lines No. 54d. 45m. Et.
64 poles to a dead box Oak, corner to JAMES FOSTER, then No. 49d. Et. 54 pol to another
box Oak, then No. 41d. Et. 79 po: to the beginning, containing One hundred and Forty
eight acres, together with all profits commodities and appurtenances belonging; To
have and to hold the part of a tract of land unto JOHN THOMAS his heirs, And JOHN FOS-
TER and CLOE his Wife for themselves and their heirs the said land against all person to
JOHN THOMAS his heirs shall warrant and forever defend by these presents; In Witness
whereof JOHN FOSTER and CLOE his Wife have hereunto set their hands and seals the day
and year first above written
Sealed and Delivered in presence of
                MOORE HOFF,   JOHN FOSTER
                FRANCIS his mark X CALVERT   CHLOE FOSTER
                LEONARD LEACHMAN
        At a Court held for prince William County the 6th day of April 1795
This Deed and the Receipt thereon endorsed from JOHN FOSTER and CLOE his wife to JOHN
THOMAS (the feme being first privily examined and consenting thereto) were acknow-
ledged by the said FOSTER to be his act and deed and ordered to be recorded
                        Teste ROBERT GRAHAM, Cl Cur

pp.   THIS INDENTURE made this (blank) day of February in year of our Lord one
491-   thousand seven hundred and ninety five Between JOHN FOSTER and CHLOE his
492   Wife of County of FAUQUIRE of one part and MOORE HOFF of County of Prince
            William of other part; Witnesseth that JOHN FOSTER and CHLOE his Wife in con-
sideration of the sum of Forty three pounds, Five shillings specie in hand paid by
MOORE HOFF, by these presents have bargained and sold unto MOORE HOFF his heirs part

of a tract of land given to said JOHN FOSTER by his Grand Father's Last Will and Testament, lying in County of Prince William, Beginning at two white Oaks on a Branch called SAVAGES corner now BERNARD HOOE Gent., then with a line of said HOFF's So. 30d. Wt. 165 po: near a Branch, thence up the TAN BRANCH and binding therewith No. 55d. Et. 3o po:, thence No. 52d. Et. 14 po., then No. 66 Et. 20 pol, then No. 60d. Et. 56 po., thence So. 76d. Et. 14 po. to a Maple in said Branch, corner to JOHN THOMAS, then leaving said Branch No. 45d. 30m. Et. 45 po. to a large Cherry tree, the said line dividing the aforesaid purchase from a purchase made by JOHN THOMAS of said FOSTER, then with another dividing line No. d50d. Wt. 90 po. to the beginning, containing Forty three acres and one Rood., together with all profits comodities and appurtenances to said Forty three acres and one Rood of land belonging; To have and to hold the tract of land unto MOORE HOFF his heirs; And JOHN FOSTER and CLOE his Wife for themselves their heirs against every person shall warrant and forever defend by these presents; In Witness whereof the said JOHN FOSTER and CHLOE his Wife have hereunto set their hands and seals the day and year first above written

Sealed and Delivered in the presence of

FRANCIS CORNWELL,	JOHN FOSTER
FRANCIS his mark X CALVERT,	CHLOE FOSTER
JOHN his mark + THOMAS	

At a Court held for Prince William County the 6th day of April 1795 This Deed and the Receipt thereon endorsed from JOHN FOSTER and CHLOE his Wife to JOHN THOMAS (the feme being first privily examined and consenting thereto) were acknowledged by said FOSTER to be his act and deed and ordered to be recorded

Teste ROBERT GRAHAM, Cl Cur

pp. 493- 494   THIS INDENTURE made the 17th day of August one thousand seven hundred and ninety three Between WILLIAM FIELDER of County of Prince William of one part and GEORGE LANE of aforesaid County of other part; Witnesseth that WILLIAM FIELDER in consideration of the sum of Fifty pounds to him in hand paid by GEORGE LANE, by these presents doth bargain sell and confirm unto GEORGE LANE his heirs all that tract of land Beginning at a Savin Bush standing on a Hill in an Old Field, near the place whereof JOHN HIGHWARDEN formerly lived, thence along the GLEEB line to the intersection with WILLIAM TYLER's line, thence along WILLIAM TYLERs line to the Long Branch of QUANTICO RUN, thence down the Branch running with TYLERs line, thence leaving ths said Long Branch and running over a Hill to the corner of said TYLER, thence leaving said TYLERs line and running to the intersection of the Cross fence with SAMUEL FIELDERs line, thence along SAMUEL FIELDERs line to the beginning, supposed to contain Eighty acres be the same more or less, Also all houses profits and appurtenances belonging; To have and to hold the said tract of land with the appurtenances unto GEORGE LANE and his heirs, And WILLIAM FIELDER for himself and his heirs will warrant and forever defend by these presents; In Witness the said WILLIAM FIELDS hath hereunto set his hand and seal the date above

Signed Sealed and Delivered in presence of

PHILIP DAWE,   WILLIAM his mark W FIELDER
SPILSBY STONE, ELIZABETH JACKSON

At a Court held for Prince William County the 6th day of Jany: 1795 This Deed and the Receipt thereon endorsed from WILLIAM FIELDS to GEORGE LANE were proved by the Oaths of PHILIP DAWE and SPILSBY STONE and ordered to be Certified; And at a Court continued and held for said County the 7th day of April 1795, the said Deed & Rect. were fully proved by the Oath of ELIZABETH JACKSON and ordered to be recorded   Teste ROBERT GRAHAM, Cl Cur

pp.   KNOW ALL MEN by these presents that we JOHN WILLIAMS, MATTHEW HARRI-
494-   SON JUNR. and GEORGE LANE are held and firmly bound unto his Excellency
495   ROBERT BROOKE Esqr., Governor of the Commonwealth of Virginia and his Suc-
        cessors in the sum of Three thousand Dollars to which payment well and truly to
be paid we bind ourselves our heirs firmly by these presents; Sealed with our seals and
dated this seventh day of April one thousand seven hundred and ninety five
  THE CONDITION of the above obligation is such that whereas the above bound JOHN
WILLIAMS hath this day been appointed CLERK of the COURT for Prince William County
by the Court of said County, Now if the above bound JOHN WILLIAMS shall faithfully
perform his duty as Clerk of the County Court during his continuance in Office, Then
the above obligation to be void else to be and remain in full force and virtue
Sealed and Delivered in presence of
        The Court   JOHN WILLIAMS
                                                          M. HARRISON JR.
                                                          GEO: LANE
  At a Court continued and held for Prince William County the 7th day of April 1795
JOHN WILLIAMS, MATTHEW HARRISON JR. and GEORGE LANE severally acknowledged
this Bond to be their act and deed which is ordered to be recorded
                           Teste JOHN WILLIAMS, Cl Cur

pp.   THIS INDENTURE made and entered into this sixth day of March in year one
495-   thousand seven hundred and ninety five Between WILLIAM McDANIEL of Coun-
496   ty of Prince William of one part and SIMON LUTTRELL and THOMAS CHAPMAN,
        acting Trustees of the Last Will and Testament of WILLIAM CARR deced., of
County aforesaid of other part: Witnesseth that WILLIAM McDANIEL in consideration of
the sum of Eighteen hundred pounds current money of Virginia to him in hand paid by
THOMAS CHAPMAN, one of the parties before mentioned, do by these presents bargain
and sell unto SIMON LUTTRELL and THOMAS CHAPMAN four lotts in the Town of DUM-
FRIES where ESME SMOCK now lives, known by the numbers Nine, Ten, Fifteen & Sixteen, (excepting a part of two of said lotts, to wit, a part of No. 15 & Sixteen sold by
ALEXANDER HENDERSON Esqr. to THOMAS CAVES at request of said WILLIAM McDANIEL
as will appear by Deed bearing date the sixth day of February one thousand seven hundred and Eighty nine), Also all houses advantages and appurtenances of every kind; To
have and to hold the four Lotts and their appurtenances unto SIMON LUTTRELL and
THOMAS CHAPMAN, Trustees as aforesaid, for the benefit of WILLIAM CARR's Heirs in
manner as directed by said WILLIAM CARR deced., reference being had to the said Will,
to that part which directs the appropriation of Debts when received to be applied to the
purchase of Lands; And WILLIAM McDANIEL for himself his heirs doth warrant and
forever defend the lotts (with the exception of the part sold to CAVES as aforesaid); In
Witness whereof WILLIAM McDANIEL has hereunto set his hand and seal the day and
year above written
Signed Sealed and Delivered in presence of
        JAMES HAYES,   M. HARRISON JR.   WM. McDANIEL
        HANSON RENO,   ALEXR: HENDERSON,
        JOHN GIBSON
  At a Court continued and held for Prince William County the 7th day of April 1795
This Deed and the receipt thereon endorsed from WILLIAM McDANIEL to WILLIAM
CARR's Trustees, were acknowledged by the said McDANIEL to be his act and deed which
were ordered to be recorded   Teste JOHN WILLIAMS, Cl Cur

pp.   KNOW ALL MEN by these presents that I JOHN TAYLOE of County of RICHMOND
497-   and State of Virginia am held and firmly bound unto LUKE CANNON, FRANCIS
498   CANNON, DANIEL CARR and ARCHIBALD CARR in the sum of Two thousand pounds
        Virginia Currency, and for the payment thereof well and truly to be made I bind
myself my heirs firmly by these presents. Sealed with my seal and dated this Seventeenth day of June in year of our Lord one thousand seven hundred and ninety three
   Whereas the said LUKE CANNON, FRANCIS CANNON, DANIEL CARR and ARCHIBALD
CARR have this day agreed with the above bound JOHN TAYLOE for the purchase of a
certain tract of land containing One thousand acres being part of a tract belonging to
said JOHN TAYLOE containing Two thousand acres situated in County of Prince William
and laying on both side of the waters of QUANTICO, the thousand acres the part whereof
is this day sold by said TAYLOE is situated on South side of North Fork of QUANTICO and if
on actual survery thereof it shall be found there is not one thouand acres on said South
side of the said Fork, then said TAYLOE is to convey so much land situated on the opposite side of the said Fork of QUANTICO as will in the whole make one thousand acres; but
if found to contain more than one thousand acres, the whole of the surplus shall also be
conveyed to said LUKE CANNON, FRANCIS CANNON, DANIEL CARR and ARCHIBALD CARR
paying for such surplus to said TAYLOE at the rate of Twenty shillings per acre;
   Now the Condition of the above obligation is such that if the above bound JOHN TAYLOE
his heirs when required shall perform by executing Deeds then the above obligation to
be void else to remain in full force and virtue in Law. In Witness whereof I have hereunto set my hand and affixed my seal this Twentieth day of June in year of our Lord one
thousand seven hundred and ninety three
Signed Sealed and Delivered in presence of
        JOHN CANNON, THOMAS CHAPMAN,   JOHN TAYLOE
        WILLM. BEALE JR., WILLIAM CARR
   At a Court continued and held for Prince William County the 7th day of April 1795
This Bond and the Receipt thereon endorsed from JOHN TAYLOE to LUKE CANNON,
FRANCIS CANNON, DANIEL CARR and ARCHIBALD CARR were proved by the Oaths of
JOHN CANNON, THOMAS CHAPMAN & WILLIAM CARR and ordered to be recorded
                 Teste JOHN WILLIAMS, Cl Cur

pp.   (On margin: Exd. & delivered Mr. J. LINTON 3d. April 1809, B. HARRISON).
498-   THIS INDENTURE made this Tenth day of December in year of our Lord one
500   thousand seven hundred and ninety four Between THOMAS LEE SENR. and
        MILDRED his Wife of County of Prince William of one part and CHARLES TYLER
of County aforesaid of other part; Witnesseth that THOMAS LEE SENR. and MILDRED LEE
in consideration of the sum of Four hundred pounds current money of Virginia to them
in hand paid by CHARLES TYLER by these presents doth bargain sell and confirm unto
CHARLES TYLER his heirs one part of a lott of land lying in Town of DUMFRIES and
bounded, Beginning at ESPIEs Corner on the Main Street and running along the Main
Street to the Cross Street by Mr. ALEXANDER LITHGOWs, thence with said Cross Street to
the line of JOSHUA BARKER deced., thence with said line to a parallel line with the
beginning, & thence in a strait line to the beginning, Together with all houses
improvement profits rights members and appurtenances bleonging; To have and to
hold lthe lot of land unto CHARLES TYLER his heirs; And THOMAS LEE SENR. and
MILDRED LEE his Wife and their heirs shall warrant and defend by these presents; In
Witness whereof the above named THOMAS LEE SENR. and MILDRED LEE his Wife hath
hereunto set their hands and affixed their seals the day month and year before written

Signed sealed and delivered in presence of
    JA: BAKER,   THOS: LEE SR.
    JAMES WHITE HERNDON,   MILDRED LEE
    CORNELIUS McCOLLY

At a Court continued and held for Prince William County the 7th day of April 1795 This Deed and the Receipt thereon endorsed from THOMAS LEE SR. and MILDRED his Wife to CHARLES TYLER were acknowledged by the said LEE to be his acts and deeds which were ordered to be recorded   Teste JOHN WILLIAMS, Cl Cur

pp. 500-503   THIS INDENTURE made (blank) in year of our Lord Christ one thousand seven hundred and ninety four Between ISAAC WILLIAMS of County of Prince William of one part and JOHN LANSDOWN of said County of other part; Witnesseth that in consideration of the sum of Fifty pounds current money of Virginia to said ISAAC WILLIAMS in hand paid by JOHN LANSDOWN; by these presents doth demise and to farm let unto JOHN LANSDOWN the whole of an undivided moiety of land lying in County of Prince William and on the Waters of CHAPPEWAMSICK RUN being the whole of the land will'd to me by WILLIAM HORTON of County of STAFFORD, and all houses and orchards profits and appurtenances belonging; To have and to hold the moiety of land and all the premises unto JOHN LANSDOWN his heirs during the full term of one whole year paying therefore the Rent of one year of Indian Corn to ISAAC WILLIAMS on the last day of the said term if lawfully demaned, to the intent that by virtue of these presents and of the Statute for transferring uses into possession the said JOHN LANSDOWN may be in the actual possession thereof and be hereby the better enable to accept a release of the reversion and inheritance thereof; In Witness whereof said ISAAC WILLIAMS hath hereunto set his hand and seal the day and year above written
Sealed and Delivered in the presence of
    JOHN CLAYTON,   ISAAC his mark X WILLIAMS
    ELIZABETH JARVEST LANSDOWN   JOHN LANSDOWN
    JAMES MURDUCK   October 29th 1794

(On pages 502, 503, and 504 appears the Release of the foregoing Lease, which adds nothing to the information found in the Lease)
At a Court continued and held for Prince William County the 7th day of April 1795 This Release from ISAAC WILLIAMS to JOHN LANSDOWN was proved by the Oaths of ELIZABETH J. JACKSON and JOHN CLAYTON and acknowledged by the parties and ordered to be recorded   Teste JOHN WILLIAMS, Cl Cur

pp. 503-506   THIS INDENTURE made and entered into this sixth day of March in year of our Lord 1795 Between ALEXANDER HENDERSON of one part and SIMON LUTTRELL and THOMAS CHAPMAN, the only acting Trustees named and constituted by the Last Will and Testament of Capt. WILLIAM CARR deced. (ROBERT LUTTRELL the other Trustee having renounced and relinquished his trust in him invested by said Will) of the other part; Witnesseth that whereas the said HENDERSON some years ago bargained and sold certain lotts in Town of DUMFRIES which are hereafter particularly described unto a certain WILLIAM McDANIEL of the County of Prince William but the same were never conveyed unto said McDANIEL, And Whereas the said McDANIEL hath bargained and sold unto said SIMON and THOMAS the aforesaid Lotts in trust for the design and uses of said Will so far as the same respects the premises, Now in Consideration of the aforesaid recited causes and for the further sum of Five shillings in hand paid by said SIMON and THOMAS, said ALEXANDER by these presents doth bargain and sell unto said SIMON and THOMAS for the design and uses of said Will in Trust and to the heirs in Trust

for the purposes aforesaid the four following lots or half acres of land lying in Town of
DUMFRIES and County of Prince William, to wit, numbers Nine and Sixteen and Ten and
Fifteen, conveyed to said HENDERSON by a certain JOHN GIBSON by Deed bearing date the
tenth day of October in year 1776, except so much of the afsd. four lotts as hath been
conveyed unto a certain THOMAS CAVE by said HENDERSON at the request of said
McDANIEL by Deed bearing date the 6th day of Feby: in year 1789, recorded in the Coun-
ty Court of Prince William, Together with all houses and all other appurtenances of
every kind appurtaining; To have and to hold the four lots (except the part thereof
conveyed unto the said CAVE) in fee simple with all appurtenances unto said SIMON and
THOMAS and their heirs In Trust for the use of the said Will its uses and objects and the
Legatees thereby intended to be benefitted; In Witness whereof the said ALEXANDER
HENDERSON hath hereunto set his hand & Seal the day and year first above written
Sealed and Delivered in the presence of

M HARRISON JR.,   ALEXR: HENDERSON
HANSON RENO, JAMES HAYES
JOHN O'CONNOR, JOHN GIBSON

At a Court continued and held for Prince William County the 7th day of April 1795
This Deed and the receipt thereon endorsed from ALEXANDER HENDERSON to WILLIAM
CARR's Trustees were acknowledged by the said HENDERSON to be his acts and deeds and
ordered to be recorded   Teste JOHN WILLIAMS, Cl Cur

pp.   (On margin: Examd. & Delivered to JNO: WILLIAMS Guardian of MURRAY FORBES
506-   June 18, 1801)
508   THIS INDENTURE made this seventh day of April in year of our Lord one thou-
       sand seven hundred and ninety five Between RODHAM BLANCETT & JEAN his
Wife of County of Prince William of one part and HUGH FORBES and MURRAY FORBES,
Son and Heir of DAVID FORBES deced., of other part; Witnesseth that RODHAM BLANCETT
and JEAN his Wife in consideration of sum of One hundred pounds current money of
Virginia to them in hand paid by HUGH FORBES and MURRAY FORBES, by these presents
they the said RODHAM and JEAN his Wife do grant sell and confirm unto HUGH FORBES
and MURRAY FORBES their heirs all that tract of land lying in County of Prince William
and is bounded; Beginning at a large white Oak on West side of CHAMPS MILL BRANCH
said to be a corner to THOMAS DAVIS, extending thence No. 80 degrees Et. 50 po. then So.
80d. E. 76 pole to the line of JOHN ORR, thence with that line and the line of JOHN NEW-
MAN No. 6 1/2d. Wt. 160 po: near a marked Spanish Oak, then No. 85d. Wt. 54 po: to a
forked red Oak near CHAMPS BRANCH, thence up said Branch South 10d. E. 96 po: to the
beginning; containing 100 acres, Together with all houses and advantages belonging;
To have and to hold the tract of land unto HUGH and MURRAY FORBES and their assigns,
free and clear from all incumbrances whatsoever, And RODHAM BLANCETT and JEAN his
Wife and their heirs shall warrant and forever defend by these presents; In Witness
whereof said RODHAM BLANCETT and JEAN his Wife have hereunto set their hands and
affixed their seals the day and year first above written
Sealed and Delivered in presence of

JAMES MITCHELL   RODHAM BLANCETT
                                              JANE BLANCETT

At a Court continued and held for Prince William County the seventh day of April 1795
This Deed and the Receipt thereon endorsed from RODHAM BLANCETT and JANE his Wife
to HUGH FORBES and MURRAY FORBES (the feme being first privily examined and thereto consenting) were acknowledged by the said BLANCETT to be his acts and deeds and
ordered to be recorded   Teste JOHN WILLIAMS, Cl Cur

pp.
509
511

THIS INDENTURE made the Twentieth day of March in year of our Lord one thousand seven hundred and ninety Between RODHAM BLANCETT, HUGH DAVIS and JOHN POSEY NEWMAN of County of Prince William of one part and TRAVIS DAVIS of the County aforesaid of other part; Witnesseth that RODHAM BLANCETT, HUGH DAVIS and JOHN POSEY NEWMAN in consideration of sum of Five shillings Sterling money to them in hand paid by TRAVIS DAVIS, by these presents doth give up and confirm unto TRAVIS DAVIS and his heirs all their rights and titles of a certain tract of land lying in County aforesaid and in QUANTICO NECK which tract of land ISAAC DAVIS deced. purchased of WILLIAM BLAND and the said ISAAC dying Intestate the said land fell to WILLIAM DAVIS JUNR., Son and heir at Law to said ISAAC, and Whereas the said WILLIAM for divers causes and good reasons made a general Deed of Gift to his Brothers and Sisters of said land, And all houses orchards profits and appurtenances to said premises belonging; To have and to hold the lands hereby conveyed unto TRAVIS DAVIS his heirs clear of all incumbrances whatsoever (the taxes hereafter to grow due and payable for the premises only excepted and foreprized) And RODHAM BLANCETT, HUGH DAVIS and JOHN POSEY NEWMAN and their heirs shall warrant and forever defend by these presents; In Witness whereof the said RODHAM BLANCETT, HUGH DAVIS and JOHN POSEY NEWMAN hath hereunto set their hands and seals the day and year first above written

Sealed and Delivered in presents of

JOHN KINCHELOE,	WREN CARTER,	RODHAM BLANCETT
BENSON DAVIS,	GEORGE SAFER.	HUGH DAVIS
		JNO: P. NEWMAN

This Deed and rect. was reacknowledged by RODHAM BLANCETT and HUGH DAVIS for themselves and JOHN POSEY NEWMAN the 4th day of November 1793 in the presence of
JOHN WILLIAMS, JNO: ATTWELL, LANGH: DADE,
WILLIAM DAVIS, PHILIP DAWE

At a Court continued and held for Prince William County the 8th day of September 1790 This Deed and the Receipt thereon endorsed from RODHAM BLANCETT, HUGH DAVIS and JOHN POSEY NEWMAN to TRAVIS DAVIS were proved by the Oath of WREN CARTER and ordered to be certified; And at a Court held for said County the second day of May 1701, the said Deed and Receipt were further proved by the Oath of JOHN KINCHELOE and ordered to be further certified; Teste ROBERT GRAHAM, Cl Cur

And at a Court continued and held for the said County the 7th day of April 1795 The Reacknowledgement of the said Deed and Receipt was proved by the Oaths of LANGHORNE DADE, PHILIP DAWE and JOHN WILLIAMS and the said Deed, Rect., and reacknowledgement were ordered to be recorded Teste JNO: WILLIAMS, Cl Cur

pp.
511-
513

THIS INDENTURE made the Eighteenth day of November in year of our Lord one thousand seven hundred and ninety four Between HUGH DAVIS and JEAN his Wife of County of Prince William of one part and CUMBERLAND WILSON of County of Prince William of other part; Witnesseth that HUGH DAVIS and JEAN his Wife for the sum of Three hundred and fourteen pounds, Twelve shillings current money to them in hand paid by CUMBERLAND WILSON, by these presents do bargain and sell unto CUMBERLAND WILSON and his heirs all those tracts of land lying in County of Prince William containing Two hundred and Thirty acres which said tracts of land were conveyed to said HUGH DAVIS by a certain WILLIAM SMITH and ANN his Wife as will more fully appear by reference to two certain Deeds duly recorded in the Office of the aforesaid County, the one bearing date the 9th day of November 1792 and the other the 30th day of June in the present year; one of the tracts contains One hundred and Thirty three acres more or less and is bounded, Beginning at a Poplar standing on the South

side of BULL RUN corner to ROBERT SPITTLE and running with his line So. 68 Wt. 125 po: to a red Oak, another corner of SPITTLE, thence So. 35 3/4 Et. 180 po. to a white Oak, corner to the Original Patent; thence with the line of the Old Patent So. 72 1/2 Et. 66 po: to a small Hickory on the bank of BULL RUN, thence up said Run according to the several meanders thereof to the beginning; The other tract is bounded, Beginning at the mouth of the North Run of OCAQUAN RIVER and running up the same No. 150 po: to a marked Hickory on the upper side of said Run, thence No. 75 Wt. 100 to a marked red Oak standing at the upper end of a piece of low ground on the River side, thence down the River the several meanders thereof to the beginning; And all houses orchards, profits and appurtenances appurtaining; To have and to hold the aforesaid tracts of land with all appurtenances unto CUMBERLAND WILSON his heirs; And HUGH DAVIS and JEAN his Wife and their heirs against all persons do by these presents warrant and defend; In Witness whereof the said HUGH DAVIS and JEAN his Wife have hereunto set their hands and seals the day and year first within written
Sealed and Delivered in presence of

| JOHN OVERALL,   WILLIAM SCOTT JUNR. | HUGH DAVIS |
| JESSE TAYLOR,   ROBERT GRAYSON | JANE DAVIS |

At a Court continued and held for prince William County the 2nd day of December 1794 This Deed from HUGH DAVIS and JEAN his Wife to CUMBERLAND WILSON was proved by the Oaths of JOHN OVERALL and JESSE TAYLOR and ordered to be Certified; And at a Court continued and held for the aforesaid County the 7th day of April 1795, the said Deed was fully proved by the Oath of ROBERT GRAYSON and ordered to be recorded
Teste JOHN WILLIAMS, Cl Cur

pp.   THIS INDENTURE made done and concluded this 28th day of August in year of
513-   our Lord one thousand seven hundred and Eighty nine Between HUGH DAVIS,
516   TRAVIS DAVIS and POSEY NEWMAN for themselves, HUGH DAVIS and TRAVIS
        DAVIS before named for WARREN DAVIS, all of County of Prince William of one part and RODHAM BLANCETT of same County of other part; Whereas WILLIAM DAVIS JUNR. by Deeds for the consideration therein mentioned did make over and convey to PRESLEY DAVIS, CORNELIUS DAVIS, ISAAC DAVIS, JOHN DAVIS, WARREN DAVIS, TRAVIS DAVIS, JANE DAVIS and MARY DAVIS, his Brothers and Sisters, several tracts of land lying in County of Prince William which descended to him said WILLIAM DAVIS JUNR. as Son and Heir at Law of his Father, ISAAC DAVIS, who died intestate, and that the said lands should be equally divided between them the said PRESLEY, CORNELIUS, ISAAC, JOHN, WARREN, TRAVERSE, JANE and MARY DAVIS as they should severally arrive to the age of twenty one years, which said Deeds are recorded among the Records of said County, the said PRESLEY, CORNELIUS, ISAAC & TRAVERSE for themselves and HUGH DAVIS, Husband to JANE DAVIS, on her part and POSEY NEWMAN, Husband to MARY DAVIS on her part, did enter and possess themselves as they severily came to the age of twenty one years of different parts of said land according to the true meaning of the recited Deeds, and JOHN DAVIS dying before the arrived to the age of Twenty one years share in said lands descended to the survivors as by the Deeds provided, and the said WARREN DAVIS after arriving to the age of twenty one years did contract and sell unto HUGH DAVIS, party to these presents, all right title and demand which should be vested in him; And the within named ISAAC DAVIS by Deed bearing date the 29th day of September one thousand seven hundred and seventy nine for the consideration therein named, did bargain sell and confirm unto RODHAM BLANCETT, party to these presents a certain tract of land which he possessed by virtue of the Deeds of Conveyance from said WILLIAM DAVIS JUNR., And the said CORNELIUS by his Deed bearing date the 29th day of September one thousand seven hundred and seventy nine for the consideration

therein mentioned did bargain sell and confirm unto RODHAM BLANCETT party to these
presents a certain part of said lands he possessed by virtue of the before recited Deeds
of Conveyance from WILLIAM DAVIS JUNR., And Whereas PRESLEY, CORNELIUS, ISAAC,
WARREN, TRAVERSE, HUGH for his Wife, JANE, and POSEY for his Wife, MARY, have
never entered into any regular agreement before the date of these presents to ascertain and divide the said lands so as to secure the respective parties the peaceable possession of their Interests and to secure the purchases and sales heretofore made so that the
same shall be valid in Law and equity; Now This Indenture Witnesseth that HUGH DAVIS
TRAVIS DAVIS and POSEY NEWMAN for themselves and HUGH DAVIS and TRAVIS DAVIS
for WARREN DAVIS as the first parties to these presents in consideration of the sum of
Seven pounds current money of Virginia to them in hand paid by RODHAM BLANCETT as
second party to these presents, doth release and discharge said RODHAM BLANCETT his
heirs the true meaning of the parties to these presents of HUGH DAVIS, TRAVERSE
DAVIS and POSEY NEWMAN for themselves and HUGH DAVIS and TRAVERSE DAVIS on
behalf of WARREN DAVIS that all bargains sales and contrcts herein before mentioned
shall be valid and of full force and effect in Law; In Witness whereof they have hereunto set their hands and seals the day and year first within written
Signed Sealed & Delivered & acknowledged in presence of
        JOHN KINCHELOE,   HUGH DAVIS,
        BARTON HAMILTON,   TRAVERS DAVIS
        JAMES FOLEY   JOHN P. NEWMAN
                                             WARREN DAVIS
    Reacknowledged by HUGH DAVIS and TRAVERS DAVIS and by them for WARREN DAVIS
and JOHN POSEY NEWMAN this 4th day of November 1793 in presence of
        JOHN WILLIAMS, LANGH: DADE, JOHN ATTWELL,
            WILLIAM DAVIS, PHILIP DAWE
    At a Court held for Prince William County the 4th day of January 1790
This Deed from HUGH DAVIS, TRAVERS DAVIS, JOHN POSEY NEWMAN and WARREN
DAVIS to RODHAM BLANCETT was proved by the Oath of JAMES FOLEY and ordered to be
Certified; And at a Court held for said County the 2d. day of May 1791, this Deed was
further proved by the Oath of JOHN KINCHELOE and ordered to be further Certified;
                        Teste ROBERT GRAHAM, Cl Cur
    At a Court continued & held for said County the 8th day of April 1795
The Reacknowledgement of the sd. Deed was proved by the Oaths of LANGHORNE DADE,
PHILIP DAWE and JOHN WILLIAMS and the said Deed and Reacknowledgement were
ordered to be recorded   Teste JOHN WILLIAMS, Cl Cur

p.   KNOW ALL MEN by these presents that I CUTHBERT HARRISON of County of
517   DUNMORE and Colony of Virginia am held and firmly bound unto BURR HARRI-
        SON of County of Prince William in full and just sum of Seven hundred and
Twenty eight pounds current money of Virginia to be paid to BURR HARRISON on demand, to the which payment well and truly to be made I bind myself my heirs firmly by
these presents; Sealed with my seal and dated this 17th day of June 1776
    THE CONDITION of the above obligation is such that whereas the above bound CUTH-
BERT HARRISON was indebted to NEILE McCOOLE the sum of Three hundred and Fourteen
pounds current money of Virginia which said debt said CUTHBERT HARRISON hath made
himself liable for and oblige himself to pay, If therefore the said CUTHBERT HARRISON
shall pay unto BURR HARRISON his heirs the sum of Three hundred and fourteen
pounds current money of Virginia on demand then the above obligation to be void and
of none effect otherwise to remain in full force power and virtue

Witness Present EDWIN YOUNG,   CUTH: HARRISON
                 GEORGE HARRISON
  1785. March 20th. Recd. of CUTHBERT HARRISON Two hundred and thirty five pounds
Eighteen shillings in part of within Bond for which he has a duplicate of this Rect.,
received per me.   BURR HARRISON
  At a Court continued and held for Prince Wm. County the 8th day of April 1795
The Signature to this Bond from CUTHBERT HARRISON to BURR HARISON deced., was
proved by the Oaths of MATTHEW HARRISON JUNR. to be the hand writing of said CUTH-
BERT HARRISON and the said Bond with the Receipt thereon were ordered to be recorded
                     Teste JOHN WILLIAMS, Cl Cur

pp.   THIS INDENTURE made the Third day of December in year one thousand seven
518-   hundred and ninety four Between WILLIAM LINTON of Town of DUMFRIES in
520   County of Prince William of one part and THOMAS BLACKBURN of County afore-
          said of other part; Witnesseth that WILLIAM LINTON for the sum of Five Shil-
lings current money of Virginia to him paid before the execution of these presents;
doth bargain and sell unto THOMAS BLACKBURN and to his heirs a tract of land lying in
County of Prince William on South side of North Fork of QUANTICO RUN, containing
eight hundred and eighteen acres as will appear by a survey thereof made by HENRY
DADE HOOE on the sixth day of May in the year 1793 which land is bounded; Beginning
at a marked Beach on North side of said North Fork of QUANTICO RUN extending thence
So. 53..30 Wt. 315 po. to a marked box Oak, thence No. 80..30 Wt. 328 po. to a small white
Oak in a Valley, thence No. 32 ( ) 339 po: to the aforesaid North Run, thence beginning
at the aforesaid Beach and running the meanders of the North Run to enclose the
aforesaid tract of land and all appurtenances to the same belonging; To have and to hold
lthe tract of land unto THOMAS BLACKBURN and to his heirs, Provided always and these
presents are upon this condition, that if WILLIAM LINTON his heirs shall pay unto
SIMON LUTTRELL and THOMAS CHAPMAN, Executors of WILLIAM CARR deced., or their
assigns, the full sum of Four hundred and Sixty eight pounds, Five shillings and Three
pence current money with legal interest for the same from the sixth day of January
1794 (and the said THOMAS CHAPMAN and SIMON LUTTRELL as Executors of said WIL-
LIAM CARR having in their possession a Bond passed by THOMAS BLACKBURN with the
said WILLIAM LINTON his security for the same), that then these presents shall cease
determine and be void; In Witness whereof the said WILLIAM LINTON hath hereunto set
his hand and affixed his seal the day and date before written
Signed Sealed acknowledged & Delivered in presence of
     LANGH: DADE   WILLIAM LINTON
  At a Court contd. and held for Prince William County the 8th day of April 1795
This Deed of Mortgage from WILLIAM LINTON to THOMAS BLACKBURN was proved by the
Oaths of LANGHORNE DADE, ALEXANDER LITHGOW and WM. BARNES and ordered to be
recorded   Teste JOHN WILLIAMS Cl Cur

pp.   KNOW ALL MEN by these presents that whereas I THOMAS BLACKBURN of Coun-
521-   ty of Prince William have sold and conveyed to a certain WILLIAM LINTON of
522   County aforesaid one certain tract of land containing upwards of Eight hundred
          acres lying in County aforesaid on the North Branch of QUANTICO RUN, which
said tract of land my Wife, CHRISTIAN BLACKBURN, hath relinquished all her right of
Dower by joining in the execution of the said Deed and her acknowledgement thereof
certified and annexed to said Deed, And whereas in consideration that said CHRISTIAN
BLACKBURN would agree to relinquish her dower in said land, I said THOMAS BLACK-
BURN have agreed to convey to her sole and seperate use the Negro slaves hereafter

named, and their future increase, Now Know ye that I THOMAS BLACKBURN in consideration of CHRISTIAN BLACKBURN having joined in the execution of the aforesaid Deed
and her relinquishing all her right of dower in the aforesaid tract of land as well as for
Five shillings to me in hand paid by LANGHORNE DADE of County of Prince William, by
these presents do bargain and sell unto LANGHORNE DADE his heirs the following Negro
slaves & their future increase, that is to say, Cathiana, otherwise called Jenny, Anna,
Doll and her Children, Julist, Patty and Patience, a sickly infant at the breast, To have
and to hold the Negro slaves and their future increase unto LANGHORNE DADE his heirs
to the use of CHRISTIAN BLACKBURN her heirs and no other use. In Witness whereof I
have hereunto set my hand and affixed my seal the 3d day of December in year of our
Lord one thousand seven hundred and ninety four
Signed Sealed & Delivered in presence of us
     ALEXR. LITHGOW,   T. BLACKBURN
     GEO: GRAHAM, WM. BARNES
  At a Court continued and held for Prince William County the 8th day of April 1795
This Deed in Trust from THOMAS BLACKBURN to LANGHORNE DADE was proved by the
Oaths of ALEXANDER LITHGOW and WILLIAM BARNES and ordered to be recorded
             Teste JOHN WILLIAMS, Cl Cur

pp.   THIS INDENTURE made this 29th day of May one thousand seven hundred and
522-   Eighty seven Between BENJAMIN BENSON of CHARLES County in the State of
524   MARYLAND of one part and WILLIAM DAVIS of County of Prince William of
       other part; Witnesseth that BENJAMIN BENSON for the sum of Fifty pounds cur-
rent money of Virginia to him in hand paid by WILLIAM DAVIS, by these presents doth
bargain sell and confirm unto WILLIAM DAVIS and his heirs all that tract of land lying
in County of Prince William granted him by WILLIAM BLAND and WILLIAM DAVIS
deced., in a larger tract Beginning at a Hickory Stump opposite BLANDS MILL DAM and
corner to THOMAS MONTGOMERIE Esqr., and ARCHIBALD CASH, thence No. 67 Wt. 76 po: to
a red Oak near OCAQUAN, thence No. 40 Wt. 56 po: to a large white Oak on PINEY BRANCH
thence down PINEY BRANCH to OCAQUAN RIVER up the same its meanders to the beginning, containing Fifty acres be the same more or less, Together with all houses
Orchards profits and appurtenances belonging; To have and to hold the tract of land
unto WILLIAM DAVIS his heirs, And BENJAMIN BENSON his heirs the parcel of land
unto WILLIAM DAVIS his heirs shall warrant and defend against the claim of me my
heirs & assigns; In Witness whereof said BENJAMIN BENSON hath hereunto set his hand
and seal the day month and year first written
Signed Sealed & Delivered in presence of
     TRAVERS DAVIS,   BENJA: BENSON
     RODHAM BLANCETT: HORATIO BLANCETT
  At a Court continued and held for Prince William County the 5th day of June 1787
This Deed and the receipt thereon endorsed from BENJAMIN BENSON to WILLIAM DAVIS
were proved by the Oaths of RODHAM BLANCETT and TRAVERS DAVIS and ordred to be
Certified;   Teste ROBERT GRAHAM, Cl Cur
  At a Court contd. and held for the said County the 9th day of April 1795
The said Deed and Receipt were fully proved by the Oath of HORATIO BLANCETT and
ordered to be recorded   Teste JOHN WILLIAMS, Cl Cur

pp.   THIS IS TO CERTIFY all people unto whom this present writing shall come, Know
524-   ye that I ELIZABETH DAVIS and MARY NELSON, for divers good causes and valu-
525   able considerations doth appoint GEORGE STONE of the Colony of Virginia and
       County of Prince William my whole and soul Gardeen and Trustee of the Lega-

tees of which the said WILLIAM NELSON of County of STAFFORD left three Children,
JAMES, WILLIAM and MARY NELSON, and that all the goods and property should be
equally divided amongs them. Now I ELIZABETH DAVIS and MARY NELSON doth freely
deliver without any manner of lett or denial of me or any other person of all goods and
property to GEORGE STONE by virtue hereof; In Witness whereof I said ELIZABETH DAVIS
and MARY NELSON have hereunto set our hands and seals this 2d. day of September 1794
Signed Sealed and Delivered in the presents of us

JOHN ANDERSON,   ELIZABETH her mark X DAVIS
WALTER his mark —— SKINNER,   MARY her mark X NELSON
JAMES LATHERIM

   At a Court continued and held for Prince William County the 9th day of April 1795
This Power of Attorney from ELIZABETH DAVIS and MARY NELSON to GEORGE STONE was
proved by the Oaths of JOHN ANDERSON and JAMES LATHERIM and ordered to be
recorded   Teste JOHN WILLIAMS, Cl Cur

pp.   THIS INDENTURE made this ninth day of April in year of our Lord one thousand
525-   seven hundred and ninety five Between JOSEPH KIRKBRIDE and MARY his Wife
529   of CITY of PHILADELPHIA and State of PENNSYLVANIA of one part and ISAAC
           McPHERSON of Town of ALEXANDRIA County of FAIRFAX of other part; Whereas
HENRY LEE Esqr. did by his Indenture bearing date the Twenty ninth day of January
one thousand seven hundred and ninety three for the consideration therein mentioned
bargain sell and confirm unto JOSEPH KIRKBRIDE and ISAAC McPHERSON their heirs as
Tenants in Common a tract of land lying upon the South side of OCCAQUAN RIVER in
County of Prince William and bounded, Beginning at an old marked red Oak on side of
OCAQUAN RIVER a corner to the tract of land known by the name of THE FURNACE
TRACT, thence along the line of said FURNACE TRACT South eleven degrees West one
hundred and seventy six poles to a Poplar by a Branch, another corner to said Tract,
thence South sixty five degrees West seventy poles to the back line of another Tract of
land known by the name of PEYTONS TRACT, thence with line of PEYTONS TRACT North
twenty three degrees West passing the corner of said Tract and continuing the same
Course through another tract of land called EWELLS TRACT and through part of another
tract called CARTERS TRACT four hundred and thirty five poles to OCAQUAN RIVER at the
mouth of HOOES CREEK, thence with a line at right angles with the last mentioned line
crossing the river to the North side thereof, thence down the River with the several
courses and meanders thereof and binding therewith until it shall reach that part of
the said River which is opposite the old red Oak, the beginning corner or boundary of
said tract of land, thence across the River to the beginning, containing Two hundred
and Fifty acres of land and the Forges and Mills and improvements and the sole right of
the River OCAQUAN contained within the said boundaries. NOW THIS INDENTURE Witnesseth that JOSEPH KIRKBRIDE and MARY his Wife for the sum of five thousand two
hundred pounds current money of Virginia to said JOSEPH KIRKBRIDE in hand paid by
ISAAC McPHERSON by these presents do bargain sell and confirm unto ISAAC McPHER-
SON his heirs one equal undivided moiety of said tract of land sold by HENRY LEE unto
said JOSEPH KIRKBRIDE and ISAAC McPHERSON as aforesaid; and one equal undivided
moiety of all Mills, Mill Houses, building and other improvements upon the tract of land
To have and to hold unto ISAAC McPHERSON his heirs, And JOSEPH KIRKBRIDE and his
heirs shall warrant and forever defend by these presents; In Witness whereof the said
parties have hereunto set their hands and seals the day and year first within written
Sealed & Delivered in presence of

ABRAM HEWES,   JOS: KIRKBRIDE
REUBEN LEIGH   MARY KIRKBRIDE

CITY of PHILADELPHIA. On the Twentieth day of April one thousand seven hundred and ninety five JOSEPH KIRKBRIDE and MARY his Wife personally appeared before me MATTHEW CLARKSON, Mayor of said City and acknowledged th preceeding Indenture to be their act and deed, the said MARY having been privately examined by me apart from and out of the hearing of said JOSEPH, her Husband, who declared she executed the Indenture freely and voluntarily; In Testimony whereof I have hereunto set my hand and caused the Seal of the City to be affixed the 20th day of April 1795

MATTH: CLARKSON, Mayor

THOMAS MIFFLIN, Governor of the Commonwealth of PENNSYLVANIA to whom these presents shall come, Greeting; Know ye that MATTHEW CLARKSON Esqr. was at the time of subscribing the same and now is Mayor of the City of PHILADELPHIA and full faith and credit is to be given to him accordingly; Given under my hand and the Great Seal of the State at PHILADELPHIA this Twentieth day of April in the year of our Lord one thousand seven hundred and ninety five and of the Commonwealth the Nineteenth

THO: MIFFLIN

By the Governor, JAMES TRIMBLE, Deputy Secy.
At a Court held for Prince William County the 4th day of May 1795
This Deed and the Receipt thereon endorsed from JOSEPH KIRKBRIDE and MARY his Wife to ISAAC McPHERSON were together with the Certificate of the Governor of PENNSYLVANIA and the Mayor of the City of PHILADELPHIA ordered to be recorded
Teste JOHN WILLIAMS, Cl Cur

pp. 529-531   THIS INDENTURE made this Tenth day of March in year of our Lord one thousand seven hundred and ninety five Between MARY CAMPBELL of one part and GEORGE GRAY TYLER of other part; Witnesseth that MARY CAMPBELL for the sum of Fourteen hundred Dollars specie to said MARY CAMPBELL in hand paid by GEORGE GRAY TYLER, by these presents do bargain and sell unto GEORGE GRAY TYLER his heirs a certain parcel of land lying in County of Prince William and bounded, Beginning at a Oak Bush and Stake, the corner of GEORGE GRAY TYLERs land, thence with the line of FRANCIS RUSSELL No. 33 Et. 95 po: to a marked Maple in or near SKINKERs line, thence No. 54 1/2 West 64 po., thence No. 35 1/2 Et. 172 po., thence No. 54 1/2 Et. 166 po., and sixteenth, thence So. 35 1/2 West 320 po: to two Gums and a white Oak in CARTERs line, and corner to GEORGE GRAY TYLERs land, thence iwth the line of said TYLERs So. 66 1/2 Et. 244 po. to the beginning, including Three hundred and forty nine and three quarter acres of land, prt of a larger tract of land devised by the Last Will and Testament of the late REVD. ISAAC CAMPBELL deceased to be divided among his Sons and Daughters which has been allotted to MARY CAMPBELL as her Dividend thereof; And all houses orchards, profits and appurtenances to the same belonging; To have and to hold the tract containing Three hundred and Forty nine and 3/4 acrs with all appurtenances unto GEORGE GRAY TYLER his heirs; And MARY CAMPBELL her heirs the tract of land unto GEORGE GRAY TYLER his heirs shall warrant and defend by these presents; In Witness whereof said MARY CAMPBELL have hereunto set her hand and seal the day and year first above written
Sealed and Delivered in presence of
BURR PEYTON,   MARY CAMPBELL
WILLIAM TYLER, JOHN LINTON
At a Court continued and held for Prince William County the 7th day of April 1795
This Deed and the Receipt thereon endorsed from MARY CAMPBELL to GEORGE GRAY TYLER was proved by the Oaths of WILLIAM TYLER and JOHN LINTON and ordered to be certified; And at a Court held for said County the 4th day of May 1795, the said Deed and Receipt were fully proved by the Oath of BURR PEYTON and ordered to be recorded

pp.   THIS INDENTURE made done and concluded this Twenty first day of November
531-   one thousand seven hundred and ninety four Between JOHN JAMESON and
533   SALLEY JAMESON his Wife of County of STAFFORD of one part and HEBRON RALLS
         of County of Prince William of other part; Witnesseth that JOHN JAMESON and
SALLY his Wife for the sum of One hundred & fifty pounds current money of Virginia
to them in hand paid by HEBRON RALLS, by these presents do bargain and sell unto
HEBRON RALLS his heirs a certain tract of land lying in County of Prince William and is
that particular tract of land which DAVID JAMESON, late deceased, purchased of a certain HADEN EDWARDS, and which land was by the Last Will and Testament of said DAVID
JAMESON deced. bequeathed to said JOHN JAMESON and is bounded; Beginning at a dead
Spanish Oak, thence No. 66 Wt. 54 po: to a Stone on a Branch, thence up said Branch So.
43 Wt. 22 po: to a Sycamore, thence West nineteen po., to a large black Oak in an Old
Field, thence So. 80 West 60 poles to a Hickory in an Old Field, thence No. 25 Wt. 66 po. to
a white Oak, then No. 83 Et. 6 po. to a red and box Oak, thence No. 8 Wt. 193 poles to a
white Oak, thence Et. 49 po., to several marked saplins, thence No. 88 Et. 78 po. to two
white Oaks, thence S. 11d. Et. 260 po. to the beginning, containing One hundred and
Sixty acres be the same more or less with the appurtenances thereunto belonging unto
HEBRON RALLS his heirs and JOHN JAMESON and SALLEY his Wife and their heirs shall
warrant and forever defend against the claim and lawful demand of all persons, In
Witness whereof the said JOHN JAMESON and SALLEY his Wife have hereunto inter-
changeably set their hands and affixed their seals the day and year first within written
Signed Sealed & Delivered in presence of
         J: RALLS, GEO: CALVERT,   JOHN JAMESON
         RAWLEIGH RALLS, CHS: RALLS   SALLY JAMESON
   At a Court held for Prince William County the 1st day of December 1794
This Deed and the Receipt thereon from JOHN JAMESON and SALLEY his Wife to HEBRON
RALLS were proved by the Oaths of CHARLES RALLS & GEORGE CALVERT and ordered to
be certified;   Teste ROBERT GRAHAM, Cl Cur
   At a Court held for Prince William County the 4th day of May 1795
The said Deed and the Receipt thereon endorsed (the feme being first privily examined
and thereto consenting) were acknowledged by the said JAMESON to be his act and deed
and ordered to be recorded   Teste JOHN WILLIAMS, Cl Cur

pp.   (On margin: Examd. & deld. Apl. 27th 1797; N. COX)
534-   THIS INDENTURE made this Eighth day of April one thousand seven hundred
535   and ninety five Between WALTER GRAHAM and SALLEY his Wife of County of
         FAUQUIRE of one part and DAVID WILSON SCOTT of County of Prince Wm. of other
part; Witnesseth that WALTER GRAHAM and SALLEY his Wife for the sum of Forty five
pounds current money to them in hand paid by DAVID WILSON SCOTT, by these presents
do bargain sell and confirm unto DAVID WILSON SCOTT his heirs a certain tract of land
lying in County of prince William which was granted to WALTER GRAHAM as Assignee
of NATHANIEL HEDGMAN TRIPLETT by BEVERLY RANDOLPH Esqr., Governor of Virginia,
by Patent bearing date the 26th day of March in year of our Lord one thouand seven
hundred and ninety, which said tract of land is bounded; Beginning at a Sycamore in
the line of said TRIPLETT on QUANTICO CREEK the lower part of a Marsh, thence with
said line and up the Creek North twenty degrees Wt. one hundred and twenty poles to
the upper part or extremity of said Marsh, and from thence round the Marsh the
several courses and meanders thereof to the beginning, containing Thirteen acres as
by a survey thereof made the sixth day of May one thouand seven hundred and Eighty
seven which will more fully appear duly recorded in the Registers Office of the Commonwealth, And all houses orchards profits and appurtenances to the same appur-

taining, To have and to hold the tract of land unto DAVID WILSON SCOTT his heirs, And
WALTER GRAHAM and SALLEY his Wife and their heirs do by these presents warrnt and
defend the tract of land unto DAVID WILSON SCOTT and his heirs against the claims of all
persons; In Witness whereof said WALTER GRAHAM and SALLEY his Wife have hereunto set their hands and affixed their seals the day and year above written
Sealed and Delivered in presence of
     THOS: THORNTON,   WALTER GRAHAM
     WM. SMITH, JOHN WILLIAMS   SALLEY GRAHAM
  At a Court held for Prince William County the 4th day of May 1795
This Deed from WALTER GRAHAM and SALLEY his Wife to DAVID WILSON SCOTT was
proved by the Oaths of WILLIAM SMITH, THOMAS THORNTON and JOHN WILLIAMS and
ordered to be recorded   Teste JOHN WILLIAMS, Cl Cur

pp.   (On margin: Examd. & Deld. Septr. 11th 1797. JOHN WILLIAMS)
536-   THIS INDENTURE made this forth day of May one thousand seven hundred and
537   ninety five Between ALEXANDER HUMES and FRANCES HUMES his Wife of Prince
       William County of one part and RUTT JOHNSTON of County aforesaid of other part;
Witnesseth that ALEXANDER HUMES and FRANCES his Wife for the sum of one hundred
and twenty pounds current money of Virginia to him in hand paid by RUTT JOHNSTON
by these presents doth bargain & sell unto RUTT JOHNSTON his heirs all that tract of
land lying in Prince William County between PINEY BRANCH and the CABIN BRANCH,
Beginning at the CABIN BRANCH at a white Oak, corner to JAMES FLORANCE, and then
with his line No. 87d. Wt. ten perches, then So: 80d. Wt. 35 perches to a Hickory near a
Branch, thence No. 65d. Wt. 17 po., to a white Oak, then No. 48d. Wt. 17 po: to another
white Oak, thence No. 63d. Wt. 24 po: to a large white Oak, then So: 37d. Wt. 48 po., to a
white Oak Bush on the point of a Hill, then So. 25d. Wt. 90 po: to the South of PINEY
BRANCH and a white Oak saplin, then So. 67d. Et., 66 po., then East 20 po. to a white Oak
Stump corner to RUTT JOHNSTON, then So. 20d. Et. 22 po., to several red Oak stumps, then
No. 76d. Et. 26 po. to three white Oaks on a point, then So. 70d. Et. 72 po: to a Hickory
Stump near a box Oak, then No. 58d. Et. 43 po. to a Stone, then No. 77d. Et. 18 po. to CABIN
BRANCH, then up the Branch and binding on MONTGOMERIEs line, thence No. 25d. Wt. 21
po. to WASHINGTONs Corner, thence No. 55d. Wt. 4 po. to a Beach, Corner to the Mill Tract
thence with the line of said Tract to the beginning; including about One hundred and
Fifty five acres more or less, Together with all rights profits and privileges thereunto
belonging; To have and to hold unto RUTT JOHNSTON his heirs, And ALEXANDER HUMES
AND FRANCES HUMES his Wife and their heirs the said land against them and their
heirs unto RUTT JOHNSTON his heirs shall warrant and forever defend by these pre-
sents; In Witness whereof the parties first to these presents hath put their hands and
fixed their seals the day and date above written
Signed Sealed and Delivered in the presence of
     GEORGE FLORANCE,   JAS: FOSTER,   ALEXR: HUME
     WILLM. MUNDAY,   GRIEF HEDGES   FRANCES her mark + HUME
(Witnesses to the Receipt: EDWD. HARDING, JAS: WIGGINTON, WM. DUNNINGTON)
  At a Court held for Prince Wm. County the 4th day of May 1795
This Deed and the Receipt thereon endorsed from ALEXANDER HUME and FRANCES his
Wife to RUTT JOHNSTON (the feme being first privily examined and thereto consenting)
were acknowledged by the sd. HUME & ordered to be recorded
           Teste JOHN WILLIAMS, Cl Cur

pp.   A Poll taken at Prince William Court House on Monday 16th day of March 1795
538-   for the Election of a Member to the House of Representatives of the United States
540   for the District composed of the Counties of LOUDOUN, FAIRFAX and Prince
         William

	Candidates		
RICHARD B. LEE	RICHARD BRENT	RICHARD BRENT	RICHARD BRENT
Voters names	Voters names	Voters names	Voters names
WILLIAM DUVAL	WILLOUGHBY TEBBS	GERRARD ALEXANDER	JOHN DYE
ALEXANDER LITHGOW	WILLIAM BROWN	WILLIAM McDANIEL	JOHN FRYER
JOHN LAWSON	ROBERT GRAHAM	JAMES FOSTER	ALEXANDER CLEVELAND
WANSFORD ARRINGTON	JAMES MUSCHETT	JOHN STIFLE	JOHN McMILLIAN
DANIEL DAUGHERTY	PHILIP DAWE	THOMAS HOOMES SENR.	GEORGE NEW: BROWN
JOHN KINCHELOE	EDMOND BROOKE	THOMAS SHANKS	JAMES NOLAND
STEPHEN HOWISON	LUKE CANNON	WILLIAM GRANT SENR.	SAMUEL KING
DAVID W. SCOTT	DANIEL LEDSON	JOHN FITZHUGH	WILLIAM LINTON
RICHARD M. SCOTT	TOWNSHEND DADE	JOHN LANSDOWN	SPILSBY STONE
ELIJAH KENT his land	THOMAS NORMOND	MOSES COCK	WILLIAM THORN
Fairfax lives Fauquier	THOMAS OLIVER	MOSES DAVIS	NATHANL. C. HUNTER
JOHN GIBSON	ANTHONY BUCKNER	ROBERT LUTTRELL	THOMAS BLACKBURN
GALVAN De BERNOUX	THOMAS THORNTON	THOMAS NEWMAN	JAMES JAMESON
JAMES JOHNTON took	WILLIAM WYATT	BENJAMIN JAMESON	JAMES GRINSTEAD
the Oath	JAMES ROACH	HUMPHREY CALVERT SENR.	FRANCIS CANNON
ROBERT CARTER	JAMES MITCHELL	BERNARD HOOE JR.	EDWARD HARDIN
LANDON CARTER JUNR.	JOSEPH GILBERT	RICHARD DAVIS	JAMES KING
JESSE EWELL SENR.	THOMAS DAVIS SENR.	JOHN MACRAE	MOSES MOSS
WILLM. ALEXANDER	GEORGE GRAHAM	DAVID LEE	JOHN GRINSTEAD
	JOHN EDRINGTON	JOHN WRIGHT	WILLIAM KEYS
	JAMES GRAHAM	ALEXANDER BRUCE	WILLIAM REAGAN
	LOFTUS NOEL	JOHN STEEL	BERNARD HOOE SENR.
	JAMES REID	JOHN THOMAS	JOHN MATTHEWS
	GEORGE HUBER	ENOCH RENO	WILLIAM SUTTLE

All the following for the Candidate RICHARD BRENT

	BENSON DAVIS	CARTY WELLS	JAMES PEAKE
LEONARD WOODYARD	THOMAS DOWDALL	BENJAMIN WHEELER	JOHN KING (livg. in FX)
WILLIAM KING JUNR.	MOORE HOFF	NATHAN WHEELER	MARK THARP
JEREMIAH DOWELL	THOMAS CAVE	JOHN DAVIS SENR.	WILLIAM BARNES
DANIEL C. BRENT	JAMES FOLEY	HENRY DOGAN	GEORGE STONE
BASIL KING	PETER COCKRELL	BENJAMIN WROE	JOHN FERGUSON
FRANCIS MONTGOMERIE	WILLIAM ATTWELL	JOHN WATERS JUNR.	AMOS DYE
JOHN SULLIVAN	CHARLES CORNWELL JUNR.	RICHARD WHEELER	LANGHORNE DADE
( )INGTON WICKLIFFE	GEORGE WILLIAMS	RICHARD WROE	WILLIAM HELM
( )ARD GALLAGHER	WILLIAM WRIGHT SENR.	JOSIAS STONE	RUTT JOHNSTON
( )TS WICKLIFFE	WILLIAM MARTIN JUNR.	ZACHARIAH BRADFIELD	JESSE REEVES
( )N THORN	OBED CALVERT JUNR.	HARGUSS KING	JOHN EDWARDS
JOHN KINCHELOE	FRANCIS RENO JUNR.	JAMES TOLIVER	THOMAS GREEN
CORNELIUS KINCHELOE	ROBERT HOWSON HOOE	RICHARD FOOTE	JONATHAN REEVES
RICHARD LEACHMAN	THOMAS LEACHMAN	GEORGE CALVERT JUNR.	WILLIAM HART
( )L. BRAWNER	JESSE CALVERT SENR.	WILLIAM JAMESON	JAMES GUINONETT
JOHN COX	PETER TRONE	JOHN POPE	SCARLETT MADDEN

WILLIAM FOSTER SENR.   JAMES WEBSTER   HENRY TYLER   BENJAMIN BRONAUGH
BENJAMIN COOPER   JOSEPH STEPHENS   ROBERT SPITTLE   CONROD WERT
( ) SMITH   EZEKIEL DONNELL   JOSEPH BRADY   HENRY DADE
JOHN LANGFITT   JOHN WILKINSON   WILLIAM HICKSON   CHARLES ADAMS
CHARLES MOTTISET   WILLIAM DAVIS (son of Isaac)   WILLIAM MONTGOMERIE   SNOWDEN HORTON
JAMES BURK   HUGH DAVIS   GEORGE FLORANCE   FRANCIS CORNWELL SR.
DANIEL GRIEVES   BENJAMIN THOMAS   RODHAM BLANCETT   JAMES EWELL SENR.
( )ANIES JACKSON   BENJAMIN WIGGINTON   JAMES GREEN   BENJAMIN PRITCHARD
WILLIAM POWELL SENR.   WILLIAM FARROW   WILLIAM TACKETT   SAMPSON LEACHMAN
THOMAS HARRIS   EDWARD CARTER   SAMUEL JACKSON   ALEXANDER LEE
WILLIAM BATISS   SAMUEL FIELDER   WILLIAM FAIRFAX   THOMAS BIRD
GEORGE RAINY   JAMES CAMPBELL   HEZEKIAH REEVES   BENJAMIN TYLER
JOSEPH PORTER living   JESSE CORNWELL   PETER HANSBROUGH JUNR.   THOMAS HART
  in Loudoun   ALEXANDER HUME   GEORGE FLORANCE SENR.   BENJAMIN STONE
HEZEKIAH FAIRFAX   DANIEL TEBBS (land   JAMES FLORANCE   JOSIAH STONE JUNR.
HENRY WASHINGTON   lying in Fairfax)   JOSHUA CARNEY (living   JOHN CUNDIFF
SAMPSON WINDSOR   WILLIAM LYNN SENR   in Stafford, Land this Co.   THOMAS BREWER
JOHN WILLIAMS   RICHD. ROBINSON (took Oath)   EDWARD COE (took Oath.   RICHARD SHIRLEY
JAMES JAMES   HEBRON RALLS   land in Loudoun, Resident P.W.   GEORGE SHIRLEY
JOSEPH BOTTS   STEPHEN FRENCH   JAMES WYATT
BURR PEYTON   JOHN STOCK   JAMES JAMES, Clerk
PRESLEY JEWELL   ISAAC FARROW   A COPY Teste GEO: LANE, D.S. for
GEORGE WEAVER   MICHAEL LYNN   THOMAS HARRISON
COLIN CAMPBELL   JAMES GWATKINS
GEORGE BARKER   JAMES GRIGSBY   All those refused to swear
GEORGE LANE   MOSES JEFFRIES   for RICHARD B. LEE   for RICHD. BRENT
GEORGE GRAY TYLER   OBED. CALVERT SENR.   ANTHONY GRAY   ELIJAH GREEN
DAVID BLACKWELL   JOHN HEDGES MINOR   ROBERT COLE   JOHN JACKSON
WILLIAM TYLER   HOWSON HOOE SENR.   JOHN F. CARTER   FRANCIS CALVERT
THOMAS ATTWELL (took Oath)   JOHN WOODYARD
WILLIAM CUNDIFF   JOHN BIGGS   JAMES JAMES, Clerk
CHARLES TYLER   HOWSON HOOE JUNR.
JOSHUA FOSTER   WILLIAM TEBBS

   At a Court contd. and held for Prince William County the 5th day of May 1795
This Poll for the Election of a Member of Congress was ordered to be recorded
      Teste JOHN WILLIAMS, Cl Cur

pp.   A Poll taken at Prince William County Court House on Monday 6th day of April
541-   1795 for the Election of Two members to the House of Representatives of the
546   State of Virginia to represent the said County in the ensuing session of Assembly
                CANDIDATES

JOHN POPE	THOMAS LEE	EDMUND BROOKE
Voters names	Voters names	Voters names
WILLIAM McDANIEL	WILLIAM McDANIEL	WILLIAM BARNES
JOHN LAWSON	JOHN LAWSON	MOSES DAVIS
MOSES DAVIS	WILLIAM BARNES	HENRY TYLER
ALEXANDER LITHGOW	ALEXANDER LITHGOW	CARR BAILEY SENR.,
HENRY TYLER	CARR BAYLEY SENR.	RICHARD M. SCOTT
WILLIAM COPIN JUNR.	WILLIAM COPIN JUNR.	CHARLES MODISETT
CHARLES MODISETT	RICHARD M. SCOTT	NATHANIEL GRIEVES

JOHN POPE	THOMAS LEE	EDMUND BROOKE
ALEXANDER HUME	NATHANIEL GRIEVES	LUKE CANNON
BENJAMIN WHEELER	LUKE CANNON	ROBERT LUTTRELL
WILLIAM FITZHUGH	ALEXANDER HUME	BENJAMIN WHEELER
SAMPSON WINDSOR	ROBERT LUTTRELL	SAMPSON WINDSOR
WILLIAM BAILIS	WILLIAM FITZHUGH	WILLIAM BAILY
ALEXANDER HENDERSON	ALEXANDER HENDERSON	JOHN HOOE
JESSE CORNWELL	JOHN HOOE	WILLIAM BROWN
WILLIAM BROWN	JESSE CORNWELL	ANTHONY BUCKNER
WILLIAM JACKSON	WILLIAM JACKSON	DANIEL LEDSOM
ANTHONY BUCKNER	THOMAS DAVIS SENR.	RICHARD WROE
DANIEL LEDSOM	JAMES NOLAND	BERNARD HOOE SENR.
RICHARD WROE	BENSON DAVIS	BENJAMIN GRIGSBY
THOMAS DAVIS SENR.	BERNARD HOOE SENR.	ALEXANDER CLEVELAND
JAMES NOLAND	JARRARD ALEXANDER	JARRARD ALEXANDER
( )NSON DAVIS	WILLIAM DAVIS (Son of Isaac)	WILLIAM RAGAN
BENJAMIN GRIGSBY	JOHN DYE SENR.	JOHN DYE SENR.
WILLIAM REAGAN	JAMES SMITH	DANIEL DAUGHERTY
WM. DAVIS (son of Isaac)	DANIEL DAUGHERTY	THOMAS BLACKBURN
JAMES SMITH	JOHN SULLIVAN	PETER TRONE
THOMAS BLACKBURN	LEONARD LEACHMAN	LEONARD BRASFIELD
PETER TROANE	BENJAMIN WIGGINTON	GEORGE FLORANCE SR.
LEONARD BRASFIELD	JOHN MATTHEWS	THOMAS NEWMAN
GEORGE FLORANCE SENR.	SAMUEL FIELDER	JAMES NEWMAN
JOHN SULLIVAN	BERNARD HOOE JUNR.	BERNARD HOOE JUNR.
LEONARD LEACHMAN	HOWSON HOOE SENR.	ROBERT GRAHAM
BENJAMIN WIGGINTON	ROBERT GRAHAM	JOHN BAILIS
JOHN MATTHEWS	JOHN THORN	JOHN BIGGS
THOMAS NEWMAN	THOMAS OLIVER	GEORGE LATHAM
SAMUEL FIELDER	JAMES REID	JAMES DENEALE
JAMES NEWMAN	JAMES DENEALE	HENRY SILKMAN
JOHN THORN	HENRY TURNBULL	JAMES McINTOSH
JOHN BAILIS	HENRY SELECTMAN JUNR.	JOHN HEDGES
JOHN BIGGS	HOWSON HOOE JUNR.	THOMAS BREWER
GEORGE LATHAM	FRANCIS RENOE	JOSHUA REEVE
THOMAS OLIVER	SIMON LUTTRELL	WILLIAM HIXON
JAMES REID	BENJAMIN COOPER	JOHN SMITH
HENRY TURNBULL	WILLIAM HART	HOWSON HOOE JUNR.
JAMES McINTOSH	ZACHARIAH ALLEN SENR.	RUTT JOHNSTON
JOHN HEDGES JUNR.	THOMAS LEACHMAN	FRANCIS RENOE
THOMAS BREWER	THOMAS HART	SIMON LUTTRELL
JOSHUA REEVE	MOSES MOSS	JOHN McCORMICK
WILLIAM HIXON	LANGHORNE DADE	WILLIAM HART
JOHN SMITH	WALTER COOE	MARK THARP
RUTT JOHNSTON SENR.	TOWNSHEND DADE	BENJAMIN TYLER
JOHN McCORMICK	JOHN EDRINGTON	JAMES FLOURANCE
BENJAMIN COOPER	GEORGE RAINEY	WALTER COOE
MARK THARP	MOSES JEFFRIES	LANGHORNE DADE
ZACHARIAH ALLEN SENR.	PHILIP DAWE	MATTHEW WHITING
THOMAS LEACHMAN	JOHN GIBSON	WILLIAM HELM

JOHN POPE	THOMAS LEE	EDMOND BROOKE
THOMAS HART	WILLIAM FOSTER	TOWNSHEND DADE
BENJAMIN TYLER	ISAAC FARROW	RICHARD FOOTE SENR.
MOSES MOSS	JOHN DAVIS	JAMES TALIAFERRO
JAMES FLORANCE	JAMES FOSTER	JAMES KING
MATTHEW WHITING	JESSE EWELL SENR.	GEORGE RAINEY
WILLIAM HELM	FRANCIS G. DebBERNOUX	JOHN FRYER SENR.
RICHARD FOOTE SENR.	ALEXANDER BRUCE	SAMPSON LEACHMAN
JAMES TALIAFERRO	JOHN McMILLIAN	JOSHUA FOSTER
JAMES KING	JAMES EWELL SENR.	SAMUEL KING
JOHN EDRINGTON	WILLIAM WRIGHT	RICHARD SHIRLEY
SAMPSON LEACHMAN	GEORGE HUBER	GEORGE SHIRLEY
JOSHUA FOSTER	BENJAMIN THOMAS	JAMES GRINSTEAD
THOMAS NEWMAN	JOHN T. FITZHUGH	FRANCIS MONTGOMERIE
MOSES JEFFRIES	JESSE BARRON	PETER LAMPKIN
PHILIP DAUGH	JOHN THOMAS	WILLIAM COPIN SENR.
JOHN GIBSON	PETER COCKRELL	BENJAMIN WROE
SAMUEL KING	FRANCIS CANNON	BENJAMIN STONE
JOHN GRINSTEAD	THOMAS CAVES	STEPHEN FRENCH
RICHARD SHIRLEY	MOORE HOFF	JOSIAS STONE
GEORGE SHIRLEY	STEPHEN HOWISON	THOMAS BIRD
WILLIAM FOSTER	JOHN CANNON	SAMUEL THOMAS
JAMES GRINSTEAD	HENRY DADE HOOE	GEORGE FLORANCE
FRANCIS MONTGOMERIE	WILLIAM DAVIS	ALEXANDER BRUCE
PETER LAMPKIN	WILLIAM ATTWELL	JOHN McMILLIAN
ISAAC FARROW	BASIL BRAWNER	WILLIAM MARTIN
WILLIAM COPIN SENR.	WILLIAM GRANT SENR.	WILLIAM FAIRFAX
BENJAMIN WROE	OBED CALVERT SENR.	WILLIAM KING
BENJAMIN STONE	OBED. CALVERT JUNR.	ROBERT SPITTLE
STEPHEN FRENCH	JAMES PEAKE	ZACHARIAH BRASFIELD
JOSIAH STONE	JAMES FOLEY	JOSIAH STONE SENR.
THOMAS BIRD	JAMES JAMES	JOHN STEEL
JOHN DAVIS	THOMAS HARRIS	JOHN MILLS
JAMES FOSTER	HUMPHREY CALVERT SENR.	BENJAMIN THOMAS
SAMUEL THOMPSON	WILLIAM TEBBS	WILLIAM JAMESON
GEORGE FLORANCE JUNR.	JOSEPH STEPHENS	WILLIAM CUNDIFF
JESSE EWELL SENR.	COLIN CAMPBELL	LOFTUS NOEL
FRANCIS G. DeBERNOUX	RICHARD ROBERTSON	WILLIAM KEES
JAMES EWELL SENR.	THOMAS DOWDALL	STEPHEN HOWISON
WILLIAM MARTIN JUNR.	JOHN KINCHELOE	HENRY THORNBERRY
WILLIAM FAIRFAX	ENOCH RENOE	ALEXANDER SCOTT
WILLIAM KING	CHARLES EWELL	HENRY D. HOOE
ROBERT SPITTLE	SENETT DUVALL	MOSES WICKLIFFE
ZACHARIAH BRADFIELD	JOHN WATERS SENR.	HEZEKIAH FAIRFAX
JOSIAH STONE SENR.	CHARLES ADAMS	BURR PEYTON
WILLIAM WRITE	THOMAS HOOMES SENR.	FRANCIS CORNWELL
JOHN WRITE	BENJAMIN BURROUGHS	CHARLES ATTWELL
GEORGE HUBER	SCARLETT MADDEN	JAMES WHITE
JOHN STEEL	MARK MANKIN	WILLIAM ATTWELL
JOHN MILLS	SAMUEL JACKSON	JOSEPH BRADY
WILLIAM JAMESON	BASIL KING	WILLIAM TACKETT

JOHN POPE

WILLIAM CUNDIFF
JOHN T. FITZHUGH
JESSE BARRON
LOFTUS NOWELL
WILLIAM KEYS JUNR.
JOHN THOMAS
PETER COCKRELL
FRANCIS CANNON
THOMAS CAVES
MOORE HOFF
HENRY THORNBERRY
JOHN CANNON
ALEXANDER SCOTT
MOSES WICKLIFFE
WILLIAM DAVIS
HEZEKIAH FAIRFAX
( )N PEYTON
FRANCIS CORNWELL
CHARLES ATTWELL
JAMES WHITE
JOSEPH BRADY
WILLIAM TACKETT
HEZEKIAH REEVES
WILLIAM ASHMORE
THOMAS THORNTON
JOHN BIGGS
GEORGE LATHAM
WILLIAM GRANT SENR.
JOHN WILKINSON
OBED CALVERT SENR.
OBED CALVERT JUNR.
JAMES PEAKE
JAMES FOLEY
JAMES JAMES
THOMAS HARRIS
WILLIAM KEYS (Younger)

GEORGE STONE

WILLIAM TEBBS
CHARLES CORNWELL
RICHARD ROBERTSON
JAMES WEBSTER
JOHN KINCHELOE
CHARLES PURCELL
CHARLES EWELL
JOSHUA CARNER
JOHN WATERS JUNR.
JOHN LOVE
JEREMIAH DOWELL
BENJAMIN BURRIS

THOMAS LEE

JAMES WEBSTER
CHARLES PURCELL
JAMES COCHRAN
ARRINGTON WICKLIFFE
BENJAMIN JAMESON
JOHN POPE
HENRY WASHINGTON
GEORGE LANE
WILLOUGHBY TEBBS

All the names following voted for JOHN POPE

SAMUEL JACKSON
JOSEPH STEPHENS
BASIL KING
WILLIAM ARNELL
JAMES BURK
WANSFORD ARRINGTON
ARRINGTON WICKLIFFE
WILLIAM PEARSON
BENJAMIN JAMESON
JOSEPH GILBERT
THOMAS HOOMES SENR.

EDMUND BROOKE

HEZEKIAH REEVES
WILLIAM ASHMORE
THOMAS THORNTON
JOHN BIGGS
GEORGE LATHAM
BASIL BRAWNER
JOHN WILKENSON
WILLIAM KEYS (Younger)
GEORGE STONE
HUMPHRY CALVERT SENR.
SNOWDEN HORTON
COLIN CAMPBELL
WILLIAM ATTWELL
JOHN FERGUSON
WANSFORD ARRINGTON
ENOCH RENOE
WILLIAM PEARSON
JOHN LOVE
JOHN HAMMITT
JOHN WOODYARD
JOHN LANGFITT
JOHN WILCOCKS
CHARLES CORNWELL
HEBRON RALLS
JAMES JAMESON
JAMES BURK
JOSHUA CARNEY
WILLIAM FARROW
JOSEPH GILBERT
JEREMIAH DOWELL
JESSE CALVERT SENR.
THOMAS LEE
JOHN POPE
NATHANIEL C. HUNTER
GEORGE WILLIAMS

SNOWDEN HORTON
HEBRON RALLS
THOMAS DOWDALL
JAMES JAMESON
JOHN FERGUSON
JAMES COCKREAN
SENETT DUVAL
WILLIAM FARROW
CHARLES ADAMS
JOHN HAMMITT
JESSE CALVERT SENR.

THOMAS LEE   WILLY: TEBBS
SCARLETT MADDEN   THOMAS NORMAN
HENRY WASHINGTON
JOHN WOODYARD   GEORGE LANE
GEORGE LANE   ALEXANDER CLEVELAND
MARK MANKIN   THOMAS NORMAN
NATHANIEL C. HUNTER
JOHN LANGFITT   This Poll was taken by GEO: LANE D. S. for
GEO: WILLIAMS   THOMAS HARRISON Sheriff
JOHN WILCOCKS

   At a Court held for Prince William County the 5th day of May 1795
This Poll for the Election of Representatives to the General Assembly of Virginia was
ordered to be recorded   Teste JOHN WILLIAMS Cl Cur

p.   WHEREAS WILLIAM HOLBOURNE formerly of the County of Prince William but
547   now of County of RICHMOND did by his certain Deed of Indenture bearing date
        the twenty first day of September in year of our Lord one thousand seven hun-
dred and Eighty five duly recorded in the Court of Prince William among other things
covenant and agree for himself his heirs to pay JOHN MACRAE party to these presents
his heirs the yearly rent of Thirty three pounds Fifteen shillings; Now this Indenture
made this Sixteenth day of October in year one thousand seven hundred and ninety
four between JOHN MACRAE of one part and WILLIAM HOLBOURNE of other part Witnesseth that JOHN MACRAE do by these presents release WILLIAM HOLBOURNE his heirs
from the payment of the said yearly rent; In Witness whereof, I have hereunto affixed
my hand & seal this Sixteenth dy of October in year of our Lord one thousand seven
hundred and ninety four
        WILLIAM SCOTT,   JNO: MACRAE
        JOHN G. HESLOP, TIMOTHY BRUNDIGE
   At a Court held for Prince William County the 1st day of June 1795
This Release from JOHN MACRAE to WILLIAM HOLBOURNE was proved by the Oaths of
WILLIAM SCOTT and TIMOTHY BRUNDIGE and acknowledged by the said MACRAE and
ordered to be recorded   Teste JOHN WILLIAMS, Cl Cur

p.   PURSUANT to an Order of the Worshipfull Court of Prince Wm. County bearing
548   date the 5th of April 1791, hereunto annexed, we the Subscribers have pro-
        ceeded to lay off the Dower of CHARLES THORNTONs Widow in the lands whereof
he died seized and the same having been surveyed we find one third part thereof contained in the lower end of the said tract of land by a Division Line begininning at a
Stone which lies 19 poles the corner of JAMES GREEN (formerly CARTERs) & in that line
running No. 65 Et. and running thence No. 34 Wt. 216 po. to the line of Capt. WM. TEBBS
to a white Oak 34 po: below his corner and CURTIS dower land, containing One hundred
and thirty seven acres which we do accordingly set apart for her said Dower, Given
under our hands this 19th day of December 1794   JA: EWELL
                                                        DAVID BLACKWELL
                                                        SAML: WATSON

   At a Court held for Prince William County the 6th day of July 1795
This Report of the alotment od Dower to the Widow of CHARLES THORNTON deced. was
areturned to the Court and ordered to be recorded
                        Teste JOHN WILLIAMS, Cl Cur

pp.   THIS INDENTURE made the 25th day of December in year of our Lord one thou-
548-   sand seven hundred and Eighty four Between THOMAS THORNTON, MARY ANN
556   his Wife, CHICHESTER CURTIS and LETTICE his Wife of County of Prince William
         of one part and ROBERT BROWN, Gentlemen, of said County of other part; Witnes-
seth that THOMAS THORNTON, MARY ANN his Wife, CHICHESTER CURTIS and LETTICE his
Wife for the sum of Five shillings current money of Virginia to them in hand paid by
ROBERT BROWN, do by these presents bargain and sell unto ROBERT BROWN all that tract
of land lying in Prince William County, Beginning at a Mulberry tree, corner to
MATTHEW MOSS deced., land and the said THORNTONs own land, thence No. 66d. Et. 29 po.
to a Birch by BROAD RUN, corner to HOLTZCLAWs new survey, thence along said line the
same course continued 230 poles to a white Oak on a barren Hill, Capt. JAMES TEBBS's
corner, thence along the said TEBBS line No. 21d. Wt. 103 poles to a white Oak on a
Stoney point, another of TEBBS's corners, thence leaving TEBBS line No. 85d. Wt. 258
poles to a heap of Stone in Captain THOMAS BLACKBURNs line, thence along said line
reversed So. 47d. 30 Wt. 39 poles to a Spanish Oak stump in the Fork of BROAD RUN, corner to the lands of Colo; CARTER & BLACKBURN, and the said THORNTONs own lands;
thence down BROAD RUN binding on Mr. THORNTONs other line So. 31d. 30m. Et. 56, po.,
So. 11 Et. 41 poles, So. 31d. Wt. 34 poles, thence to the beginning, containing Three hundred and one acres more or less together with one other tract of land on West side of
BROAD RUN beginning at the butment of THORNTONS MILL DAM, running thence to
where the STONEY BRANCH intersects CHARLES THORNTONs line, thence Easterly with
the said land to the Mulberry tree, the beginning of the other tract, thence to the
beginning, containing Ten acres more or less; And all houses orchards profits and
appurtenances belonging; To have and to hold the land and premises unto ROBERT
BROWN his heirs, during the full term of one whole year paying therefore the rent of
one pepper corn if demanded to the intent that by virtue of these presents and of the
Statute for transferring uses into possession said ROBERT BROWN may be in actual possession of the premises and may thereby be enabled to accept a release of the reversion & inheritance thereof; In Witness whereof the said THOMAS THORNTON, MARY
ANN his Wife, CHICHESTER CURTIS and LETTICE his Wife have hereunto set their hands
and affixed their seals the day and year first above written
Sealed and Delivered in the presence of

HENRY HOPE,	THOMAS THORNTON
CHARLES TYLER,	MARY ANN her mark (THORNTON
JOHN BROWN	CHICHESTER CURTIS
ANTHONY BUCKNER, SEIERS HAMRICK	LETTICE CURTIS

At a Court held for Prince William County the 7th day of May 1785
This Lease and the receipt thereon endorsed from THOMAS THORNTON, MARY ANN his
Wife and CHICHESTER CURTIS and LETTICE his Wife to ROBERT BROWN was proved by the
Oath of CHARLES TYLER and ordered to be Certified; And at a Court held for the said
County the 6th day of October 1794, the said Deed and Receipt were proved by the Oath of
HENRY HOPE and further certified; Teste ROBERT GRAHAM, Cl Cur
   At a Court held for the said County the 6th day of July 1795
The said Lease and Receipt were fully proved by the Oath of ANTHONY BUCKNER and
were together with the Dedimus for the privy examinations of the femes returned
executed and ordered to be recorded Teste JOHN WILLIAMS, Cl Cur

       THIS INDENTURE made this 27th day of December in year of our Lord one thou-
sand seven hundred and Eighty four Between THOMAS THORNTON and his Wife, MARY
ANN, CHICHESTER CURTIS and his Wife, LETTICE, of County of Prince William of one part
and ROBERT BROWN Gentleman of the same County of other part; Witnesseth that said

THOMAS THORNTON and MARY ANN his Wife and CHICHESTER CURTIS and LETTICE his
Wife for the sum of Four hundred fifty pounds current money of Virginia to them in
hand paid by ROBERT BROWN, by these presents do bargain sell release and confirm
unto ROBERT BROWN (in his actual possession now being by virtue of a bargain and sale
to him thereof made for one whole year and by force of the Statute for transferring
uses into possession, and his heirs (the two tracts of land as in the foregoing Lease are
described as in the Lease); To have and to hold the premises unto ROBERT BROWN his heirs
free and clear from all incumbrances whatsoever; And THOMAS THORNTON and MARY
ANN his Wife and CHICHESTER CURTIS and LETTICE his Wife their heirs will warrant and
forever defend by these presents; In Witness whereof (they) have hereunto set their
hands and affixed their seals the day and year first within written
Sealed & Delivered in presence of
          HENRY HOPE,   T. THORNTON
          CHARLES TYLER,   MARY ANN her mark (THORNTON
          JOHN BROWN, ANTHONY BUCKNER,   CHICHESTER CURTIS
          SEIERS HAMRICK   LETTICE CURTIS
   The Commonwealth of Virginia to WILLIAM EDWD. WYATT, ALEXANDER BROWN and
JOHN TYLER, Gentlemen, Greeting, Whereas (the Commission for the privy Examinations of
MARY ANN, the Wife of THOMAS THORNTON and LETTICE the Wife of CHICHESTER CURTIS); Witness
ROBERT GRAHAM Clerk of our said Court at the Courthouse the 27th day of December
1784   ROBERT GRAHAM
   Prince William County to wit; By virtue of the within dedimus to us directed, we the
subscribers went to the within named LETTICE CURTIS and MARY ANN THORNTON and
examined them seperately from their Husbands (the return of the execution of the privy
examination of MARY ANN THORNTON and LETTICE CURTIS); As Witness our hands and seals
this Twenty eighth day of December one thousand seven hundred & Eighty four
                              WM. E. WYATT
                              ALEXR. BROWN
   At a Court held for Prince William County the 7th day of March 1785
This Release and the Receipt thereon endorsed from THOMAS THORNTON and MARY ANN
his Wife and CHICHESTER CURTIS and LETTICE his Wife to ROBERT BROWN were proved
by the Oath of CHARLES TYLER & ordered to be certified; And at a Court held for said
County the 6th day of October 1794, the Deed and Receipt were proved by the Oath of
HENRY HOPE and further certified;   Teste ROBERT GRAHAM, Cl Cur
   At a Court held for said County the 6th day of July 1795
This said Deed and Receipt were fully proved by the Oath of ANTHONY BUCKNER and together with the Dedimus for the privy examination of the femes returned executed,
ordered to be recorded   Teste JOHN WILLIAMS, Cl Cur

pp.   TO ALL TO WHOM these presents shall come, SPENCE GRAYSON of County of
556-   Prince William sendeth Greeting. Know ye that I SPENCE GRAYSON in consider-
557   ation of the natural love and affection which I have and bear unto my Daughter
          SUSANNA WASHINGTON as also for divers other good causes me at this time es-
pecially moving, by these presents do give & confirm unto LUND WASHINGTON JUNR.
the Husband of said SUSANNA, his heirs the following Negro slaves, to wit, Aggey & Ben
and the future increase of Aggey, To have & to hold the Negro slaves with the future
increase of Aggey unto LUND WASHINGTON his heirs without any manner of challenge
of me said SPENCE GRAYSON or any other person; In Testimony whereof I have hereunto set my hand and affixed my seal this second day of March 1795

Sealed and Delivered in presence of
    HENRY LEE, WILLIAM HUSKINS,   SPENCE GRAYSON
    WILLIAM LINDSAY
  At a Court held for Prince William County the 6th day of July 1795
This Deed of Gift from SPENCE GRAYSON to LUND WASHINGTON JUNR. was proved by the
Oath of WILLIAM HUSKINS and ordered to be recorded
            Teste JOHN WILLIAMS, Cl Cur

pp.   TO ALL TO WHOM these presents sahll come, SPENCE GRAYSON of County of
557-   Prince William sendeth Greeting; Know ye that I said SPENCE GRAYSON as well
558   for the natural love and affection which I have and do bear unto my Daughter,
     MARY DERMOTT, as also for divers other good causes and consideration me at this
time especially moving, by these presents do give and confirm unto JAMES R. DERMOTT
(the Husband of said MARY) his heirs the following Negro slaves, to wit, Clara and her
two Children, Sarah & Alice, and their future increase; To have & to hold the said Negro
slaves together with their future increase unto said JAMES his heirs, without any
matter of challenge of me said SPENCE GRAYSON; In Witness whereof I have hereunto
set my hand and affixed my Seal the second day of March seventeen hundred & ninety
five
Sealed & Delivered in presence of
    HENRY LEE, WILLIAM HUSKINS,   SPENCE GRAYSON
    WILLIAM LINDSAY
  At a Court held for Prince William County the 6th day of July 1795
This Deed of Gift from SPENCE GRAYSON to JAME R. DERMOTT was proved by the Oath of
WILLIAM HUSKINS & ordered to be recorded
            Teste JOHN WILLIAMS, Cl Cur

pp.   THIS INDENTURE made this third day of January in year of our Lord one thou-
558-   sand seven hundred and ninety five Between GEORGE GRAY TYLER of one part
561   and THOMAS COLLIS and THEODOSHE his Wife of other part; Witnesseth that
     GEORGE GRAY TYLER in consideration of the Rents and Covenants herein after
reserved on part of said THOMAS COLLIS and wife to be paid and performed, by these
presents doth demise and to farm let unto THOMAS COLLIS Three hundred and fifty acres
of land with the appurtenances except one fourth of an acre reserved by GEORGE GRAY
TYLER in wood never to be cut down or cultivated, lying in County of Prince William on
the BROAD RUN, part of a tract of land of the Revd. ISAAC CAMPBELL deced., and
bounded Beginning at a Hickory and a red Oak on BROAD RUN, thence No. 20 1/4 East 385
poles to a Stake in the dividing line, thence No. 66 1/2 Wt. 113 poles to a red Oak and
Spanish Oak in CARTERs line, thence with CARTERs line So. 35 1/2 Wt. 330 poles to a
marked Locus and Ash on BROAD RUN, thence down the Run and binding therewith to
the first station; including Three hundred and fifty acres; To have and to hold the said
premises except as before excepted unto THOAMS COLLIS and THEODOSHE his Wife during
their natural lives, paying yearly to GEORGE GRAY TYLER his heirs the sum of Thirty
pounds specie, together with the Taxes of the demised premises; the first of which pay-
ments to commence the first day of January next; In Witness whereof the said GEORGE
TYLER and said THOMAS COLLIS and THODOSHE his Wife have interchangeably set their
hands and seals the day and year above written
Signed Sealed & Delivered in the presence of
    CHARLES his mark + OWENS,   _GEORGE GRAY TYLER
    REUBEN SHURLEY,   THOS: COLLIS
    GEORGE his mark X SHURLEY

At a Court held for Prince William County the 6th day of July 1795
This Lease for Lives was acknowledged by the parties thereto to be their act and deed
and ordered to be recorded   Teste JOHN WILLIAMS, Cl Cur

pp.   THIS INDENTURE made this Twenty first day of March in year of our Lord one
561-   thousand seven hundred and ninety five Between WALTER GRAHAM and SALLEY
564   his Wife, late of the County of Prince William, of one part, and JOHN WILLIAMS
         of the County aforesaid of other part; Witnesseth that WALTER GRAHAM and
SALLEY his Wife for the sum of Forty pounds current money to them in hand paid by
JOHN WILLIAMS, by these presents do bargain and sell unto JOHN WILLIAMS his heirs a
certain lott or half acre of land in the Town of DUMFRIES, Number Seventy, which lot
hereby conveyed was sold to WALTER GRAHAM together with three others by a certain
ELIAS EDMONDS as will appear by certain Deeds of Lease and Release dated the 25th &
26th days of August 1788 duly recorded in or among the Records of the aforesaid County,
and a part thereof Leased to a certain PETER MILLER for the annual rent of Four pounds
current money, as will appear by the Lease dated the third day of September one thousand seven hundred and ninety one; also duly recorded among the Records of the aforesaid County; And all houses orchards profits and appurtenances to the same in any wise
appurtaining; And WALTER GRAHAM and SALLY his Wife and their heirs do by these
presents warrant and defend the tract of land against the claim of all persons; In Witness whereof the said WALTER GRAHAM and SALLEY his Wife have hereunto set their
hands and affixed their seals the day and year first within written
Sealed and Delivered in presence of
         WM. SMITH, WM. ATTWELL,   WALTER   GRAHAM
         GEO: TEBBS, WM. BEALE JR.,   SALLEY   GRAHAM
         JAMES JOHNSTON (Witness to WALTER GRAHAM)
         LANGH. DADE
   The Commonwealth of Virginia to JOSEPH BLACKWELL, JOHN JAMES & THOS: HELM.
Gentlemen, Greeting, Whereas (the Commission for the privy Examination of SALLEY, the Wife
of WALTER GRAHAM); Witness ROBERT GRAHAM Clerk of our said Court the 23rd day of
March 1795, & in the 19th year of the Commonwealth   ROBT. GRAHAM
   FAUQUIER County to wit; We JOSEPH BLACKWELL and JOHN JAMES in obedience to the
within, we the Subscribers have caused to come before us the within named SALLEY
GRAHAM and examined her privily (the return of the execution of the privy Examination of
SALLEY GRAHAM); Given under our hands and Seals this 15th day of August 1795
                              JOSEPH BLACKWELL
                              JOHN JAMES
   At a Court held for Prince William County the 7th day of September 1795
This Deed from WALTER GRAHAM and SALLEY his Wife to JOHN WILLIAMS (a Dedimus
for the examination of the feme returned executed) was proved by the Oath of LANG-
HORNE DADE, WILLIAM BEALE JUNR. and WILLIAM ATTWELL and ordered to be recorded
                    Teste JOHN WILLIAMS, Cl Cur

pp.   (On margin: Examd. & deld. Apl. 27, 1797, N. COX).
564-   THIS INDENTURE made this Twentieth day of March in year of our Lord one
566   thousand seven hundred and ninety five Between WALTER GRAHAM and SALLEY
         his Wife, late of County of Prince William of one part and JAMES MITCHELL of
County of STAFFORD of other part; Witnesseth that WALTER GRAHAM and SALLEY his
Wife for the sum of One hundred and fifty pounds current money to them in hand paid
by JAMES MITCHELL, by these presents do bargain and sell unto JAMES MITCHELL his
heirs a certain lott or half acre of land lying in Town of DUMFRIES and County afore-

said and laid down in a plan of the Town by the number Sixty Four, which said lott
hereby conveyed was sold to WALTER GRAHAM together with three others by a certain
ELIAS EDMONDS as will more fully apear by certain Deeds of Lease and Release bearing
date the 25th and 26th days of August one thousand seven hundred & Eighty eight and
duly recorded among the Records of aforesaid County, And all houses orchards, profits
and appurtenances to the same in any wise appurtaining; To have and to hold the tract
of land with its appurtenances unto JAMES MITCHELL his heirs, And WALTER GRAHAM
and SALLEY his Wife and their heirs do by these presents warrant and defend the lott of
land unto JAMES MITCHELL against the claim of any person; In Witness whereof the
said WALTER GRAHAM and SALLEY his Wife have hereunto set their hands and seals the
day and year first within written
Sealed and Delivered in the presence of
      NATHL. C. HUNTER, GEORGE LANE,   WALTER GRAHAM
      GEO: WILLIAMS, JOHN WILLIAMS,   SALLEY GRAHAM
      JOHN FRISTOE
   The Commonwealth of Virginia to JOSEPH BLACKWELL and JOHN JAMES Gentlemen,
Greeting, Whereas (the Commission for the privy Examination of SALLEY, the Wife of WALTER
GRAHAM); Witness ROBERT GRAHAM, Clerk of our said Court this 21st day of March 1795
and in the 19th year of the Commonwealth   ROBT. GRAHAM
   FAUQUIER County to wit, We JOSEPH BLACKWELL and JOHN JAMES in obedience to the
within, we the subscribers have caused to come before us the within named SALLEY
GRAHAM and examined her privily (the return of the execution of the privy Examination of
SALLEY GRAHAM); Given under our hands and seals this 15th day of August 1795
                       JAS: BLACKWELL
                       JNO: JAMES
   At a Court held for Prince William County the 7th day of September 1795
This Deed with the receipt thereon from WALTER GRAHAM and SALLEY his Wife to
JAMES MITCHELL (a Dedimus for the privy examination of the feme being returned
executed) were proved by the Oaths of JOHN WILLIAMS, JOHN FRISTOE and GEORGE LANE
and ordered to be recorded   Teste JOHN WILLIAMS, Cl Cur

pp.   KNOW ALL MEN by these presents that I YELVERTON PEYTON of County of
567-   FREDERICK in Commonwealth of Virginia for the sum of Thirty pounds current
568   money of Virginia to me in hand paid by JAMES MITCHELL of Town of DUMFRIES
        by these presents do release and discharge the said JAMES MITCHELL and assigns
from all right title and demand in Law or Equity which I have unto a certain Lott in
Town of DUMFRIES and County of Prince William conveyed to JAMES MITCHELL by
WALTER GRAHAM on the Twentieth day of last March and which is the same Lott the
said WALTER GRAHAM Mortgaged to me on the 12th day of July one thousand seven
hundred and ninety two for securing the payment of Twenty seven pounds, Eight Shillings with legal Interest thereon from the 12th day of July 1792 which said lott is
known by the number Sixty Four; To have and to hold the lott to said MITCHELL his
heirs against the claim of me ye sd. YELVERTON PEYTON my heirs; In Witness whereof I
have hereunto set my hand and affixed my seal the thirteenth day of May in year of
our Lord one thouand seven hundred & ninety five
Sealed & Delivered in presence of
      JOHN WILLIAMS, WM. ATTWELL,   Y: PEYTON
      JOHN GIBSON, JOHN OVERALL,
      MUNGO HANCOCK
   At a Court held for Prince William County the 7th day of Septr. 1795
This Deed from YELVERTON PEYTON to JAMES MITCHELL was proved by the Oaths of

JOHN GIBSON, WILLIAM ATTWELL and JOHN WILLIAMS and ordered to be recorded
Teste JOHN WILLIAMS, Cl Cur

pp   THIS INDENTURE made this 27th day of March in year of our Lord one thousand
568-   seven hundred & ninety five Between DANIEL DAUGHERTY and BARBARA
570   DAUGHERTY his Wife of County of Prince William of one part and JOHN FISHER
            of same County of other part; Witnesseth that DANIEL DAUGHERTY and BAR-
BARA his Wife for the sum of One hundred and Eighty three pounds, Five shillings current money to them in hand paid by JOHN FISHER, by these presents do bargain sell and
confirm unto JOHN FISHER his heirs all that tract of land lying in County of aforesaid
on OCAQUAN RIVER which is bounded, Beginning at A., two Sycamores on South side of
OCAQUAN RIVER, corner to the land sold by HENRY LEE Esqr. to JOSEPH KIRKBRIDE and
ISAAC McPHERSON, thence the several courses and meanders of the said River and
binding therewith to B., a Branch emptying into the River OCAQUAN between a Chesnut Oak and Poplar marked as a Corner, thence up the Branch Wt. 93 1/2 poles to C.,
near a small white Oak, black Oak and two Pines on South side of a Branch, thence down
said Branch So. 88d. Et. 67 po: to D., a pile of Rocks near a black Oak white Oak and
Hickory on North side of the Branch, thence still down the said Branch some distance S.
58d. Et. 96 poles to E., a Chesnut Oak on North side of WHORES CREEK, then down the
meanders of said Creek and binding therewith to F. the intersection of KIRKBRIDE and
McPHERSONs line, thence with their line No. 23d. Wt. 16 po., to the beginning, including
Eighty three acres and one quarter of an acre being part of a tract of land containing
One hundred and fifty six acres conveyed by HENRY LEE Esqr. to said DANIEL DAUGHER-
TY by Deed recorded in County Court of Prince William on second day of February one
thousand seven hundred and ninety five; And all houses orchards profits and appurte-
nances to the same in any wise appurtaining: To have and to hold the tract of land unto
JOHN FISHER his heirs; And DANIEL DAUGHERTY and BARBARA his Wife and their heirs
do by these presents warrant the tract of land unto JOHN FISHER against the claim of
every person; In Witness whereof the said DANIEL DAUGHERTY and BARBARA his Wife
have hereunto set their hands and affixed their seals the day and year first written
Sealed & Delivered in presence of
        AMOS FISHER,   DANIEL DAUGHERTY
        THOMAS FISHER, WILLIAM TALBUTT   BARABRA her mark ✝ DAUGHERTY
    At a Court held for Prince William County the 7th day of September 1795
This Deed and the Receipt thereon from DANIEL DAUGHERTY and BARBARA his Wife to
JOHN FISHER (the feme being first privily examined and consenting thereto) were
acknowledged by the said DANIEL and BARBARA and ordered to be recorded
                    Teste JOHN WILLIAMS Cl Cur

pp.   (On margin: Examd. & Delivered the 22nd day of Feby. 1796 to Mr. ABRAM
570-   HEWES, J. WILLIAMS)
575   THIS INDENTURE made this 10th day of April in year of our Lord one thousand
            seven hundred and ninety five Between ISAAC McPHERSON of Town of ALEXAN-
DRIA in State of Virginia of one part and JOSEPH KIRKBRIDE of CITY of PHILADELPHIA
in the State of PENNSYLVANIA of other part; Whereas ISAAC McPHERSON in and by
several obligations or writings obligatory bearing date respectively the Twenty
seventh day of August one thousand seven hundred and ninety four stands bound unto
JOSEPH KIRKBRIDE by one of them in the sum of Twelve hundred and Thirty three
pounds, Six shillings and Eight pence gold and silver money as the same is now current
in Virginia, conditioned for the payment of Six hundred and Sixteen pounds, thirteen
shillings and four pence gold and silver money on or before the first day of December

one thousand seven hundred & ninety five; together with lawful Interest for the same in the like coin; And by by one of the Writings Obligatory in the further sum of Twelve and Thirty three pounds, Six shillings and eight pence money as aforesaid; conditioned for the payment of Six hundred and Sixteen pounds Thirteen shillings and four pence on or before the first day of May in year one thousand seven hundred and Ninety seven; together with lawful Interest in like coin, And by the other Writing Obligatory in the further sum of Ten hundred and Fifty three pounds Six shillings and eight pence gold and silver money as aforesaid, conditioned for the payment of Five hundred & twenty six pounds, thirteen shillings and four pence gold and silver money aforesaid; on or before the first day of May one thousand seven hundred and ninety eight together with lawful Interest for the same in like coin without any fraud or further delay upon the back of each of which several Writings Obligatory was endorsed and duly acknowledged a covenant that if ISAAC McPHERSON his heirs should pay unto JOSEPH KIRKBRIDE or assigns the sum of money by said Writings Obligatory conditioned to be paid upon the day therein stipulated; This Indenture witnesseth that ISAAC McPHERSON as well for the aforesaid Debts and for securing the payment thereof unto JOSEPH KIRKBRIDE by these presents doth bargain sell and confirm unto JOSEPH KIRKBRIDE his heirs an equal moiety of a tract of land lying upon South side of OCAQUAN RIVER in County of Prince William containing Two hundred and fifty acres (being the same premises which said JOSEPH KIRKBRIDE and MARY his Wife by Indenture bearing date the ninth day of April one thousand seven hundred and ninety five granted unto said ISAAC McPHERSON his heirs together with one equal undivided moiety of all Mills, Mill Houses, Buildings and other Improvements upon the said Tract of land; To have and to hold unto JOSEPH KIRKBRIDE his heirs, Provided always that if ISAAC McPHERSON his heirs shall pay unto JOSEPH KIRKBRIDE and assigns the aforesaid several sums of money amounting to One thousand seven hundred and sixty pounds Virginia currency at the times appointed for payment thereof the said Writings Obligatory shall cease and determine and become void; In Witness whereof the parties have hereunto set their hands and seals the day and year first within mentioned
Sealed & Delivered in presence of

ABRAM HEWES, EDWARD FENWICK,   ISAAC McPHERSON
GEO: GRAHAM, JAMES DENEALE,   JOSEPH KIRKBRIDE
DAVID W. SCOTT, JAMES REID

At a Court held for Prince William County the 7th day of September 1795 This Deed of Mortgage from ISAAC McPHERSON to JOSEPH KIRKBRIDE was acknowledged by the said ISAAC McPHERSON and togehter with the Mayor of PHILADELPHIA's Certificate respecting the acknowledgement of JOSEPH KIRKBRIDE were ordered to be recorded   Teste JOHN WILLIAMS Cl Cur

pp.   (On margin: Examined and Delivered March 17th 1796, J. WILLIAMS)
576-   THIS INDENTURE made this ninth day of May in year of our Lord one thousand
579   seven hundred and ninety five Between ISAAC McPHERSON of Town of ALEXAN-
        DRIA and County of FAIRFAX of one part and NATHANIEL ELLICOTT of County of
Prince William of other part; Whereas HENRY LEE by his Indenture bearing date the Twenty ninth day of January one thousand seven hundred and ninety three for the consideration therein mentioned did bargain sell and confirm unto ISAAC McPHERSON and a certain JOSEPH KIRKBRIDE their heirs a tract of land lying on South side of OCCA-QUAN RIVER and bounded, Beginning at an old red marked Oak on South side of OCCA-QUAN RIVER a corner of the tract of land known by the name of the FURNACE TRACT, thence along the line of said FURNACE TRACT South eleven degrees West one hundred and seventy five poles to a Poplar by a Branch, another corner of said Tract, thence

South sixty five degrees West seventy poles to the back line of another Tract of land known by the name of PEYTONs TRACT, thence with the line of PEYTONs TRACT No. 23d. West (passing the corner of said Tract) and continuing the same course through another tract of land called EWELLs TRACT and through part of another Tract called CARTERs TRACT, four hundred and thirty five poles to OCAQUAN RIVER, at the mouth of HOOES CREEK, thence with a line at right angles with the last mentioned line crossing the River to the North side, thence down said River with the several course and meanders thereof and binding therewith until it shall reach that part of said River which is opposite the old red Oak the beginning Corner Boundary of said tract of land, thence across the River to the place of beginning; containing Two hundred and Fifty acres and all the houses and improvements thereupon made, And whereas JOSEPH KIRKBRIDE and his Wife for the consideration therein mentioned did sell unto ISAAC McPHERSON his heirs one equal undivided moiety of said tract of land Mills, Mill Houses buildings and improvements and Whereas ISAAC McPHERSON did sell unto a certain DANIEL DAUGHERTY his heirs two acres of the aforesaid tract of land which two acres of land are in the last mentioned Indenture distinctly described; Now This Indenture Witnesseth that ISAAC McPHERSON in consideration of the sum of Five thousand Two hundred pounds current money of Virginia to him in hand paid by NATHANIEL ELLICOTT by these presents doth bargain sell and confirm unto NATHANIEL ELLICOTT his heirs one equal undivided moiety of the aforesaid tract of land conveyed by HENRY LEE unto said ISAAC McPHERSON and JOSEPH KIRKBRIDE their heirs after deducting therefrom the two acres of land conveyed unto DANIEL DAUGHERTY, To have and to hold the premises unto NATHANIEL ELLICOTT his heirs free and clear from all incumbrances whatsoever; And ISAAC McPHERSON and his heirs shall warrant and forever defend by these presents; In Witness whereof the said parties have hereunto set their hands and seals the day and year first before mentioned
Sealed & Delivered in presence of
    JAS: KEITH,   GEO: GRAHAM,   ISAAC McPHERSON
    EDWARD FENWICK,   ESME SMOCK,
    HANSON RENO,   CHARLES TYLER JR.,
    JAMES MUSCHETT, JOHN M. MUSCHETT
  At a Court held for Prince William County the seventh day of Septr: one thousand seven hundred and ninety five   This Deed and the receipt thereon endorsed from ISAAC McPHERSON to NATHANIEL ELLICOTT were acknowledged by said ISAAC McPHERSON to be his acts and deeds and ordered to be recorded
                Teste JOHN WILLIAMS, Cl Cur

pp.   (On margin: Examined & deld. 29th Octr. 1796; J. WILLIAMS)
580-   THIS INDENTURE made and entered into this fourth day of September in year
581   of our Lord one thousand seven hundred and ninety five Between JOHN GRIN-
        STEAD and ANN his Wife of County of Prince William of one part and JAMES GRINSTEAD SENR. of County aforesaid of other part; Witnesseth that JOHN GRINSTEAD and ANN his Wife for the sum of One hundred and Ten pounds current money of Virginia to them in hand paid by JAMES GRINSTEAD SENR., do by these presents bargain sell and confirm unto JAMES GRINSTEAD SENR. his heirs a certain tract of land in Prince William County, the same which said JAMES GRINSTEAD by a Deed of Gift bearing date the 11th day of May 1793 had conveyed to said JOHN GRINSTEAD; Beginning at a white Oak Stump and Rock Stone in the North side of QUANTICO RUN and running No. 60d. Et. 118 poles to a corner, thence No. 27d. W. 134 poles, thence So. 88 Wt. 83 poles to a Turkey Oak and box Oak hear the head of the Branch, thence So. 12d. Wt. 116 poles down said Branch, thence So. 43d. Wt. 30 poles still keeping down the meanders of said Branch

to the Run, thence down the Run So. 35d. Et. 6 poles, So. 57d. Et. 24 poles, thence leaving
the said Run and running So. 72 Et. 22 poles, No. 80 Et. 48 poles to some marked bushes
then unto the beginning, Also all houses profits with the appurtenances; To have and
to hold unto JAMES GRINSTEAD SENR. his heirs, And JOHN GRINSTEAD and ANN his Wife
& their heirs doth warrant forever defend the premises unto JAMES GRINSTEAD SENR.
his heirs against all claims of any person; In Witness whereof the said JOHN GRINSTEAD
and ANN his Wife hath hereunto set their hands and seals the day and year first written
Signed Sealed and Delivered in the presence of

THOMAS CHAPMAN SENR.,   JOHN GRINSTEAD
WILLIAM SMITH, PHILIP DAWE,   ANNEA GRINSTEAD
SAML. HOWISON

At a Court held for Prince William County the seventh day of September 1795
This Deed and the Receipt thereon endorsed from JOHN GRINSTEAD and ANN his Wife to
JAMES GRINSTEAD SENR. (the feme being first privily examined and consenting thereto) were acknowledged by the said JOHN GRINSTEAD to be his acts and deeds and ordered
to be recorded   Teste JOHN WILLIAMS, Cl Cur

p.   (On margin: Examd. & deld. Apl. 27th 1797, N. COX)
582   Mr. JAMES JOHNSTON Sir. You will please pay Mr. JOHN LINTON the purchase
         and consideration money of the Deed for two lotts of land situate in Town of
DUMFRIES formerly the property of Mr. JOHN LINTON deced., the said money amounts to
the sum of Two hundred and Thirty one pounds, for making the said payment unto said
LINTON this shall be your power warrant and justification and the same shall be
binding and obligatory on me my heirs; Given from under my hand this Eighth day of
August in the year of our Lord 1795
In presence of MARY CAMPBELL,   MARGARET TYLER, Admrx. of
         GEO: G: TYLER,   JOHN TYLER deced.
         M. HARRISON JR.,   WILLIAM TYLER
To Mr. JAMES JOHNSTON
         DUMFRIES 10th of August 1795. Received of JAMES JOHNSTON Two hundred and
Thirty one poudns which is the amount of the above Order
Teste JOHN WILLIAMS   JNO: LINTON
At a Court held for Prince William County the 7th day of September 1795
This Order drawn by MARGARET TYLER, Admrx. of JOHN TYLER deced., (in favor of JOHN
LINTON) on JAMES JOHNSTON was proved by the Oath of MATTHEW HARRISON JUNR. and
the Receipt of the said JOHN LINTON thereon endorsed by the Oath of JOHN WILLIAMS 7
the said Order and Receipt were ordered to be recorded
                    Teste JOHN WILLIAMS, Cl Cur

pp.   THIS INDENTURE made this Seventh day of September in year of our Lord one
583-   thousand seven hundred and ninety five Between WILLIAM DAVIS and ELIZA-
585   BETH his Wife of County of Prince William of one part and GEORGE FLORANCE,
         Son of JOSEPH, of other part; Witnesseth that for the sum of Fifty pounds in
hand paid by GEORGE FLORANCE in Silver Dollars at Six shillings each or Gold by weight
as it currently passes to said WILLIAM DAVIS in hand paid by GEORGE FLORANCE, by
these presents said WILLIAM DAVIS and ELIZABETH his Wife have bargained and sold
unto GEORGE FLORANCE his heirs all that tract of land containing Fifty acres be the
same more or less, it being part of a tract of land taken up by WILLIAM BLUND & WIL-
LIAM DAVIS in said County containing Three hundred and seventy six acres and devi-
ded between them, it also being a piece of land formerly belonging to BENJAMIN BEN-

SON of MARYLAND and sold by him to said WILLIAM DAVIS, it lying and binding on the North side of OCAQUAN joining said GEORGE FLORANCEs land and THOMAS MONT-GOMERIEs deceast, it also being a piece of land that Mr. CLEMAN FAIR has lived on some time and his Wife now lives on the said Land, Together with all houses profits and appurtenances to the Fifty acres belonging; To have and to hold the Fifty acres of land be the same more or less, unto GEORGE FLORANCE, Son of JOSEPH, his heirs without the disturbance of WILLIAM DAVIS and ELIZABETH his Wife their heirs; In Witness whereof the said WILLIAM DAVIS and ELIZABETH his Wife hath hereunto set their hands and affixed their seals the dand and year first above written
Signed Sealed and Delivered in presents off

MUNGO HANCOCK,   WILLIAM DAVIS
JOHN M. MUSCHETT,   ELIZABETH DAVIS
ARRINGTON WICKLIFF   her X mark

At a Court held for Prince William County the 7th day of September 1795
This Deed and the Receipt thereon endorsed from WILLIAM DAVIS and ELIZABETH his Wife to GEORGE FLORANCE (the feme being first privily examined and consenting thereto), were acknowledged by the said WILLIAM DAVIS to be his acts and deeds and ordered to be recorded   Teste JOHN WILLIAMS, Cl Cur

pp.   KNOW ALL MEN by these presents that I MARGARET TYLER of County of Prince
585-   William for the sum of Sixty pounds to me in hand paid by these presents do
586   bargain and sell three small Negroes by the name of Matilda, Romio and John
           unto SARAH BALL CAMPBELL, FLORA CAMPBELL and DONALD CAMPBELL, To
have and to hold the said Negroes unto SARAH, FLORA and DONALD CAMPBELL to them their heirs; And I MARGARET TYLER my heirs the bargained premises do warrant and forever defend against the claim of all persons claiming under me; In Witness whereof I have hereunto set my hand and seal this Seventh day of April Anno Domini 1795
Signed Sealed and Delivered in the presence of us by

WM. TYLER Agent for MARGARET TYLER,   MARGARET TYLER Admrx.
WM. BARNES, RACHEL her mark X HEWITT

At a Court held for Prince William County the 7th day of September 1795
This Bill of Sale from MARGARET TYLER, Admrx. of JOHN TYLER deced., to SARAH B. CAMPBELL, FLORA CAMPBELL and DONALD CAMPBELL was proved by the Oath of RACHAEL HEWITT and ordered to be recorded
                          Teste JNO: WILLIAMS, Cl Cur

p.   A Return of the Situation of QUANTICO WAREHOUSE the Quantity of Tobacco
586   taken in this year and the Quantity they will contain at one time;
           The situation of the Warehouse is not good but are now repairing; The Quantity
of Tobacco taken this year -1037 Hhds., The Quantity we suppose they will contain at this time with safety, about 900 Hhds.
At a Court held for Prince William County the 7th day of September 1795
This Return of the Situation of QUANTICO WAREHOUSE was presented to the Court and ordered to be recorded   Teste JOHN WILLIAMS, Cl Cur

pp.   THIS INDENTURE made this Twentieth dy of June one thouand seven hundred
587-   and ninety five Between NANCY CHICK POWELL of County of SPOTSYLVANIA of
588   one part and SAMUEL CORNWELL of County of Prince William of other part; Wit-
           nesseth that NANCY CHICK POWELL for the sum of Twenty five pounds current
money to her in hand paid by SAMUEL CORNWELL, by these presents do bargain sell and confirm unto SAMUEL CORNWELL his heirs all that parcel of land given by JOHN CHICK

to the said NANCY CHICK POWELL by his last Will and Testament duly recorded in the
County Court of Prince William on the 8th day of September 1789; which land is
bounded Beginning at a white Oak the beginning corner of a larger tract of land divi-
ded by GEORGE CALVERT deced. between his Sons, GEORGE CALVERT and HUMPHREY
CALVERT, and continuing along the line to a small box Oak, a corner to the Dividing
Line or Middle between said GEORGE and HUMPHREY, thence across the land along the
Middle Line to a red Oak a corner tree, and along the first old line to a box Oak, to con-
tain Fifty acres, be the same more or less, which tract of land conveyed was granted by
Deed of Gift duly recorded from GEORGE CALVERT deced. to his Son, the aforesaid GEORGE
CALVERT, who did by Deed bearing date the sixth day of September one thouand seven
hundred and Eighty five convey the land to JOHN CHICK, And all houses orchards pro-
fits and appurtenances; To have and to hold unto SAMUEL CORNWELL his heirs; And
NANCY CHICK POWELL and her heirs doth by these presents warrant and defend the
tract of land unto SAMUEL CORNWELL his heirs against the claim of every person; In
Witness whereof the said NANCY CHICK POWELL hath hereunto set her hand and affixed
her seal the day and year above written
Sealed and Delivered in the presence of
     THOMAS DAVIS, WILLIAM BRUNTIN   NANCY CHICK her mark ✝ POWELL
     HUMPHREY his Cross ✝ CALVERT   ANN ✝ CHICK her Cross
   At a Court held for Prince William County the 7th day of September 1795
This Deed from NANCY CHICK POWELL to SAMUEL CORNWELL was proved by the Oaths of
HUMPHREY CALVERT WM. BRUNTIN and THOMAS DAVIS and ordered to be recorded
               Teste JNO: WILLIAMS, Cl Cur

p.   KNOW ALL MEN by these presents that we WILLIAM LINTON and TIMOTHY
589   BRUNDIGE of Prince William County for the sum of Seventy five pounds current
       money to us in hand paid by WALTER GRAHAM of FAUQUIER County by these
presents do for ourselves our heirs release and discharge WALTER GRAHAM his heirs
from all right title and demand in Law or Equity which we have unto a certain tract of
land to us by the aforesaid WALTER GRAHAM on the 13th day of October 1791 in trust for
the purpose of discharging a Debt due to Mr. BERNARD GALLAGHER, In Witness whereof
we have hereunto set our hands and affixed our seals this Twenty first day of March
one thousand seven hundred and ninety five
Sealed and Delivered in presence of
     (no witnesses recorded)   WILLIAM LINTON
                                           TIMOTHY BRUNDIGE
   At a Court continued and held for Prince William County the 8th day of September 1795
This Deed of Surrender from WILLIAM LINTON and TIMOTHY BRUNDIGE to WALTER
GRAHAM was acknowledged by the said LINTON & BRUNDIGE to be their acts and deeds
and ordered to be recorded   Teste JNO: WILLIAMS, Cl Cur

p.   KNOW ALL MEN by these presents that we WILLIAM LINTON and JOHN McMIL-
590   lian are held and firmly bound unto ROBERT BROOKE Esquire, Governor of Vir-
       ginia or his successors for the use of the Commonwealth in the sum of Four
thousand Dollars to which payment well and truly to be made we bind ourselves our
heirs firmly by these presents; Sealed with our seals and dated this 8th day of September 1795
   THE CONDITION of the above obligation is such that whereas the above bound WILLIAM
LINTON at a Court held for the County of Prince William the 7th day of September (Inst.)
was by said Court recommended to be continued an INSPECTOR of Tobacco at QUANTICO
WAREHOUSE; Now if said WILLIAM LINTON shall truly and faithfully perform the duties

of an Inspector at the aforesaid Warehouse agreeable to an Act of Assembly intitled,
"An Act for reducing into one the several Acts of Assembly for the Inspection of Tobac-
co," then the above obligation to be void else to be and remain in full force & virtue
Sealed & Delivered in presence of
          The Court   WILLIAM LINTON
                                                           JOHN McMILLIAN
     At a Court contd. and held for Prince William County the 8th day of Septr: 1795
This Bond from WILLIAM LINTON and JOHN McMILLIAN to ROBERT BROOKE Esqr., Governor of Virginia, was acknowledged by the said LINTON and McMILLIAN and ordered to
be recorded   Teste JNO; WILLIAMS, Cl Cur

p.   KNOW ALL MEN by these presents that we WILLIAM CARTER and ALEXANDER
591   HENDERSON are held and firmly bound unto ROBERT BROOKE Esqr., Governor of
          Virginia or his successors for the use of the Commonwealth in the sum of Four
thousand Dollars to which payment well and truly to be made we bind ourselves our
heirs firmly by these presents; Sealed with our seals and dated this 8th day of
September 1795
     THE CONDITION of the above obligation is such that whereas the above bound WILLIAM
CARTER at a Court held for the County of Prince William the seventh day of September
instant, was by the said Court recommended to be continued an INSPECTOR of Tobacco at
QUANTICO WAREHOUSE; Now if said WILLIAM CARTER shall truly and faithfully perform
the duties of an Inspector at the aforesaid Warehouse agreeable to an Act of Assembly
intitled, "An Act for reducing into one the severals Acts of Assembly for the Inspection
of Tobacco," Then the above obligation to be void else to be and remain in full force and
virtue Sealed and Delivered in the presence of
          The Court   WILLIAM CARTER
                                                           ALEXR: HENDERSON
     At a Court continued and held for Prince William County the 8th day of September 1795
This Bond from WILLIAM CARTER and ALEXANDER HENDERSON to ROBERT BROOKE Esqr.,
Governor of Virginia, was acknowledged by the said CARTER and HENDERSON and
ordered to be recorded   Teste JNO: WILLIAMS, Cl Cur

p.   DUMFRIES 26th May 1795
592   Gentlemen. You will please to reinstate Mr. WALTER GRAHAM in his Estate
          which you had in trust on my Account as Mr. DAVID WILSON SCOTT has given
me his Obligation for the balance due me. I am Gent.
To Messrs. LINTON & BRUNDIGE   BERNARD GALLAGHER
     At a Court continued and held for Prince William County the 8th day of September 1795
This Missive from BERNARD GALLAGHER to WILLIAM LINTON and TIMOTHY BRUNDIGE
was acknowledged by the said GALLAGHER to be his act and deed and ordered to be
recorded   Teste JOHN WILLIAMS, Cl Cur

pp.   WHEREAS I JOSEPH CARR of RANDOLPH County and DISTRICT of NORTH CARO-
592-   LINA have bargained and contracted for a certain tract of land in County of
593   NORTHUMBERLAND and State of Virginia with a certain JOHN LYNN of Prince
          William County And Whereas it will not be in my power to transact the said
business, I therefore authorize and impower said JOHN LYNN my lawful Attorney and
assignee to survey the said land, grant Deeds for the same in fee simple in my name,
likewise to demand recover and receive the said land in my name and to and for the use
of himself his heirs &c. by all lawful ways of and from all persons whom it may con-
cern with such further power and authorities as are needful and convenient for the

recovering of the said land; Given under my hand and seal this 19th day of August 1795
Teste WILLIAM LYNN   JOSEPH his mark X CARR
        JAMES HOLLADAY, ELIZABETH JACKSON
    At a Court held for Prince William County the 7th day of September 1795
This Power of Attorney from JOSEPH CARR to JOHN LYNN was proved by the Oaths of
WILLIAM LYNN and JAMES HOLLADAY and ordered to be Certified; And at a Court con-
tinued and held for the said County the 8th day of September 1795, the said Power of
Attorney was fully proved by the Oath of ELIZABETH JACKSON and ordered to be
recorded   Teste JNO: WILLIAMS, Cl Cur

p.   Prince William County Sct.
593   I hereby certify that this day Mr. GEORGE WASHINGTON GRAYSON came before
         the Subscriber, one of the Justices for the County aforesaid, and made Oath on
the Holy Evangelist, that he removed a Negroe man named Robin from CHARLES County
in the State of MARYLAND into the County of Prince William on the thirteenth instant,
that he did not remove the Negro Robin with the intention of evading the Acts of
Assembly to prevent the further importation of slaves into this Commonwealth and did
not remove the said Negroe with intent to sell him and that the Negroe slave named
Robin was not imported from Africa or any of the West India Islands; Given under my
hand this 14th day of Jany. 1795   WM. BARNES
    At a Court held for Prince William County the 5th day of October 1795
This Certificate from WILLIAM BARNES Gent. to GEORGE W. GRAYSON was ordered to be
recorded   Teste JOHN WILLIAMS, Cl Cur

pp.   THIS INDENTURE made the first day of August one thousand seven hundred and
593-   ninety five Between THOMAS LEACHMAN & ELIZABETH his Wife of Prince Wil-
595   liam County of one part and JAMES FOSTER of County aforesaid of other part;
         Witnesseth that THOMAS LEACHMAN and ELIZABETH his Wife in consideration of
One hundred pounds specie to the said LEACHMAN in hand paid by JAMES FOSTER, by
these presents doth bargain & sell unto JAMES FOSTER his heirs part of that tract of land
whereon said LEACHMAN now lives which he holds by the Last Will & Testament of
WILLIAM FOSTER deced., bearing date 1777, and lying in County aforesaid, on the small
Drain of BROAD RUN and OCCOQUAN; Begining at a Water and Box Oak in the Dividing
Branch between said LEACHMAN & FOSTER, then E. 134 po: to a white Oak on the top of
Hill in an Island in or near WASHINGTONs Line, then up the Branch and binding there-
with and also with WASHINGTONs Line No. 10d. W. 70 po: to a corner in said Branch,
thence with another of said lines W. 110 po: to the Dividing Branch between the partys
to this Deed, then down the sd. Dividing Branch and binding therewith S. 46 po., then S.
76d. W. 22 po: to the begining, including Fifty acres, the said Branch still continues to
Divide the remainder of sd. LEACHMANs Land and FOSTERs untill you get to a marked
Maple near the mouth of the said LEACHMANs Spring Branch, then South 80d. E. 17 po.
to a stooped white Oak near LEACHMANs Spring, then S. 55d. E. 14 po: to a Spanish red
Oak, then S. 24 E. 26 po: to a large Willow Oak in the head of a Branch, then down the
Branch & binding therewith to the line of CANNON, also all trees profits commodities
and appurtenances belonging; To have and to hold the tenement and every of the
appurtenances unto JAMES FOSTER his heirs; And THOMAS LEACHMAN & ELIZABETH his
Wife & their heirs against all persons unto JAMES FOSTER will warrant and forever
defend by these presents; In Witness whereof the said THOMAS LEACHMAN and ELIZA-
BETH hath hereunto set their hands and seals the date above written
                                        THOMAS LEACHMAN
                                        ELIZABETH LEACHMAN

At a Court held for Prince William County the 5th day of October 1795
This Deed and Receipt thereon from THOMAS LEACHMAN and ELIZABETH his Wife to
JAMES FOSTER, the feme being first privily examined and consenting thereto, were
acknowledged by the said THOMAS LEACHMAN & ELIZABETH his Wife and ordered to be
recorded   Teste JOHN WILLIAMS, Cl Cur

pp.   Virginia   In the High Court of Chancery
595-   Between WILLOUGHBY TEBBS and BETSEY his Wife, devisees of WILLIAM CARR
596   deceased, Plts. and CARR CHAPMAN, CHARLES CHAPMAN and JENNY CARR CHAP-
        MAN, Children and Devisees of THOMAS CHAPMAN deceased, and Infants under
age of Twenty one years by JESSE EWELL, their Guardian, and JAMES JENETT and SUSAN-
NAH his Wife, which SUSANNAH was Widow and Relict of said THOMAS CHAPMAN, Defts.
  This Cause came on this fifth day of June in yer of our Lord one thouand seven hundred and ninety five to be heard on the Bills, answer exhibits and examinations of witnesses and was agreed by Counsil; on consideration whereof the Court doth order that
the Indentures of Lease and Release made the twenty first day of December in the year
one thousand seven hundred and Sixty two between THOMAS CHAPMAN by the name of
THOMAS CHAPMAN of Prince William County and Colony of Virignia of one part and
WILLIAM CARR by the name of WILLIAM CARR, Gentleman, of the Town of DUMFRIES of
other part, for conveyance of Four lots or two acres of land situate in that Town, numbered Eleven, Twelve, Thirteen and Fourteen, and attested by DOUGLASS WILLIAM
BENNETT and JAMES NELSON be recorded togeather with the examinations taken and
returned in this Cause to WILLIAM TEBBS, GEORGE TEBBS and CUMBERLAND WILSON, in
the Clerks Office of the County Court of Prince William and that the Infant Defts. do
within six months after they shall attain their full ages respectively convey to the Plts.
their heirs and assigns the lots of land aforesaid in fee simple
             A Copy   Teste PETER TINSLEY, C. H. C.

pp.   (On margin: Exd. & Deld. to WY. TEBBS Apl. 27th 1797; N. COX)
596-   THIS INDENTURE made the 21 day of December in the year one thousand seven
600   hundred and Sixty two Between THOMAS CHAPMAN of Prince William County &
         Colony of Virginia of one part and WILLIAM CARR Gent. of Town of DUMFRIES of
other part; Witnesseth that for the sum of Five shillings current money of Virginia to
said THOMAS CHAPMAN in hand paid by WILLIAM CARR, by these presents doth demise
and to farm lett unto WILLIAM CARR Four lotts or two acres of Land situated in Town of
DUMFRIES numbered Eleven, Twelve, Thirteen and Fourteen, which Four lotts or two
acres of land was conveyed to THOMAS CHAPMAN by the Trustees of said Town by Deed
bearing date the third day of July one thousand seven hundred and Sixty, And all
houses orchards profits commodities and appurtenances to the same belonging; To have
and to hold the lands and premises unto WILLIAM CARR during the full term of one
whole year paying therefore the Rent of one Ear of Indian Corn to THOMAS CHAPMAN
on the last day of said term if lawfully demanded to the intent that by virtue of these
presents and of the Statute for transferring uses into possession said WILLIAM CARR
may be in the actual possession of the premises and thereby be the better enabled to
accept a release of the reversion and inheritance thereof; In Witness whereof the said
THOMAS CHAPMAN hath hereunto set his hand and seale the day and year above written
Sealed and Delivered in the presents of
         JAMES DOUGLASS,   THOMAS CHAPMAN
         WM. BENNETT, JAMES NELSON

THIS INDENTURE made the 21st day of December in year of our Lord one thousand seven hundred and Sixty two Between THOMAS CHAPMAN of Prince William County and Colony of Virginia of one part and WILLIAM CARR Gent. of Town of DUMFRIES of other part Witnesseth that for the sum of Forty pounds current money of Virginia to THOMAS CHAPMAN in hand paid by said WILLIAM CARR; by these presents doth bargain sell and confirm unto WILLIAM CARR (in his actual possession now being by virtue of a bargain and sale to him thereof made for one whole year and by force of the Statute for transferring uses in possession) and to his heirs all those four lotts or two acres of land situate in Town of DUMFRIES numbered Eleven, Twelve, Thirteen and Fourteen which said four lotts of land were conveyed to said THOMAS CHAPMAN by the Trustees of said Town bearing date the third day of July one thousand seven hundred and Sixty; To have and to hold the said lands unto WILLIAM CARR his heirs free and clear from all incumbrances; And THOMAS CHAPMAN and his heirs the premises hereby released unto WILLIAM CARR and his heirs against all persons shall warrant and for ever defend by these presents; In Witness whereof the said THOMAS CHAPMAN hath hereunto set his hand and seale the day and year first above written
Sealed and Delivered in presents of
    JAMES DOUGLASS,   THOMAS CHAPMAN
    WM. BENNETT, JAMES NELSON

    THE DEPOSITION of WILLIAM TEBBS SENR. in a suit now depending in the High Court of Chancery between WILLOUGHBY TEBBS and BETTY his Wife, devisees of WILLIAM CARR Plts. and CARR CHAPMAN, CHARLES CHAPMAN & JENNY CARR CHAPMAN, Children of THOMAS CHAPMAN deced. and Infants under the age of Twenty one years by JESSE EWELL their Guardian specially appointed and JAMES GENETT and SUSANNA his Wife, the said SUSANNA was Widow and Relict of said THOMAS CHAPMAN.
    1st Question by the Complainants. Do you believe that THOMAS CHAPMAN signed and sealed the Deeds here presented dated in December 1762 for four lotts of land in the Town of DUMFRIES numbers 11, 12, 12 & 14. Answereth and saith that he doth believe the same to be the hand written of said THOMAS CHAPMAN and did execute the said Writing. 2d. Question. Do you know or believe that the Signature of WILLIAM BENNETT is in his own hand writing; Answereth and saith yes. 3d. Question. Do you believe that to be the hand writing of JAMES DOUGLASS who attested the said Deeds, Answereth yes and further saith not.   WILLIAM TEBBS
  Prince William County to wit; Agreeable to a Dedimus to us directed and a notice to that purpose, we have taken the within Deposition which was signed subscribed and sworn to before us; Given under our hands this 5th day of May 1795.
                  ALEXANDER LITHGOW
                  HENRY WASHINGTON

    THE DEPOSITION of GEORGE TEBB of full age taken in a suit now depending in the High Court of Chancery between (the same heading is repeated as in the foregoing Deposition);
  Question by Complainant. Do you believe that the signatures of THOMAS CHAPMAN, JAMES DOUGLASS, WM. BENNETT and JAMES NELSON to the Deeds hereunto annexed were severally wrote and subscribed by the aforesaid CHAPMAN, DOUGLASS, BENNETT & NELSON, answereth and saith yes for that the said Deponent was well acquainted with the hand writing of the aforesaid Gentlemen and further saith not.
                  GEO; TEBBS
  Prince William Court to wit: Agreeable to a Dedimus to us directed and a notice to that purpose which are herewith returned, we have taken the Deposition of GEORGE TEBBS

which was acknowledged and sworn to before us. Given under our hands this 5th day of May 1795   ALEXR: LITHGOW
                                                    J. LAWSON

        THE DEPOSITION of CUMBERLAND WILSON Esqr. taken in a suit (the same heading is repeated as in the Deposition of WILLIAM TEBBS); Question by the Complainants. Do you believe that JAMES DOUGLASS, WILLIAM BENNETT and JAMES NELSON subscribed and witnessed in their own hand writing Deeds of Lease and Release dated the 21st of December one thousand seven hundred and Sixty two from THOMAS CHAPMAN to WILLIAM CARR for Four lotts or two acres of land in Town of DUMFRIES described and known by the numbers 11, 12, 13 & 14, which Deeds are here annexed, Answereth and sayeth I do believe the same to be their hand writing and that they did sign and subscribe the same as I was perfectly well acquainted with each of the said JAMES DOUGLASS, WM. BENNETT & JAMES NELSON and the hand write of all of them was familiar and well known to the Deponent.   CUMBERLAND WILSON
    Prince William Sct. Agreeable to a Dedimus to us directed and a notice for that purpose at the Court House of said County took the above deposition which was signed and sworn to before us the 6th day of August 1793.   CHARLES TYLER
                                                    JAMES SMITH

        A Copy Teste PETER TINSLEY, C. H. C.
    At a Court held for Prince William County the fifth day of October 1795
Agreeable to a Decree of the High Court in Chancery made between WILLOUGHBY TEBBS and BETSEY his Wife, devisees of WILLIAM CARR deced. Plantiffs and Representatives of THOMAS CHAPMAN deced., Defendants, It is ordered that the said Decree and the Deeds and the Depositions in the said Decree mentioned be recorded
                        Teste JOHN WILLIAM, Cl Cur

p.   (On margin: Examd. & deld. to THORN Octr. 1816, LAWSON)
601   TO ALL WHOM these presents shall come I JOHN THORN do send Greeting. Know
        ye that I JOHN THORN in the County of Prince William in consideration of the love good will and affection which I have and do bear towards my loving Son, WILLIAM THORN of the same County aforesaid by these presents do give and grant unto said WILLIAM THORN a certain parcel of land containing by estimation One hundred acres be the same more or less lying in County aforesaid on a Branch called the LICK BRANCH a Branch of OCCOQUAN, being part of a certain tract of land taken up by my deceased Father, WILLIAM THORN, the same one hundred acres by estimation being boundedd, Begining at the mouth of a small Drane where said Drane emties into said LICK BRANCH the said small drane being the dividing line between the said land and the land of PETER COTTRELL, thence up the meanders of said LICK BRANCH on East side thereof unto the land of JOHN SULLIVAN, thence with the line of said SULLIVANs land unto the line of JAMES KING, thence with JAMES KINGs land unto the line of Capt. WILLIAM BROWN thence with said BROWNs land unto the Dividing Line between the said tract of land and the Land of PETER COTTRELL to the same mentioned Drane, thence down the Drane the meanders thereof to the begining; To have and to hold the said land with all appurtenances thereunto belonging from thence forth as his proper rite and title without any manner of condition; In Witness whereof I have hereunto set my hand and seale this fifth day of October in year of our Lord one thousand seven hundred and ninety five
                                                    JOHN THORN
    At a Court held for Prince William County the fifth day of October 1795
This Deed of Gift from JOHN THORN to WILLIAM THORN was acknowledged by the said JOHN THORN and ordered to be recorded   Teste JOHN WILLIAMS, Cl Cur

p.   TO ALL WHOM these present shall come, I JOHN THORN do send Greeting. Know
602   ye that I JOHN THORN in the County of Prince William in consideration of the
         love good will and affection which I have and do bear unto my Son, AUGUSTINE
THORN of County aforesaid, by these presents do freely give and grant unto AUGUSTINE
THORN a certain parcel of land containing by estimation One hundred acres be the same
more or less lying in County of Prince William on West side of a Branch aclled the LICK
BRANCH of OCCOQUAN, being part of a certain tract of land taken up bymy deced. Father,
WM. THORN, and said one hundred acres of land bounded; Begining at the mouth of a
small Drane on West side of said LICK BRANCH, thence up the meanders of the same,
thence to a marked Chesnut, COCKRELLs line, thence with COCKRELLs line to MICHAEL
KOAHNs line, thence with KOAHN line of land to WILLIAM LANEs line of land to a certain small drane in line of land to where I have rented to CHARLES ARNOLD, thence
with said Drane down the meanders thereof to said LICK BRANCH, thence down said
LICK BRANCH the meanders thereof to the begining; To have and to hold as his proper
rite and every appurtnances thereunto belonging from henceforth without any
manner of condition; In Witness whereof I have hereunto set my hand and Seal this
fifth day of October one thousand seven hundred and ninety five
                                        JOHN THORN
  At a Court held for Prince William County the fifth day of October 1795
This Deed of Gift from JOHN THORN to AUGUSTINE THORN was acknowledged by said JOHN
THORN and ordered to be recorded   Teste JOHN WILLIAMS, Cl Cur

pp.   THIS INDENTURE made this Tenth day of July one thousand seven hundred and
603-   ninety four Between FRANCIS BERRYMAN & ELIZABETH NEWTON his Wife of
605   County of FAUQUIER of one part and JOHN KINCHELOE of County of Prince Wil-
         liam of other part; Witnesseth that FRANCIS BERRYMAN & ELIZABETH NEWTON
his Wife for the sum of One hundred pounds specie in hand paid by JOHN KINCHELOE, By
these presents have bargained and sold unto JOHN KINCHELOE his heirs all that tract of
land containing One hundred & six acres of land be the same more or less situate in
County of Prince William and lying on both sides of a Branch called BUCKNALL
adjoining the lands of HOWSON HOOE Gent., ROBERT MOSLEY, JOHN LAWSON & JOHN
HAMMETT, which tract of land WILLIAM BARR deced., purchased of JOSEPH BUCKHANAN
and sd. BARR having but the only Daughter, ELIZABETH NEWTON, who marry'd said
FRANCIS BERRYMAN, party to these presents, Togeather with all houses profits and
appurtenances belonging; To have and to hold the one hundred & six acres of land with
the appurtenances unto JOHN KINCHELOE his heirs; And FRANCIS BERRYMAN and
ELIZABETH NEWTON his Wife their heirs shall warrant and for ever defend by thes
presents; In Witness whereof said FRANCIS BERRYMAN and ELIZABETH NEWTON his
Wife hath hereunto set their hands and seals the day month & year first above written
Signed Sealed and Delivered in presents of
        WILEMAN KINCHELOE,   FRANCIS BERRYMAN
        JOHN KINCHELOE JUNR.   ELIZABETH NTN. BERRYMAN
        MOSES WICKLIFF, ROBERT WICKLIFF,
        WILLIAM KINCHELOE, JOSEPH his mark X BOBO,
        JOHN his mark X MILSTED
  The Commonwealth of Virginia to JOHN BLACKWELL, JOHN THOMAS CHINN & WILLIAM
CLARKSON, Gentlemen, Greeting, Whereas (the Commission for the privy Exami-nation of
ELIZABETH NEWTON, the Wife of FRANCIS BERRYMAN), Witness ROBERT GRAHAM Clerk of the
said Court the 26th day of August 1794 and in the nineteenth year of the
Commonwealth   ROBERT GRAHAM

FAUQUIER County, to wit, In Obedience to the within, we the Subscribers have caused
to come before us the within named ELIZABETH NEWTON BERRYMAN and have examined
her privately (the return of the execution of the privy Examination of ELIZABETH NEWTON
BERRYMAN); Given under our hands & seals this 26th day of August 1794
                                    JOHN THOS: CHINN
                                    WM. CLARKSON
    At a Court held for Prince William County the sixth day of October 1794
This Deed and the Receipt thereon from FRANCIS BERRYMAN & ELIZABETH NEWTON his
Wife to JOHN KINCHELOE was proved, the Deed by the Oaths of WILEMAN KINCHELOE &
MOSES WICKLIFF, and the Receipt by the Oath of WILEMAN KINCHELOE, and ordered to be
certifyed; And at a Court held for said County the fifth day of October 1795, This Deed
was fully proved by the Oath of ROBERT KINCHELOE and togeather with the Receipt
thereon and a Commission for the examination of ELIZABETH NEWTON, Wife of the
aforesaid FRANCIS BERRYMAN returned executed, ordered to be recorded
                                    Teste JOHN WILLIAMS, Cl Cur

p.   (On margin: Examd. & Deld. Apl. 27th 1797, N. COX)
606   KNOW ALL MEN by these presents that I THOMAS MASON of CITY of RICHMOND
        & State of Virginia have appointed by these presents JAMES JOHNSTON of the
Town of DUMFRIES State aforesaid, my true and lawfull Attorney for me and in my name
to demand & receive of all my Tenants in the County of Prince William all such Rent &
arrearages of Rent which now are or hereafter shall grown due & on receipt thereof to
give sufficient discharges, and in default of payment to commence & prosecute according to Law any action for the speedy recovering of my said Rents and by my said
Attorney shall be thought fit; hereby ratifying whatsoever my said Attorney shall
lawfull do in the premises, In Witness whereof I have hereunto set my hand and seal
the Sixth day of July 1795
Signd. Seald. & Delivered in presents of
        WILLIAM WISHART   THOMAS MASON
        JNO: MACRAE
    At a Court held for Prince William County the fifth day of October 1795
This Power of Attorney from THOMAS MASON to JAMES JOHNSTON was proved by the Oath
of WILLIAM WISHARD and ordered to be recorded
                                    Teste JOHN WILLIAMS, Cl Cur

pp.   (On margin: Examd. & deld. 25th Oct. 1798; W. H.)
606-   THIS INDENTURE made this sixth day of September in year of our Lord one
610   thousand seven hundred and ninety five Between WILLIAM POWELL and MARY
        SMITH, his Wife, of Prince William County, of one part and BERNARD HOOE SENR.
of the same County of other part; Witnesseth that WILLIAM POWELL and MARY SMITH
his Wife for the sum of Five shillings current money of Virginia to them in hand paid
by BERNARD HOOE by these presents do bargain & sell unto BERNARD HOOE one certain
tract of land in Prince William County, it being that tract of land PEYTON POWELL sold
and conveyed to the aforesaid WILLIAM POWELL and is bounded, Beginning at a small
red Oak being corner tree to BERNARD HOOE and others, the sd. HOOE being one of the
parties to these presents, thence with sd. HOOEs line North 28 West 74 poles to another
corner of sd. BERNARD HOOE's standing in BENJAMIN DULANY's line, thence South 33
1/2 West 134 poles along the said DULANY line to the MAPLE BRANCH, thence down said
Branch with said DULANYs line South 98 poles to a dead Hickory, thence South 15 West
10 1/4 poles to the mouth of a Branch, thence up said Branch and binding therewith

North 70 East 6 poles, North 37 East 26 poles, North 46, East 16 poles, North 38 1/2 East 52 poles, North 46 East 22 poles to a white Oak, from thence to the begining, containing Seventy five acres of land and all houses orchards profits & appurtenances to said premises belonging; To have and to hold the land hereby conveyed unto BERNARD HOOE hisheirs during the full term of one whole year paying therefore the Rent of one pepper Corn on Lady Day next if lawfully demanded to the intent that by virtue of these presents and of the Statute for transferring uses into possession, the said BERND: HOOE may be in actual possession of the premises and be thereby enabled to except and take a release of the reversion and inheritance thereof; In Witness whereof the said WILLIAM POWELL & MARY SMITH his Wife hath hereunto set their hands and affixed their seals the day and year first above written
Signd. Sealed and Delivered in presents of us
    ENOCK S. LANE, JOHN WILLIAMS,   WILLIAM POWELL
    GEORGE LANE, LANGH: DADE   MARY SMITH POWELL
  At a Court held for Prince William County the fifth day of October 1795
This Lease from WILLIAM POWELL and MARY SMITH his Wife to BERNARD HOOE was proved by the Oaths of LANGHORNE DADE, GEORGE LANE and JOHN WILLIAMS and ordered to be recorded   Teste JOHN WILLIAMS, Cl Cur.

      THIS INDENTURE made the Seventh day of September in year of our Lord one thousand seven hundred and ninety five Between WILLIAM POWELL and his Wife of Prince William County of one part and BERNARD HOOE SENR. of the same County of the other part; Witnesseth that for the sum of One hundred and Thirty one pounds, Five shillings current money of Virginia to WILLIAM POWELL and MARY SMITH his Wife in hand paid by BERNARD HOOE, by these presents do bargain sell release & confirm unto BERNARD HOOE in his actual possession now being by virtue of a bargain and sale to him thereof made for one whole year and by force of the statute for transferring uses into possession, and his heirs one tract ofland in Prince William County it being that tract of Land PEYTON POWELL sold & conveyed to the aforesaid WILLIAM POWELL, and is bounded (the bounds of the land are repeated as in the foregoing Lease); To have and to hold the land hereby conveyed with appurtenances unto BERNARD HOOE his heirs free & clear from all other gifts grants bargains sales dower right and title of dower judgments executions titles troubles charges and incumbrances whatsoever suffered by said WILLIAM POWELL & MARY SMITH his Wife; and WILLIAM POWELL & MARY SMITH his Wife and their heirs the premises hereby granted unto BERNARD HOOE his heirs against every person whatsoever shall warrant and for ever defend by these presents; In Witness the said WILLIAM POWELL and MARY SMITH his Wife hath hereunto set their hands and seals the day and year first above written
Signed Sealed and Delivered in presents of us
    ENOCH S. LANE, JOHN WILLIAMS,   WILLIAM POWELL
    GEORGE LANE, LANGH: DADE   MARY SMITH POWELL
  The Commonwealth of Virginia to HENRY WASHINGTON, CHARLES EWELL, ALEXANDER BRUCE & CHARLES TYLER or any two or more of you, Gentlemen, Greeting. Whereas (the Commission for the privy Examination of MARY SMITH, Wife of WILLIAM POWELL); Witness JOHN WILLIAMS Clerk of our said Court this 8th day of September 1795 & in the Twentyeth year of the Commonwealth   JOHN WILLIAMS
  Prince William County to wit; In Obedience to the within, we the Subscribers have caused to come before us the within mentioned MARY SMITH POWELL and have examined her privately (the return of the execution of the privy Examination of MARY SMITH

POWELL) Given under our hands & seals this twenty first day of Sept. 1795
                                          HENRY WASHINGTON
                                          CHAS: EWELL
At a Court held for Prince William County the fifth day of October 1795
This Release and the Receipt thereon from WILLIAM POWELL and MARY SMITH his Wife
to BERNARD HOOE were proved by the Oaths of LANGHORNE DADE, GEORGE LANE & JOHN
WILLIAMS and Togeather with a Dedimus for the privy Examination of the said MARY
SMITH POWELL returned executed, ordered to be recorded
                          Teste JOHN WILLIAMS, Cl Cur

p.   KNOW ALL MEN by these presents that I EZEKIEL DUNAWAY of Prince William
611   County do sell unto GEORGE WHITECOTTON one Negro man nam'd Peter, one
          Negroe wench nam'd Grace & her Child, nam'd Cate, for the consideration of One
hundred & twenty pounds current money to me in hand paid by GEORGE WHITECOTTON
and I hereby warrent & for ever defend the aforesaid Negroes unto GEORGE WHITE-
COTTON his heirs against the claim of every person; In Witness whereof I have hereun-
to set my hand & seal this 15th day of June 1795
Sign'd Seal'd & Delivered in the presents of
          NANCEY her mark X WHITECOTTON,   EZEKIEL DUNAWAY
          JESSE   X THRELKELD
At a Court continued and held for Prince William County the 5th day of November 1795
This Bill of Sale from EZEKIEL DUNAWAY to GEORGE WHITECOTTON was proved by the
Oath of JESSE THRELKELD and ordered to be recorded
                          Teste JOHN WILLIAMS, Cl Cur

p.   KNOW ALL MEN by these presents that we SAMUEL WATSON, WALTER COE &
611   THOMAS LEE SENR. are held and firmly bound unto ROBERT BROOKE Esqr., Gover-
          nor of Virginia & his successors for the use of the Commonwealth in the full
sum of Fifteen hundred Dollars current money of Virginia to which payment well &
truly to be made we bind ourselves our heirs firmly by these presents; Sealed with our
seals and dated this fifth day of November 1795
THE CONDITION of the above obligation is such that the above bound SAMUEL WATSON,
Minister of the METHODIST EPISCOPAL CHURCH having under the Act of the General
Assembly entitled, "An Act to regulate the Solemnization of Marriages prohibiting such
as are incestuous or otherwise unlawfull to prevent forcible or stolen Marriages and
for the Punishment of the Crime of Bigamy," this day on producing his Letters of Ordi-
nation and also having made Oath of Allegiance to this State, obtained a Licence from
the County of Prince William authorizing him to join togeather any persons within this
Commonwealth in the holdy state of Matrimony according to the rites and cerimonies of
said Church that shall apply, they having first produced a lawfull Licence. Now if the
said SAMUEL WATSON shall in all things as in the said Act is directed & required, discharge the duties of said Office, then the above obligation to be void
Sealed & Deliver'd in presents of
          The Court   SAMUEL WATSON
                                               WALTER COE
                                               THOS: LEE SENR:
At a Court continued & held for Prince William County the fifth day of November 1795
SAMUEL WATSON, WALTER COE & THOMAS LEE SENR. severally acknowledged this Bond
to be their act & deed which was ordered to be recorded
                          Teste JOHN WILLIAMS, Cl Cur

p.
612

(On margin: Examd. & deld. Mr. JNO. MADDOX June 8th 1804, P. D. DAWE)
KNOW ALL MEN by these presents that I GEORGE PURCELL of Prince William
County for divers good causes and consideration by these presents do appoint
my trusty Friend, JOHN MADDOX, of County afsd. my true and lawful Attorney for me and in my name to sue for recover and receive all that part of my Father, WILLIAM PUR-CELLs Estate which I am as one of his lawful heirs justly entitled to granting my Attorney my full power and authority to take and follow such legal courses and methods for the obtaining of the same as I my own self might or could do were I personally present Ratifying and confirming whatsoever my said Attorney shall do about the premises; In Virtue whereof I have hereunto set my hand and affixed my seal this Twenty Eighth day of November one thousand seven hundred and ninety five
Signed Sealed and Delivered in the presents of

CHS. EWELL, QUINTON RATCLIFFE,   GEORGE his mark ✝ PURCELL
PETER HANSBROUGH JUNR.,

Prince William Sct. Personally appeared before us GEORGE PURCELL and acknow-ledged that this Power of Attorney was his act & dead 28th of November 1795

CHS: EWELL
P. HANSBROUGH JR.

At a Court held for Prince William County the seventh day of December 1795
This Letter of Attorney from GEORGE PURCELL to JOHN MADDOX was proved by the Oath of PETER HANSBROUGH and ordered to be recorded

Teste JOHN WILLIAMS, Cl Cur

pp.
612-
613

THIS INDENTURE made the Twenty first day of September in year of our Lord one thousand seven hundred and ninety five Between HOUSON HOOE JUNIOR and JANE his Wife of Prince William County of one part and ROBERT COLE of the County aforesaid of other part; Witnesseth that HOWSON HOOE and JANE his Wife for the sum of Nineteen pounds Nine shillings current money of Virginia to them in hand paid by ROBERT COLE, by these presents do bargain & sell unto ROBERT COLE his heirs all that parcell of land lying on North side of LITTLE CREEK in aforesaid County bounded, Begining at a dead Pine, corner tree of WARD's Land, runing thence North 5d. East 34 po: to a Stake at the intersection of JOHN BOON LUCKETTs line, thence with his line South 45d. east 98 poles to another State on a Hill in a Field in the line of CARR's land formerly TRIPLETTs, thence with a line with said CARRs land South 45d. West 17 po: to a third Stake, thence with another of sd. lines So. 45d. East 16 po: to the bank of LITTLE CREEK, then up the said Creek and binding therewith North 59d. 30 West 15 po., North 77 West 6 poles, North 70d. West 14 po. to two marked Saplings on the sd. Creek side, thence West 55 po. to the begining, containing Fourteen acres & 37 poles and also all houses commodities and appurtenances to sd premises belonging; To have and to hold the said tenement with the appurtenances unto ROBERT COLE his heirs; And HOW-SON HOOE and JANE his Wife for themselves and their heirs the premises against them & their heirs to ROBERT COLE his heirs shall warrant and forever defend by these pre-sents; In Witness whereof the said HOWSON HOOE and JANE his Wife hath hereunto set their hands and seals the day and year first above written
Signed Sealed and Delivered in presence of

HENRY D. HOOE, JOHN MADDOX,   HOWSON HOOE
RHODA his mark ϟ LOVLESS,   JANE HOOE
JOHN HOOE, ANTHONY C. GRAY,
JOHN COLE, WILLIAM MARTIN

At a Court held for Prince William County the seventh day of December 1795
This Deed and the Receipt thereon from HOWSON HOOE & JANE his Wife to ROBERT COLE
was proved by the Oaths of JOHN MADDOX, JOHN COLE & WILLIAM MARTIN and ordered
to be recorded   Teste JOHN WILLIAMS, Cl Cur

pp.   (On margin: Examd. & Deld. the 15th day July 1799, W. H.)
614-   THIS INDENTURE made the Twenty second day of July in year of our Lord one
616   thousand seven hundred and ninety five Between WILLIAM SKINKER & MARY
         his Wife of County of Prince William of one part and WILLIAM ROBINSON of
aforesd. County of other part; Witnesseth that WILLIAM SKINKER for the sum of Thirty
pounds Virginia currencey paid by WILLIAM ROBINSON, by these presents doth bargain & sell unto WILLIAM ROBINSON his heirs all that parcell of Land situate in County
of Prince William near the RED HOUSE, Beginning on the South side of the Road leading
to DUMFRIES, thence along the side of said Road South 61 degrees East 20 pole, thence
South 29 degrees West 8 pole, thence North 61 degrees West 20 pole, thence North 29 degrees East 8 pole to the beginning; containing One acre by actual survey made there by
WILLIAM CUNDIFF, And also all trees commons, profits, commodities and appurtenances
belonging; To have and to hold the tenement unto WILLIAM ROBINSON his heirs; And
WILLIAM SKINKER and MARY his Wife & their heirs the premises against them and all
persons to WILLIAM ROBINSON his heirs shall warrant and for ever defend by these
presents; In Witness whereof the said WILLIAM SKINKER and MARY his Wife hath
hereunto set their hands and seals the day and year above written
Signed Sealed and Delivered in presence of
         JAMES GARDINER,   WM. SKINKER
         WM. CUNDIFF, ENOCK SMITH LANE,   MARY SKINKER
         GEORGE JONES, THOMAS ATTWELL,
         RICHD. his mark + SHURLEY, NATHL. ROBINSON
         BENJN: WHEELER, EDW: ROBINSON
The Commonwealth of Virginia to HENRY WASHINGTON, CHARLES TYLER & JOHN
BROWN, Gentlemen, Greeting, Whereas (the Commission for the privy Examination of MARY,
the Wife of WILLIAM SKINKER); Witness JOHN WILLIAMS Clerk of our sd. Court this 3d day
of September 1795 and in the 20th year of our Foundation JOHN WILLIAMS
 Prince William County, to wit, In Obedience to the within, we the Subscribers have
caused to come before us the within named MARY SKINKER and have examined her
privily (the return of the execution of the privy examination of MARY SKINKER); Given under
our hands and seals this 10th day of Octr: 1795   HENRY WASHINGTON
                                                     CHARLES TYLER
   At a Court held for Prince William County the seventh day of December 1795
This Deed and the Receipt thereon from WILLIAM SKINKER & MARY his Wife to WIL-
LIAM ROBINSON was proved, the Deed by the Oaths of ENOCK S. LANE, EDWARD ROBINSON
and GEORGE JONES and the Receipt by the Oath of EDWARD ROBINSON and together with a
Dedimus for the privy Examination of the sd. MARY returned executed, were ordered to
be recorded   Teste JOHN WILLIAMS, Cl Cur

pp.   (On margin: Examd. & Deld. NATH. ELLICOTT March 17th 1796, J. WILLIAMS)
616-   THIS INDENTURE made this Eighteenth day of September in year of our Lord
618   one thousand seven hundred and ninety five Between NATHANIEL ELLICOTT of
         County of Prince William of one part and JAMES CARY of the Town of BALTI-
MORE in the State of MARYLAND of other part; Whereas ISAAC McPHERSON of the Town
of ALEXANDRIA in the State of Virginia being seized of a tract of land lying & being
upon the RIVER OCCOQUAN in the said County and those Mills & Improvements there-

upon made and erected commonly called by the name of OCCOQUAN MILLS, said ISAAC McPHERSON did by Indenture for the consideration therein mentioned sell & convey unto NATHANIEL ELLICOTT his heirs one equal undivided moiety of said tract of land, Mills & Improvements which tract of land is in and by the said Indenture fully plainly and distinctly meted and bounded, And Whereas the said NATHANIEL ELLICOTT and ISAAC McPHERSON did afterwards enter into certain articles of Copartnership by which the said Lands, Mills & Improvements are by them made part of their Stock in Business in which articles it is among other things stipulated and agreed upon between them that there shall be annually during the continuation of the Copartnership a valuation made by them of the said tract of land Mills & Improvements and that in the case of the death of either of them during the continuation of the Copartnership the surviver should have the option of taking the said lands Mills & Improvements at the last valuation thereupon set by them; And Whereas NATHANIEL ELLICOTT by his Intermarriage with ELIZABETH, the Daughter of JOHN ELLICOTT, late of said County of BALTIMORE in the State of MARYLAND deceased hath and will receive a very considerable sum of money as the portion of her the said ELIZABETH which sum of money said NATHANIEL ELLICOTT ia anxious of securing unto her the said ELIZABETH in case she shall survive him and in case of the death of her during his life of securing the sum of money to the issue of them the said NATHANIEL ELLICOTT and ELIZABETH his Wife; Therefore, this Indenture Witnesseth that NATHANIEL ELLICOTT as well to secure the payment of the sum of Two thousand seven hundred and thirty two pounds 4/9 current money of Virginia the sum of money received and to be received by him the said NATHANIEL as the port of said ELIZABETH unto her said ELIZABETH and in consideration of One Dollar to him paid by JAMES CARY doth bargain and sell unto said JAMES CAREY his heirs all that equal undivided moiety of that tract of land Mills & Improvements lying and being upon the RIVER OCCOQUAN in the County of Prince William sold and conveyed unto NATHANIEL ELLICOTT by ISAAC McPHERSON. To Hold in Trust for the uses and purposes herein after mentioned that is to say JAMES CAREY or his heirs shall after the death of NATHANIEL ELLICOTT as soon as conveniently be done raise from off the premises by sale or otherwise the sum of Two thousand Seven hundred and thirty two pounds 4/9 current money of Virginia and pay the same unto said ELIZABETH, but in case said ELIZABETH have departed this life before NATHANIEL ELLICOTT then JAMES CAREY and his heirs shall pay the same in equal proportions to the several Children begotten between said NATHANIEL ELLICOTT and ELIZABETH his Wife; In Witness whereof the said several parties have hereunto set their hands and seals the day and year first before mentioned

Signed Sealed and Delivered in presence of
    JOHN RANDELL   NATHANIEL ELLICOTT
    JAMES MUSCHETT (as to NATHANIEL ELLICOTT)   JAMES CAREY
    MUNGO HANCOCK (as to NATHANIEL ELLICOTT)

   At a Court held for Prince William County the Seventh day of Decemberr 1795 This Deed in Trust from NATHANIEL ELLICOTT to JAMES CAREY was acknowledged by the said ELLICOTT to be his act and deed and ordered to be recorded

pp.   (On margin: Examd. & Deld. 17th March 1796, J. WILLIAMS)
618-   THIS INDENTURE made the ninth day of October in the year of our Lord one
621   thousand seven hundred and ninety five Between JOHN TAYLOE and ANN his
       Wife of County of RICHMOND of one part and ARCHIBALD CARR of County of
Prince William of other part; Witnesseth that JOHN TAYLOE and ANN his Wife for the sum of Three hundred and Fifty pounds current money of Virginia to them in hand

paid by ARCHIBALD CARR, by these presents do bargain and sell unto ARCHIBALD CARR his heirs all that parcell of land lying on North Run of QUANTICO in County of Prince William and bounded, Beginning at a marked white Oak sappling on South side of said Run, corner to LUKE CANNON, running thence with his line So. 76 Wt. 90 poles to a marked red Oak on North side of a small Branch, thence up said Branch No. 63 Wt. 20 poles to a marked Dogwood and Hickory, thence South 52d. 15m. Wt. 30 poles to a heap of Stones in said CANNONs Line, corner to DANIEL CARR, thence with DANIEL CARRs line No. 22 Wt. 286 poles to a marked red Oak sapling in the out line of the Patent, thence with that line No. 53 1/2 Et. 115 poles to a marked Poplar and Beech on South side of said Run, thence down the run and binding therewith on the South side of said Run, thence down the Run and binding therewith to a marked red Oak saplin on the South side thereof, the beginning corner of JOHN SOWDENs Land, then with his line No. 55 Et. crossing the Run 6 poles to a marked Mulberry tree, thence No. 68 Et. 22 poles, thence So. 88 1/2 Et. 80 poles crossing KEYES's Road to SOWDENs Corner Hickory, thence So. 25 Et. 121 poles 17 links to a marked Hickory red Oak and Gum saplings, thence No. 74 1/2 Wt. 165 poles to the first station, including by a late Survey Three hundred & fifty acres together with all houses commons profits and appurtenances; To have and to hold the tenement with the appurtenances unto ARCHIBALD CARR his heirs; And JOHN TAYLOE & ANN his Wife and their heirs the said premises against all persons to said ARCHIBALD CARR his heirs will warrant and for ever defend by these presents; In Witness whereof the said JOHN TAYLOE and ANN his Wife have hereunto set their hands & seals the day and year above written

Signed Sealed and Delivered in the presence of

WILLIAM CARR,	JOHN TAYLOE
THOMAS TRIPLETT,	ANN TAYLOE
JAMES WALLACE, LUKE CANNON	

The Commonwealth of Virginia to ROBERT WORMLEY CARTER, GEORGE LEE TURBER-VILLE & VINCENT REDMAN, Gentlemen, Greeting; Whereas (the Commission for the privy Examination of ANN, the Wife of JOHN TAYLOE); Witness JOHN WILLIAMS Clerk of our said County Court this ninth day of October 1795 & in the twentyeth year of the Common-wealth   JOHN WILLIAMS

RICHMOND County, to wit; In Obedience to the within, we the Subscribers have caused to come before us the within named ANN TAYLOE and have examined her privately (the return of the execution of the privy Examination of ANN TAYLOE); Given under our hands and seals this ninth day of October 1795   GEORGE LEE TURBERVILLE
                                                                                                                   VINCENT REDMAN

At a Court held for Prince William County the seventh day of December 1795 This Deed from JOHN TAYLOE and ANN his Wife to ARCHIBALD CARR was proved to be the act and deed of said JOHN TAYLOE by the Oaths of WILLIAM CARR, THOMAS TRIPLETT and LUKE CANNON and together with a Dedimus for the privy Examination of Ann returned executed, ordered to be recorded   Teste JOHN WILLIAMS, Cl Cur

pp.   THIS INDENTURE made the ninth day of October in year of our Lord one thou-
621-   sand seven hundred and ninety five Between JOHN TAYLOE and ANN his Wife of
623   County of RICHMOND of one part and DANIEL CARR of County of Prince William
           of other part; Witnesseth that JOHN TAYLOE & ANN his Wife for the sum of Three hundred & fifty pounds current money of Virginia to them in hand paid by DANIEL CARR, by these presents do bargain & sell unto DANIEL CARR his heirs all that parcell of land lying on South side of North Fork of QUANTICO RUN in County of Prince William & bounded; Beginning at a large marked box Oak on a Path side runing thence S. 24 E.

299 poles to a heap of Stones, corner to LUKE CANNON, thence with his line No. 52 1/4 Et.
250 poles to another heap of Stones, corner to ARCHIBALD CARR, thence with his line
No. 22 Wt. 286 poles to a marked red Oak his corner, thence So. 53 1/2 Wt. 200 poles to the
first station, including Three hundred and Fifty acres together with all houses trees
commons profits and appurtenances; To have and to hold the tenement unto DANIEL
CARR his heirs; And JOHN TAYLOE and ANN his Wife and their heirs against all persons
to DANIEL CARR his heirs shall warrant and for ever defend by these presents; In Wit-
ness whereof the said JOHN TAYLOE & ANN his Wife have hereunto set their hands and
seals the day & year above written
Signed Sealed and Delivered in presence of
              WILLIAM CARR,   THOMAS TRIPLETT,   JOHN TAYLOE
              JAMES WALLACE,   LUKE CANNON   ANN TAYLOE
   The Commonwealth of Virginia to ROBERT WORMELEY CARTER, GEORGE LEE TURBER-
VILLE & VINCENT REDMAN, Gentlemen Greeting; Whereas (the Commission for the privy
Examination of ANN, the Wife of JOHN TAYLOE); Witness JOHN WILLIAMS Clerk of the said
Court the sixth day of October 1795 and in the 20th year of the Commonwealth
   RICHMOND County, to wit; In Obedience to the within, we the Subscribers have caused
to come before us the within named ANN TAYLOE and have examined her privately (the
return of the execution of the privy Examination of ANN TAYLOE); Given under our hands and
seals this ninth day of October 1795   GEORGE LEE TURBERVILLE
                                             VINCENT REDMAN
   At a Court held for Prince William County the seventh day of December 1795
This Deed from JOHN TAYLOE and ANN his Wife to DANIEL CARR was proved to be the act
and deed of said JOHN TAYLOE by the Oaths of WILLIAM CARR, THOMAS TRIPLETT &
LUKE CANNON and together with a Dedimus for the privy Examination of the said Ann
returned executed, ordered to be recorded   Teste JOHN WILLIAMS, Cl Cur

pp.   THIS INDENTURE made this ninth day of October in year of our Lord one thou-
623-   sand seven hundred and ninety five Between JOHN TAYLOE Esqr. & ANN his Wife
624   of County of RICHMOND of one part and JOHN CANNON of County of Prince Wil-
            liam of other part; Witnesseth that JOHN TAYLOE & ANN his Wife in considera-
tion of Eighty pounds to them in hand paid, by these presents doth bargain & sell unto
JOHN CANNON his heirs all that parcel of land lying in County of Prince William & contained within the following bounds; Begining at a marked white Oak in or near Mr.
TAYLOEs line about 3 poles from a stooping white Oak, formerly marked as a corner to
JOHN CANNON & JOHN GIBSON, now call'd McDANIELs corner, runing thence No. 73 West
227 poles to a Stake, thence N. 17 Et. 96 poles to several marked Hickory bushes, thence
S. 73d. Et. 93 poles to sundry marked saplings, thence S. 49 E. 80 poles to a marked Gum,
thence S. 26 1/2 Et. 85 poles to the first station, including One hundred acres of land be
the same more or less; and all rents and services thereof; To have and to hold the said
tract of land with the appurtenances unto JOHN CANNON his heirs; And JOHN TAYLOE &
ANN his Wife and their heirs the tract of land against all persons to JOHN CANNON his
heirs shall warrent and for ever defend by these presents; In Witness whereof the said
JOHN TAYLOE & ANN his Wife hath hereunto set their hands & seals the day & year
above written
Signed Sealed & Delivered in presence of
              WILLIAM CARR,   THOMAS TRIPLETT,   JOHN TAYLOE
              JAMES WALLACE THANE, LUKE CANNON
   At a Court held for Prince William County the 7th day of December 1795
This Deed from JOHN TAYLOE & ANN his Wife to JOHN CANNON was proved by the Oaths of

WILLIAM CARR, THOMAS TRIPLETT & LUKE CANNON and ordered to be recorded
Teste JOHN WILLIAMS, Cl Cur

pp.   (On margin: Examined & deld. J. GILBERT 113th March 1797, N. COX).
624-   THIS INDENTURE made this thirtieth day of July one thousand seven hundred
626   and ninety five Between JOHN LANGFITT & SARAH his Wife of County of Prince
William of one part and JOSEPH GILBERT of same County of other part; Witnesseth that JOHN LANGFITT and SARAH his Wife for the sum of Three hundred pounds
specie current money to them in hand paid by JOSEPH GILBERT, by these presents do
bargain sell & confirm unto JOSEPH GILBERT and to his heirs all that part of a lott lying
in Town of DUMFRIES laid down in plan of said Town by the number Twenty Five which
part of the lott hereby conveyed is bounded by ROCKY RUN or Branch on the East, the
Main or WATER STREET on the South, the Lott No. Twenty Six on the North and the Lott
No. Thirty four on the West; And is the same lott which was conveyed to said SARAH by
her Father, ISRAEL FOLSOM, by Deed bearing date the twenty sixth day of July in year of
our Lord one thousand seven hundred and Seventy one; and duly recorded among the
Records of the County Court of Prince William on the seventh day of September one
thousand seven hundred & seventy one; And all hoses orchards, profits commodities
and appurtenances to the same in any wise appurtaining; and the Rents issues & profits
thereof; To have and to hold the aforesaid piece of a lott of land unto JOSEPH GILBERT
his heirs; And JOHN LANGFITT and SARAH his Wife and their heirs do by these presents
warrent and defend the peice of a lott of land against the claim of all persons; In Witness whereof the said JOHN LANGFITT & SARAH his Wife have herunto set their hands
and affixed their seals the day & year above written
Sealed and Delivered in presents of
      ALEXR. LITHGOW,   JOHN LANGFITT
      WILLIAM SMITH, JOHN WILLIAMS   SARAH LANGFITT
      J. LAWSON, ELIJAH BIGBE
The Commonwealth of Virginia to ALEXANDER LITHGOW, JOHN LAWSON and JAMES
SMITH Gentlemen, Greeting, Whereas (the Commission for the privy Examination of SARAH,
the Wife of JOHN LANGFITT); Witness JOHN WILLIAMS Clerk of our said Court this 30th day
of July 1795 & in the Twentieth year of the Commonwealth   JOHN WILLIAMS
  Prince William County to wit; In obedience to the within, we the Subscribers have
caused to come before us the within named SARAH LANGFITT and have examined her
privily (the return of the execution of the privy examination of SARAH LANGFITT); Given under
ur hands & seals this 31st day of July 1795   ALEXR: LITHGOW
                                      J. LAWSON
At a Court held for Prince William County the 7th day of December 1795
This Deed from JOHN LANGFITT and SARAH his Wife to JOSEPH GILBERT was proved by
the Oaths of WILLIAM SMITH, JOHN WILLIAMS & ALEXANDER LITHGOW, with a Dedimus
for the privy examination of the said SARAH returned executed, ordered to be recorded
Teste JOHN WILLIAMS, Cl Cur

pp.   THIS INDENTURE made the 2d. day of June 1795 Between CHARLES TYLER of
626-   County of Prince William of one part and RICHARD KING of said County of other
627   part; Witnesseth that in consideration of the Rents ariseing annually, the said
    CHARLES TYLER doth demise farm & lease unto RICHARD KING a certain tract of
land lying in said County containing Three hundred acres bounding on ROCKY RUN and
Capt. TEBBS's Old Plantation, formerly the property of WILLIAM HENDERSON; To have
and to hold the said land and premises unto RICHARD KING his heirs during the natural

life of sd. RICHARD KING, SARAH KING & JOHN BAYS or the life of the longest liver of them, paying annually during the sd. term unto CHARLES TYLER his heirs, the reasonable Rent of Three thousand pounds of Crop Tobacco containing casks, together with all the land tax which may be due on the said land, And further RICHARD KING is to reserve one fourth part of the Wood Land where sd. CHARLES shall point out to him and keep the Apple and Peach Orchard in good rapair during the term; The parties to these Indentures have interchangably set their hands & affixed their seals this day & year first above mentioned

Teste GEO: G. TYLER,   CHARLES TYLER
      WILLIAM ALLEN,   RICHD: KING
      ELIZABETH her mark X SMITH

At a Court held for Prince William County the 7th day of December 1795
This Lease from CHARLES TYLER to RICHARD KING was acknowledged by the said parties to be their acts and deeds and ordered to be recorded
                        Teste JOHN WILLIAMS, Cl Cur

pp.   THIS INDENTURE made the 19th day of August in year of our Lord one thousand
627-   seven hundred & ninety five Between ARCHIBALD CARR of County of Prince
628   William of one part and JOHN SOWDEN of County aforesaid of other part; Witnes-
         seth that ARCHIBALD CARR for the sum of Five pounds current money of Vir-
ginia to him in hand paid by JOHN SOWDEN, by these presents do bargain & sell unto
JOHN SOWDEN his heirs a certain tract of land lying in Prince William County on the
North Fork of QUANTICO RUN bounded, Begining at the mouth of a small Branch making
into the North Run of QUANTICO opposite the Mill now a building intended for a PAPER
MILL, runing thence So. 56 1/2 Wt. 4 poles to a white Oak on South East side of said
Branch, thence North 37 Wt. 15 po., thence North 20 Wt. 12 poles, thence No. 48 1/2 Wt. 6
poles, thence North 12 Et. 12 poles; thence North 35 Et. 15 poles to the aforesaid Run including in the whole One acre of land, the same being part of a tract of land granted by
WILLIAM BERKLEY, Governor, to WILLIAM BEACH & RICHARD HALOST by Ded bearing
date 22nd March 1665/6, for Two thousand Two hundred acres and the said HALOST
having assigned his right by Deed bearing date the 16th February 1666 to RICHARD
NORMANSEL by the said RICHARD NORMANSEL & WILLIAM BEACH conveyed to a certain
ABRAHAM JENSON by Deed bearing date 27th May 166() all which conveyances are
recorded in the County of STAFFORD and the said tract was by ABRAHAM JENSON conveyed to the Revd. EMANUEL JONES & by said JONES to JOHN TAYLOE deceased, from
whom it descended to JOHN TAYLOE JUNR., who conveyed part thereof to LUKE CANNON,
FRANCIS CANNON, DANIEL CARR & ARCHIBALD CARR, party to these presents; And also
all trees proffits commodities and appurtenances belonging; To have and to hold the
tenement and all the said premises unto JOHN SOWDEN his heirs; And ARCHIBALD CARR
and his heirs to JOHN SOWDEN his heirs shall warrant & forever defend by these presents; In Witness whereof the said ARCHIBALD CARR hath hereunto set his hand and
seal the day and year first above written
Signed Sealed and Delivered in presence of
      W. GRANT,   ARCHIBALD CARR
      WILLIAM TAITT, CARTY WELLS

At a Court held for Prince William County the 7th day of December 1795
This Deed from ARCHIBALD CARR to JOHN SOWDEN was proved by the Oaths of WILLIAM
GRANT, WILLIAM TACKETT and CARTY WELLS and ordered to be recorded
                        Teste JOHN WILLIAMS Cl Cur

pp.   THIS INDENTURE made this Seventh day of December in year of our Lord one
629-   thousand seven hundred & ninety five Between ARCHIBALD CARR of Prince Wil-
630   liam County of one part and CARTY WELLS of County aforesaid of other part;
         Witnesseth that ARCHIBALD CARR for the sum of Two hundred pounds current
money of Virginia to him in hand paid by CARTY WELL, by these presents doth bargain
sell and confirm unto CARTY WELLS his heirs a certain tract of land containing One
hundred acres, it being part of Three hundred and fifty acres which ARCHIBALD CARR
pourchased of JOHN TAYLOE Esqr., and also part of a Thousand acre tract bought of said
TAYLOE by LUKE CANNON, FRANCIS CANNON, DANIEL CARR and ARCHIBALD CARR, party to these presents; the whole lying in County of Prince William situate on the North
Run of QUANTICO CREEK and bounded; Begining at a Hickory marked on three sides
standing in the Dividing Line between DANIEL CARR and said ARCHIBALD CARR, thence
No. 56 deg. East 87 poles to the North Run of QUANTICO CREEK to a marked Dogwood,
thence down said North Run with the several meanders threof South 76 East 22 poles,
North 8 East 17 poles, North 80 East 12 poles, North 74 East 26 poles, North 47 1/2 East 28
poles, South 67 1/2 West 22 poles, South 3 East 28 poles, South 57 1/2 East 44 poles, South
56 West 24 poles to two marked Dogwoods and two red Oaks standing on the Run side on
the West side thereof, thence into the Woods South 48 1/2 West 139 1/2 poles to the
intersection of the aforesaid Dividing Line to a marked red Oak, Poplar, Chesnut, red Oak
and Hickory, thence with the Dividing Line to the begining; to contain One hundred
acres, Togeather with all buildings profits to the same belonging; To have and to hold
the One hundred acres of land with the appurtenances unto CARTY WELLS his heirs;
And ARCHIBALD CARR and his heirs the within granted premises unto CARTY WELLS
his heirs shall warrant and for ever Defend by these presents; In Witness whereof the
said ARCHIBALD CARR hath hereunto set his hand and affixed his seal the day & year
first above written
Signed Sealed and Delivered in presence of
     W. GRANT,   ARCHIBALD CARR
     JOHN SOWDEN, WILLIAM TAITT
  At a Court held for Prince William County the seventh day of December 1795
This Deed from ARCHIBALD CARR to CARTY WELLS was proved by the Oaths of WILLIAM
GRANT, JOHN SOWDEN & WILLIAM TACKETT & ordered to be recorded
                         Teste JOHN WILLIAMS, Cl Cur

p.   TO ALL WHOM these presents shall come, I JOSEPH FLORENCE do send Greeting:
631   Know ye that I JOSEPH FLORENCE of County of Prince William in consideration of
         the love good will and affection which I have and do bear towards my loving
Son in Law, JAMES NOLEN, and MARY his Wife of County aforesaid by these presents do
freely give & grant unto JAMES NOLEN and MARY his Wife their heirs one Negroe girl
nam'd Sarah; To have and to hold said Negroe Sarah from henceforth as his proper
right & title without any manner of condition; In Witness whereof I have hereunto set
my hand and seal this second day of December in year of our Lord one thousand seven
hundred and Ninety five
Signed Sealed and Delivered in presence of
     JAMES WIGGENTON   JOSEPH his mark X FLORENCE
     WILLIAM FLORENCE,
     CELAH her mark X CLEAVAN:
  At a Court held for Prince William County the seventh day of December 1795
This Deed of Gift from JOSEPH FLORENCE to JAMES NOLEN was proved by the Oath of
JAMES WIGGINTON and ordered to be recorded
                         Teste JOHN WILLIAMS, Cl Cur

pp.   THIS INDENTURE made and entered into this seventeenth day of November in
631-   the year of our Lord one thousand seven hundred & ninety five Between
632   EZEKIEL DONNELL of County of Prince William of one part and THOMAS JACOB of
        County aforesaid of other part; Witnesseth that EZEKIEL DONNELL for the sum of
six hundred and twenty five pounds current money to Virginia to him in hand paid by
THOMAS JACOBS, by these presents do bargain sell and confirm unto THOMAS JACOBS
and his heirs one Lott or half acre of Land lying in Town of DUMFRIES and County
aforesaid laid down in a platt of said Town by the number One hundred and Eighty, and
was conveyed to EZEKIEL DONNELL by JOHN DONNELL by Deed executed the Sixteenth day
of March one thousand seven hundred and ninety three and duly recorded among the
Records of aforesaid County, Also all that piece of Ground in said Town by WATER
STREET and QUANTICO CREEK and adjoining to the aforesaid lott numbered One hundred
and Eighty, which piece of ground was conveyed to EZEKIEL DONNELL by HENRY LEE
Esquire by Deed bearing date the twenty seventh day of August one thousand seven
hundred and ninety three and duly recorded among the Records of the DISTRICT COURT
held at the Town of DUMFRIES; To have and to hold the bargained premises unto THO-
MAS JACOB his heirs; And EZEKIEL DONNELL his heirs doth warrant and for ever defend
the bargained premises unto THOMAS JACOB and his heirs against all claims of any
person; In Witness whereof said EZEKIEL DONNELL hath hereunto set his hand & seal
the day and year first written
Signed Sealed and Delivered in the presence of
      JOHN WILLIAMS, WY: TEBBS,   EZEKIEL DONNELL
      WM. SMITH, WM. ATTWELL,
      JNO: W. WIGGINTON, JAS: JOHNSTON
  At a Court held for Prince William County the 7th day of December 1795
This Deed from EZEKIEL DONNELL to THOMAS JACOB was proved by the Oaths of WILLIAM
SMITH, JOHN WILLIAMS & WILLIAM ATTWELL & ordered to be recorded
             Teste JOHN WILLIAMS, Cl Cur

pp.   (On margin: Examd. & deld. CHS. LOVE the 5th April 1796, J. WMS.)
632-   THIS INDENTURE made this Fourteenth day of July Seventeen hundred and
635   ninety four Between AUGUSTINE LOVE & MARY his Wife of County of FAUQUIER
        of one part and SAMUEL LOVE of County of LOUDOUN of other part; Witnesseth
that AUGUSTINE LOVE and MARY his Wife for the sum of Four hundred pounds to them
in hand paid by the said SAMUEL LOVE, have bargained sold & confirmed unto
SAMUEL LOVE his heirs all those two tracts of land adjoining each other lying in County
of Prince William on BROAD RUN (one of those tracts is a WATER GRIST MILL), the land
intended to be conveyed by this Deed is the Land bought by SAMUEL LOVE of ROBERT
BROWN & Wife, and afterwards sold by SAMUEL LOVE to the abovesaid AUGUSTINE LOVE
which is recorded in the Office of the DISTRICT COURT of DUMFRIES; said Deed bearing
date the seventh day of October in year Seventeen hundred & ninety one containing
Three hundred and ten acres together with all houses orchards and water courses belonging; To have and to hold the aforesaid Land according to the bounds as described in
the Deeds above referenced with all appurtenances unto SAMUEL LOVE his heirs free
and clear from all Incumbrances whatsoever; And AUGUSTINE LOVE and MARY his Wife
and their heirs the premises hereby sold unto SAMUEL LOVE his heirs will warrent and
for ever defend by these presents; In Witness whereof the said AUGUSTINE LOVE and
MARY his Wife have hereunto set their hands and affixed their seals the day and year
first above written

Signed sealed and delivered in presence of

JAMES NISBETT, GEO: LEE,
FRANCIS ADAMS, ISAAC HUTCHISON,
CHARLES J. LOVE, JOSEPH GRANT,
ROBERT BROWN, AMBROSE BARNETT

AUGUST: LOVE
MARY LOVE

The Commonwealth of Virginia to THOMAS DIGGS, AMBROSE BARNETT & ROBERT BROWN Gentlemen, Greeting, Whereas (the Commission for the privy Examination of MARY, the Wife of AUGUSTINE LOVE); Witness ROBERT GRAHAM Clerk of said Court the 3rd day of October 1794 & in the 19th year of the Commonwealth   ROBERT GRAHAM

FAUQUIER County to wit; In Obedience to the within, we the Subscribers have caused to come before us the within named MARY LOVE and have examined her privately (the return of the execution of the privy Examination of MARY LOVE); Given under our hand & seals this 27th day of November 1794   AMBROSE BARNETT
ROBERT BROWN

At a Court held for Prince William County the fifth day of Jany: 1795
This Deed from AUGUSTINE LOVE and MARY LOVE his Wife to SAMUEL LOVE was proved by the Oath of CHARLES J. LOVE and ordered to be Certified; And at a Court held for said County the sixth day of July in year aforesaid, this Deed was further proved by the Oath of JAMES NISBETT and ordered to be further Certified; And at a Court continued and held for the said County the eighth day of December in the year aforesaid, this same Deed was fully proved by the Oath of GEORGE LEE and together with the Commission for the examination of the said feme returned executed, ordered to be recorded
Teste JOHN WILLIAMS, Cl Cur

pp.
635-
636

KNOW ALL MEN by these presents that we ANN ATTWELL, Administratrix, and CHARLES B. ATTWELL, Administrator, with the Will annexed of THOMAS ATTWELL deceased, of County of Prince William by these presents do appoint WILLIAM ATTWELL of County aforesaid our true and lawful Attorney for us and in our names to ask demand sue for recover and receive all debts and dues which shall be due or owing to us on account of THOMAS ATTWELL deced., confirming all our said Attorney shall lawfully do concerning the premises; In Witness whereof we have hereunto set our hands and affixed our seals this Thirtieth day of December in year of our Lord one thousand seven hundred and ninety five
Signed Sealed and Acknowledged in presence of

GEORGE TEBBS,
JOHN LINTON, THOMAS SMITH

ANN ATTWELL
CHARLES B. ATTWELL

At a Court held for Prince William County the 6th day of Jany. 1796
This Letter of Attorney from ANN ATTWELL, Administratrix, and CHARLES B. ATTWELL, Administrator, with the Will annexed of THOMAS ATTWELL deceased, to WILLIAM ATT-WELL was proved by the Oaths of JOHN LINTON & THOMAS SMITH and ordered to be recorded   Teste JOHN WILLIAMS, Cl Cur

pp.
636-
637

(On margin: Examined & Delivered DANL. GRANT pr. Order of JOHN LANSDOWN, Exor. of JNO: LANSDOWN, A. HAYES)
THIS INDENTURE made the Eighteenth day of September in year of our Lord Christ one thousand seven hundred and ninety two Between JOHN LANSDOWN of County of Prince William of one part & BENJAMIN HARRISON & MARY his Wife of County of FAUQUIRE of other part; Witnesseth that BENJAMIN HARRISON in consideration of the tract of land lying on GOOSE RUN which JOHN POPE and Wife bartered and exchanged with said HARRISON for the within mentioned premises, said BENJAMIN HARRISON and MARY his Wife have granted demised & to farm lett unto JOHN LANS-

DOWN a certain tract of land lying in County of Prince William and on the Waters of
CHAPERWAMSICK and LUCKEY RUNs, containing Two hundred and seventy five acres
bounded, Beginning at four white Oaks on the said CHAPERWAMSICK RUN at the mouth
of a small Branch three of which sd. white Oaks stand on the upper or South side of a
small Branch and the other on South side of said CHAPERWAMSICK, thence No. 87 W. 186
poles to two red Oaks & a black Oak in HELM's line thence with HELM's line S. 11 W. 46
poles to a Stake on LUCKY RUN near KENDALS STILL HOUSE, thence So. 4. W. 234 poles to
a Hickory red Oak and black Oak, thence with an antient marked line S. 51 E. 262 poles to
a white Oak in BRIDWELLs line, thence with BRIDWELLs line No. 34 Et. 18 poles to two
white Oaks by some call'd Box Oaks near ACQUIA ROAD and corner to WM. GERRARD,
thence No. 40 W. 176 poles to two Persimmons, two Maples and a white Oak in East Fork
of North Branch of CHAPERWAMSICK RUN thence down the several meanders of said
CHAPERWAMSICK RUN to the begining, containing Two hundred and seventy five acres
and all houses orchards profits commodities and appurtenances to said premiese belonging; To have and to hold the Two hundred and Seventy five acres of land granted
and demised unto JOHN LANSDOWN his heirs dureing the full term of one whole year
paying therfor the Rent of one Ear of Indian Corn to said BENJAMIN and MARY his Wife
on the last day of said term if the same shall be lawfully demanded to the intent that by
virtue of these presents and of the Statute for transferring uses into possession the said
JOHN LANSDOWN may be in the actual possession of the premises and be thereby the
better enabled to accept a release of the reversion and inheritance thereof; In Witness
whereof the said BENJAMIN HARRISON & MARY his Wife hath hereunto set their hands
and seals the day and year first above written
Sealed and Delivered in presence of

JOHN BURROUGHS,		BEN: HARRISON
BENJAMIN GRIGORY,	JAMES HOMES	MARY HARRISON

At a Court continued and held for Prince William County the 4th day of Jany. 1796
This Lease from BENJAMIN HARRISON and MARY his Wife to JOHN LANSDOWN was
proved by the Oaths of JOHN BURROUGHS and BENJAMIN GRIGORY and ordered to be
recorded

pp.   (On margin: Examined and Delivered DANIEL GRANT 8th day of Febry. 1813 per
638-   order JOHN LANSDOWN, A. HAYES)
641   THIS INDENTURE made the Nineteenth day of September in year of our Lord
           Christ one thousand seven hundred and ninety two Between BENJAMIN HARRI-
SON and MARY his Wife of County of FAUQUIER of one part and JOHN LANSDOWN of
County of Prince William of other part; Witnesseth that BENJAMIN HARRISON and
MARY his Wife in consideration of one tract of land lying on GOOSE RUN which JOHN
POPE and Wife bartered and exchanged with said HARRISON for the within mentioned
premises have bargained and sold unto JOHN LANSDOWN (in his actual possession now
being by virtue of a bargain and sale for one whole year and by force of the Statute for
transferring uses into possession) and his heirs a certain tract of land lying in County
of Prince William containing Two hundred and Seventy five acres lying on the North
Fork of CHAPERWAMSICK and bounded; (the description of the bounds of the land repeated as
in the foregoing Lease); To have and to hold the Two hundred and Seventy five acres of
land unto JOHN LANSDOWN his heirs free and clear from all incumbrances whatsoever
And BENJAMIN HARRISON and MARY his Wife their heirs shall warrent and for ever
defend by these presents; In Witness whereof said BENJAMIN HARRISON & MARY his
Wife hath hereunto set their hands & seals the day & year first above written

Sealed and Delivered in presence of
        JOHN BURROUGHS,   BEN: HARRISON
        BENJAMIN GRIGORY, JAMES HOMES   MARY HARRISON
    The Commonwealth of Virginia to JOHN BLACKWELL, ORIGINAL YOUNG & SAML.
BLACKWELL Gentlemen, Justices, Greeting, Whereas (the Commission for the privy Examina-
tion of MARY the Wife of BENJAMIN HARRISON); Witness ROBERT GRAHAM Clerk of our said
Court the 17th day of September in the 17th year of the Commonwealth 1792
    Prince William County, to wit; We SAMUEL BLACKWELL and ORIGINAL YOUNG pursuant
to the within Dedimus, we have apart from her Husband examined the within named
MARY HARRISON (the return of the execution of the privy Examination of MARY HARRISON);
Given under our hands & seals this nineteenth day of September A. D. 1792
                            SAML. BLACKWELL
                            ORIGINAL YOUNG
    At a Court continued and held for Prince William County the 8th day of January 1793
This Release from BENJAMIN HARRISON and MARY his Wife to JOHN LANSDOWN was
proved by the Oaths of JOHN BURROUGHS and BENJAMIN GRIGORY and the Receipt
thereon endorsed by JOHN BURROUGHS and the said Release and Receipt were ordered to
be Certfied;   Teste ROBT. GRAHAM, Cl Cur
    At a Court held for Prince William County the 4th day of January 1796
This Release was fully proved by the Oath of JAMES HOMES together with the receipt
thereon endorsed & the Dedimus for the privy examination of the feme returned executed were ordered to be recorded   Teste JOHN WILLIAMS, Cl Cur

pp.   THIS INDENTURE made this Sixteenth day of October one thousand seven hun-
641-   dred and ninety five Between HENRY DAVIS & MARY his Wife of one part &
643   CORNELIUS KINCHELOE of other part; Witnesseth that HENRY DAVIS & MARY his
           Wife for the sum of Nine pounds current money of Virginia to said HENRY
DAVIS in hand paid by CORNELIUS KINCHELOE, by these presents doth bargain & sell
unto CORNELIUS KINCHELOE hisheirs all the tenement of land lying in Prince William
County in QUANTICO NECK, it being part of a tract of land held by NATHANIEL WICKLIFF
deced. who dyed without Will, therefore his Estate by a late Act of Assembly was divided
between the heirs of BENJAMIN WICKLIFF, half Brother to sd. NATHANIEL, and Father to
said MARY DAVIS, and the heirs of ELIZABETH KINCHELOE deced., Sister to aforesaid
NATHANIEL, containing Eleven acres more or less, Also all houses profits and apperte-
nances; To have and to hold the tenement with the appertanances unto CORNELIUS
KINCHELOE his heirs; And HENRY DAVIS and his heirs the said tenement against every
person to CORNELIUS KINCHELOE & his heirs shall warrant and for ever defend by these
presents; In Witness whereof HENRY DAVIS & MARY his Wife have hereunto set their
hands and seals the day above written
Signd. Sealed & Deliverd. in presents of
        CHS: EWELL, JOSHUA DAVIS,   HENRY DAVIS
        JOHN BEAVERS, JNO: KINCHELOE,   MARY DAVIS
        HUGH DAVIS
    The Commonwealth of Virginia to ROBERT H. HOOE & CHARLES EWELL Gentlemen,
Greeing, Whereas (the Commission for the privy Examination of MARY, the Wife of HENRY
DAVIS); Witness JOHN WILLIAMS Clerk of our said Court this 16th of October in the 20th
year of the Commonwealth 1795   J. WILLIAMS
    Prince William Sct., Pursuant to the within, we have caused the within named MARY to
come before us and have examined her privily (the return of the execution of the privy Examination of MARY DAVIS); Witness our hands and seals this 16th day of October 1795

ROBT. H. HOOE
CHS: EWELL
At a Court held for Prince William County the fourth day of January 1796
This Deed and the receipt thereon from HENRY DAVIS & MARY his Wife to CORNELIUS
KINCHELOE (a Dedimus for the privy Examination of the feme being returned executed)
were proved by the Oaths of JOHN KINCHELOE, CHARLES EWELL & HUGH DAVIS and
ordered to be recorded   Teste JOHN WILLIAMS, Cl Cur

pp.   THIS INDENTURE made and entered into this Sixteenth day of December in year
643-   of our Lord one thousand seven hundred and ninety five Between RICHARD
645   MARSHALL SCOTT and JOHN FRISTOE and FRANKY his Wife of Town of DUMFRIES
           County of Prince William of one part and PEGGY CARR of Town & County afore-
said of other part; Witnesseth that RICHARD MARSHALL SCOTT, JOHN FRISTOE &
FRANKY his Wife for the sum of Five hundred and Fifty pounds current money of Virginia to them in hand paid by said PEGGY CARR, do by these presents bargain sell and
confirm unto PEGGY CARR her heirs two lotts in Town of DUMFRIES, the same which
HENRY LEE JUNR. conveyed unto DAVID WILSON SCOTT and RICHARD MARSHALL SCOTT
by Indenture of bargain & sale bearing date the twenty fifth of March one thousand
seven hundred & ninety one, and afterwards conveyed by DAVID WILSON SCOTT to
RICHARD MARSHALL SCOTT by Indenture bearing date the sixth day of October one
thousand seven hundred and ninety three, And also a Deed of bargain and sale from
RICHARD MARSHALL SCOTT and MARY his Wife to said JOHN FRISTOE dated the fifteenth
day of Oct. 1795; Also all houses profits with the appurtenances; To have and to hold the
bargained premises with the appurtenances unto PEGGY CARR her heirs; And RICHARD
MARSHALL SCOTT, JOHN FRISTOE & FRANKY his Wife their heirs doth warrant and for
ever defend the aforesaid bargained premises unto PEGGY CARR her heirs against all
claims of any person; In Witness whereof the said RICHARD MARSHALL SCOTT, JOHN
FRISTOE & FRANKY his Wife hath hereunto set their hands and seals the day and year
first within written
Signed Sealed and Delivered in presence of
     JAMES R. BAILEY, THOMAS CHAPMAN,   JOHN FRISTOE
     GEORGE HUPBER, LUKE CANNON,   FRANKY FRISTOE
                                                RICHD. M. SCOTT
     The Commonwealth of Virginia to ALEXANDER LITHGOW, WILLIAM BARNES and JOHN
LAWSON Gentlemen Greeting; Whereas (the Commission for the privy Examination of FRANKY,
the Wife of JOHN FRISTOE); Witness JOHN WILLIAMS Clerk of our said Court the 16th day of
December 1795 & in the 20th year of the Commonwealth
     Prince William County to wit: In Obedience to the within, we the Subscribers have
caused to come before us the within named FRANKY FRISTOE and have examined her
privately (the return of the execution of the privy Examination of FRANKY FRISTOE); Given
under our hands and seals this 16th day of December 1795
                         ALEXR: LITHGOW
                         WM. BARNES
     At a Court held for Prince William County the 4th day of January 1796
This Deed & the Receipt thereon from RICHARD MARSHALL SCOTT, JOHN FRISTOE &
FRANKY his Wife to PEGGY CARR (a Dedimus for the privy examination of the feme
being returned executed) were proved by the Oaths of GEORGE HUPBER, THOMAS CHAP-
MAN and LUKE CANNON and ordered to be recorded
                         Teste JOHN WILLIAMS, Cl Cur

pp.   THIS INDENTURE made this Thirtieth day of December one thousand seven
645-   hundred and Ninety five Between ARCHIBALD CARR of Town of DUMFRIES in
647   the County of Prince William of one part and JOHN GIBSON of the same Town &
       County of other part; Witnesseth that ARCHIBALD CARR for the sum of One hun-
dred and Thirty pounds current money of Virginia to him in hand paid by JOHN GIBSON,
by these presents doth bargain & sell unto JOHN GIBSON his heirs one tract of land
lying in County of Prince William on East side of the North Run of QUANTICO, containing Seventy three acres (excepting and reserving therefrom for the use of my
Mother during her life Four acres including the House she now lives in to be laid of in
a square on South East side of the Road leading to JAMES DENEALEs MILL), which said
tract of land is part of Three hundred and Fifty acres conveyed by JOHN TAYLOE Esquire
unto ARCHIBALD CARR and is of Record in County Court of Prince William and is
bounded; Beginning at a marked red Oak saplin on South West side of North Run of
QUANTICO, corner to the land sold by JOHN TAYLOE Esqr. to JOHN SOWDEN, thence with
the said SOWDENs lines North fifty five degrees East six poles, crossing the Road to a
marked Mulberry Tree; thence Northerly sixty eight degrees East twenty two poles,
thence South eighty eight and a half degrees East eighty poles crossing KEYES's ROAD to
a marked Hickory, corner to said SOWDEN, thence South twenty five degrees East one
hundred and thirty one poles and seven links to a marked Hickory, red Oak and Gum,
thence North twenty four and a half degrees West one hundred & sixty five poles to a
marked white Oak saplin on South West side of said North Run of QUANTICO, a corner to
LUKE CANNONs land; which he purchased of said JOHN TAYLOE Esquire, thence up the
North Run of QUANTICO and binding therewith to the beginning; containing Seventy
three acres, Together with all houses orchrds profits and appurtenances belonging; To
have and to hold the land and premises (except as before excepted) with every of their
rights members and appurtenances unto JOHN GIBSON his heirs; And ARCHIBALD CARR
his heirs against the claim of every person unto JOHN GIBSON his heirs shall warrant
and for ever defend by these presents; In Witness whereof ARCHIBALD CARR hath
hereunto set his hand and seal the dy and date first herein mentioned
Sealed and Delivered in presence of
    JOHN G. HENDERSON,   ARCHD: CARR
    HECTOR ALEXANDER, CARTY WELLS,
    JOHN O'CONNOR
 At a Court continued and held for Prince William County the fifth day of January 1796
This Deed and the Receipt thereon from ARCHIBALD CARR to JOHN GIBSON was proved
by the Oaths of JOHN G. HENDERSON, HECTOR ALEXANDER and JOHN O'CONNOR and
ordered to be recorded   Teste JOHN WILLIAMS, Cl Cur

pp.   KNOW ALL MEN by these presents that I WILLIAM FARROW of County of Prince
647-   William for the sum of Sixty pounds specie current money by these presents do
648   bargain sell and deliver unto GEORGE LANE of County aforesaid the following
       slaves, to wit, Henny & Pegg & her Child, Franky, Together with the futute in-
crease of the said Henny & Pegg; To have and to hold the said Henny & Pegg & her
Child, Franky, together with the future increase of said Henny & Pegg unto GEORGE
LANE his heirs; And I said WILLIAM FARROW for my self my heirs the said Henny &
Pegg & her Child, Franky, and the future increase of said Henny & Pegg unto GEORGE
LANE his heirs against the claim of every person will for ever warrant and defend by
these presents; Provided Nevertheless and upon this express condition that if WILLIAM
FARROW do well and truly pay to GEORGE LANE his heirs the just sum of Sixty pounds
current money on or before the fifth day of December next for which sum I have given

GEORGE LANE my Bond bearing date with these presents and payable the Twenty fifth
day of December next then these presents shall be void otherwise to be and remain in
full force power & virtue. In Witness whereof I have hereunto set my hand and seal
this Twenty fifth day of September one thousand seven hundred and ninety five
Sealed and Delivered in presence of
    JOHN WILLIAMS, NATHANIEL COX   WILLIAM FARROW
  At a Court held for Prince William County the first day of February 1796
This Bill of Sale from WILLIAM FARROW to GEORGE LANE was proved by the Oath of JOHN
WILLIAMS & ordered to be recorded Teste JOHN WILLIAMS, Cl Cur

pp.   We the Subscribers do agree that these plats do contain a true account of the
648-   Lands left by the Last Will and Testament of our Father, DAVID JAMESON deced.,
650   to us the Legatees of said Will; Therefore in order to avoid all contentions that
      may arise in future, we obligate ourselves our heirs to stand to the hereafter
mentioned corners as being the true intent and meaning of said Last Will and Testament of our Father, DAVID JAMESON, deced., therefore agreeable to a Survey made by
WILLIAM OREAR, the land lies as follows; to wit, for BENJAMIN JAMESON, Begining at a
white Oak thence S. 32 W. 58 poles to a large red Oak, thence S. 35 E. 98 poles to a Box Oak
on East side of a Branch, thence N. 40 E. 100 poles to a Hickory on East side of a Branch,
thence N. 50 E. 61 poles to a small red Oak on a Ridge, thence N. 40 W. 126 poles to a small
white Oak on a Branch, thence down said Branch Wt. 11 poles to a small Dogwood on sd.
Branch, thence S. 47, W. 96 poles to a red Oak on a Ridge, thence S. 165 E. 26 poles to the
begining; For DAVID JAMESON, Beginning at a white Oak (no landmarks or individuals are
noted in the metes and bounds given); For WILLIAM JAMESON, Begining at a red Oak (no land
marks or individuals are noted in the metes and bounds given); To JOHN JAMESON Begining at a
dead Spanish Oak (no landmarks or individuals are noted in the metes and bounds given); For
JAMES JAMESON, Begining at a small white Oak (no landmarks are noted but the land of WM.
RENO is mentioned in the metes and bounds given); We the Subscribers being so well
acquainted with the appointment of our Father for the Division of the before
mentioned Land amongst us the Legatees to the before mentioned land that we think
proper to avoid difference or disputes hereafter to establish these courses to stand as
being the true intent and meaning of our Father, DAVID JAMESON deed., in his Last Will
and Testament, and in order to set and put in further Testamony we have hereunto set
our hands and seals this first day of February in the year of our Lord one thousand
seven hundred and ninety six
Sealed Signed & Delivered in presents of
    TIMOTHY BRUNDIGE,   BENJAMIN JAMESON
    WM. W. DUNNINGTON   DAVID JAMESON
                                WILLIAM JAMESON
                                JAMES JAMESON
  At a Court held for Prince William County the 1st day of Feby: 1796
This Agreement between BENJAMIN JAMESON, DAVID JAMESON, WILLIAM JAMESON &
JAMES JAMESON was acknowledged by the said BENJAMIN, DAVID, WILLIAM & JAMES
and ordered to be recorded   Teste JOHN WILLIAMS, Cl Cur.
(Note: JOHN JAMESON does not appear among those signing nor those mentioned in the recording.)

pp.   THIS INDENTURE made this Fifth day of November in year of our Lord one thou-
650-   sand seven hundred and ninety five Between CHARLES BRENT ATTWELL of
651   County of Prince William of one part and ANN ATTWELL of same County of other
     part; Witnesseth that CHARLES B. ATTWELL in consideration of the natural love

& filial affection which he bears to his Mother, the said ANN ATTWELL, by these presents doth give & confirm unto said ANN ATTWELL all that tract of land lying in County of Prince George which was formerly conveyed to THOMAS ATTWELL by Deeds of Lease & Release from REDMAN GRIGSBY & ELIZABETH his Wife bearing date the 4th & 5th days of December 1778; which said Deeds are duly recorded in the sd. County Court and which tract of land was by THOMAS ATTWELL deeded to his Son, said CHARLES B. ATTWELL, as will appear by the Last Will & Testament of said THOMAS ATTWELL, which is also of Record in the said County Court; containing One hundred acres be the same more or less; To have and to hold the hereby conveyed lands & premises with the appurtenances unto ANN ATTWELL, & her assigns during the term of her natural life and said CHARLES B. ATTWELL for himself and his heirs during the term aforesaid will warrant and defend against the claims of every person; In Witness whereof said CHARLES B. ATTWELL hath hereunto set his hand & seal the day & year herein first above written
Sealed & Delivered in presence of
  JOHN WILLIAMS, MUNGO HANCOCK,   CHARLES B. ATTWELL
  T. CHAPMAN JR., WM. ATTWELL,
  JOHN W. WIGGINTON, THOMAS ATTWELL
At a Court held for Prince William County the 1st day of February 1796
This Deed from CHARLES B. ATTWELL to ANN ATTWELL was proved by the Oaths of WILLIAM ATTWELL, JOHN WILLIAMS & JOHN W. WIGGINTON and ordered to be recorded
      Teste JOHN WILLIAMS, Cl Cur

p. 651 MEMORANDUM of an Agreement made the first day of February in year of our Lord 1796 Between JAMES & GEORGE DENEALE of one part, GEORGE LANE, Guardian of JOHN HUTCHISON of other part & JOHN HUTCHISON of last part; Witnesseth that said HUTCHISON of the age of Seventeen years on the seventh day of November last with his own free will and by the advice and consent of said LANE agrees to serve the said DENEALEs as an apprentice until he arives to the age of twenty three years; in consideration of which service the said DENEALEs agree to cloth him & feed him in a suitable manner and treat him with humanity and to learn or cause him to be taught & learnt the Trade of a Cooper and to send him to School until he can read & write & cypher so far as to understand the Rule of Three and at the expiration of the service to give him a good suit of cloths and Twenty Dollars specie. Given under our hands & seals in Open Court the day & year above written
In the presence of the Court   JAMES & GEO: DENEALE
          GEORGE LANE
          JOHN his mark X HUTCHISON
At a Court held for Prince William County the first day of February 1796
This Agreement of Indenture and Apprenticeship between GEORGE LANE, Guardian to JOHN HUTCHISON, the said JOHN HUTCHISON & JAMES & GEO: DENEALE was acknowledged by said parties and being approved of by the Court ordered to be recorded; & the said JOHN HUTCHISON is ordered to be bound by his said Guardian according to the said Agreement. Teste JOHN WILLIAMS, Cl Cur

pp. 652-653 (On margin: Examd. & Deld. the 17th May 1796, J. WMS:)
THIS INDENTURE made and entered into this ninth day of September in year of our Lord one thousand seven hundred & ninety five Between the REVERD. SPENCE GRAYSON of County of Prince William of one part & SIMON LUTTRELL & THOMAS CHAPMAN, Exors. & Trustees of WM. CARR deced., of the County aforesaid of other part; Witnesseth that SPENCE GRAYSON for the sum of five hundred pounds cur-

rent money of Virginia to him in hand paid by SIMON LUTTRELL & THOMAS CHAPMAN
do by these presents bargain sell & confirm unto SIMON LUTTRELL & THOMAS CHAP-
MAN, Exors. & Trustees as aforesaid, their heirs for the benefit of WM. CARR's heirs,
three several tracts of land lying in Prince William County whereon said SPENCE GRAY-
SON at present resides, it being the same three tracts of land adjoining each other
which SPENCE GRAYSON's Father, BENJAMIN GRAYSON, devised by his Last Will and
Testament in manner following, Vizt., I give & bequeath to my Son, SPENCE GRAYSON,
and the heirs of his body lawfully begotten, Two hundred acres of land where I now
live which I bought from WILLIAM CROUCH, I also give unto my Son, SPENCE GRAYSON,
and the heirs of his body lawfully begotten, One hundred & ninety acres of land adjoining the aforesaid Two hundred acres, the same being granted to me by Deed from
the Proprietors Office dated June the Twenty second Seventeen hundred & forty three;
Item I give & bequeath to my Son, SPENCE GRAYSON, and the heirs of his body lawfully
begotten a tract of land I had from JOHN McMILLIAN which joins the land I now live
on, also all houses profits advantages hereditaments ways waters with the appurtenances of every kind and nature whatever thereunto belonging; To have and to hold
the aforesaid bargained premises with their appurtenances unto said SIMON LUTTRELL
& THOMAS CHAPMAN for the benefit of WILLIAM CARR's heirs agreeable to the Will of
WILLIAM CARR deced. directing the apropriation of his undevised Estate; And SPENCE
GRAYSON his heirs doth warrant and for ever defend the bargained premises unto
SIMON LUTTRELL & THOMAS CHAPMAN, Executors and Trustees as aforesaid, against all
claims of any persons, the intention of the said SPENCE GRAYSON and SIMON LUTTRELL
& THOMAS CHAPMAN parties hereto is that the recited land and premises is conveyed
for the sole purpose of secureing to WILLIAM CARR's heirs the sum of Two hundred and
Twenty eight pounds. Four shillings & five pence current money of Virginia which on
settlement this day is to be justly due and for which SPENCE GRAYSON hath passed two
Bonds each bearing Interest, if said Bonds to be settled and paid by SPENCE GRAYSON in
two years from this date the aforesaid Principal & Interest being paid within the time
mentioned then this Deed of Mortgage to be nul & void otherwise to remain in full force
& virtue. In Witness whereof the said SPENCE GRAYSON hath hereunto set his hand &
seal the date before written
Signed Sealed & Delivd. in presence of
    JESSE EWELL, W. SMITH   SPENCE GRAYSON
    JAMES HAYES, MOSES DAULTON
  At a Court held for Prince William County April the 4th 1796
This Deed of Mortgage from SPENCE GRAYSON to SIMON LUTTRELL & THOMAS CHAPMAN,
Executors and Trustees of WILLIAM CARR deced., was proved by the Oaths of JESSE
EWELL, WILLIAM SMITH & JAMES HAYES and ordered to be recorded
              Teste JOHN WILLIAMS, Cl Cur

pp.   THIS INDENTURE made the first day of October in year of our Lord one thousand
653-   seven hundred & ninety five Between GERARD ALEXANDER SENR. of one part
654   & GERARD ALEXANDER JUNR. of other. Witnesseth that GERARD ALEXANDER
         SENR. in consideration of the natural love and affection which has has for his
Son, GERARD, and of the sum of five pounds to him in hand paid by GERARD ALEXANDER
JUNR., by these presents doth bargain and sell unto GERARD ALEXANDER JUNR. and to
his heirs one moiety of that tract of land which he holds by purchase from PHILLIP
FITZHUGH being part of the BRENTON TRACT, lying in County of Prince William containing Five hundred & Sixty one acres two roods & nineteen poles as follows, vizt., on
the North side by the lands of JOHN FITZHUGH Esqr., on the West by RICHARD BRENT

Esqr., and on the South by W. HOWARD, Together with all houses Mills, Mill Seats woods and water courses to the same belonging; To have and to hold the said tract of land unto GERARD ALEXANDER JUNIOR and to his heirs; In Witness whereof the said GERARD ALEXANDER SEGNIOR hath hereunto set his hand and affixed his seal the day and year above written
Signed Sealed and Delivered in presents of
    LANGH: DADE;   GERARD   ALEXANDER
    DAVID WILSON SCOTT,   JOHN WILLIAMS
  At a Court held for Prince William County April the 4th 1796
This Deed from GERARD ALEXANDER SENR. to GERARD ALEXANDER JUNIOR was proved by the Oaths of DAVIS WILSON SCOTT, JOHN WILLIAMS and LANGHORNE DADE & ordered to be recorded   Teste JOHN WILLIAMS, Cl Cur

pp.   (On margin: Examd. & delivered Mr. ABM. BUSH JR., Son & Atto: in fact to
654-   ABRAHAM BUSH not living in GUILFORD County, NORTH CAROLINA, the
656   17th May 1801. J. WILLIAMS Cl Cur)
THIS INDENTURE made this Twenty second day of October in year of our Lord one thousand seven hundred and ninety four Between PEYTON BYRN, CLARY BYRN & SALLY BLAND of Prince William County of one part & ABRAHAM BUSH of County of LOUDOUN of other part; Witnesseth that PEYTON BYRN, Executor to his Father, SAMUEL BYRN's, Last Will & Testament, CLARY BYRN & SALLY BLAND for the sum of Two hundred & Sixty eight pounds, Four shillings specie, in hand paid by ABRAHAM BUSH, by these presents doth bargain sell & confirm unto ABRAHAM BUSH his heirs all that tract of land in Prince William County on both sides of the Middle Fork of POWELLS RUN, as by Deed granted by the Lord Proprietor to WILLIAM BLAND in or about the year 1726, and by him devised to his Son, THOMAS BLAND, who by his Last Will & Testament duly recorded in the County Court of FAUQUIER did devise the said tract of land containing by estimation Five hundred & Seventy seven acres to THOMAS BLAND, his Son, who sold the same to SAMUEL BYRN, excepting One hundred & Thirty acres to be laid of where WILLIAM (   ) Plantation is and to the upper end of the tract which he devised to his younger Son, JAMES BLAND, and the said SAMUEL BYRN by his last Will and Testament left the said land to be sold by his Exr. PEYTON BYRN, party to these presents, which tract of land is bounded, Beginng. at a fork'd white Oak now dead and marked black Gum on a Branch of CHAMPS MILL BRANCH, and extending thence S. 42d. E. 126 po: to a small white Oak on levil ground, then So. 20d. W. 182 po. on West side of a small Branch of POWELLS RUN, then S. 58d. W. 154 po. crossing the Middle Fork of POWELLS RUN to a blazed red Oak saplin, proved by WILLIAM LYNN to be within ten feet of where stood a marked white Oak and agreeing with the courses & distances from the begining, then No. 50d. W. 380 po., then N. 75d. E. 410 po: to the begining, containing Five hundred and Seventy seven acres, except as before excepted, And all houses orchards, profits and appurtenances; To have and to hold the Four hundred & forty seven acres of land with the appurtenances unto ABRAHAM BUSH his heirs free and clear from all Incumbrances whatsoever, And PEYTON BYRN, CLARY BYRN and SALLY BLAND and their heirs the premises hereby sold unto ABRAHAM BUSH his heirs shall warrant and for ever defend by these presents; In Witness whereof the said PEYTON BYRN, CLARY BYRN and SALLY BLAND hath hereunto set their hands and seals the day & year first within written
Signed Sealed & Delivered in presence of
    JOHN KINCHELOE,   WM. MITCHELL,   PEYTON BYRN
    WM. KINCHELOE, JOHN KINCHELOE JUNR.   CLARY BYRN
                                                    SALLY BLAND

At a Court continued and held for Prince William County the 5th day of May 1795
This Deed and the Rect. thereon from PEYTON BYRN, CLARY BYRN & SALLY BLAND to
ABRAHAM BUSH, Deed was proved by the Oaths of JOHN KINCHELOE & WM. KINCHELOE &
the Rect. by JOHN KINCHELOE & were ordered to be recorded
                        Teste JOHN WILLIAMS, Cl Cur
   At a Court held for Prince William County the 4th day of April 1796
This Deed and Receipt thereon was fully proved by the Oath of WILLIAM MITCHELL and
ordered to be recorded   .   Teste JOHN WILLIAMS, Cl Cur

pp.   (On margin: Examd. & Deld. the 17th May 1796, J. WILLIAMS)
656-   THIS INDENTURE made and entered into this seventh day of January in year of
657   our Lord one thousand seven hundred & ninety six Between WILLIAM DOWELL
         & MOLLY his Wife of County of FREDERICK and State of Virginia of one part and
JEREMIAH DOWELL of County of Prince William of other part; Witnesseth that WILLIAM
DOWELL & MOLLY his Wife for the sum of Thirty pounds current money of Virginia to
them in hand paid by JEREMIAH DOWELL, do by these presents bargain sell and confirm
unto JEREMIAH DOWELL and to his heirs all their right title & interest of in and to the
remainder part of the Land lately belonging to JOHN DOWELL, deceased, Father of said
WILLIAM & JEREMIAH , which by a clause in said JOHN DOWELL's Will recorded in the
said County Court on the second day of July 1781, was devised to said WILLIAM DOWELL,
JEREMIAH DOWELL & ISAAC DOWELL their Brother, the said clause before recited is in
these words, Vizt., "Item. I give and bequeath the remainder part of my Land to my
three Eldest Sons, Vizt. my loving Sons, WILLIAM DOWELL, JEREMIAH DOWELL & ISAAC
DOWELL to be equally divided between them in quantity and quality or if they disagree
in the Division, that it may be sold and equally divide the money between them;" And
also all houses profits with the appurtenances; To have and to hold the bargained premises unto JEREMIAH DOWELL and his heirs and WILLIAM DOWELL and MOLLY his Wife
for themselves their heris do warrant and for ever defend unto JEREMIAH DOWELL and
his heirs against the claim of any person; In Witness whereof the said WILLIAM
DOWELL and MOLLY his Wife have hereunto set their hands and affixed their seals the
day & year first within written
Signed Sealed and Delivered in the presence of
         ALEXR. LITHGOW, WM. BARNES,   WILLIAM DOWELL
         NATHANIEL E. COX, THOMAS TRIPLETT   MOLLY DOWELL
         JOHN WILLIAMS
   The Commonwealth of Virginia to ALEXANDER LITHGOW, WILLIAM BARNES and JOHN
MACRAE, Gentlemen, Greeting; Whereas (the Commission for the privy Examination of MOLLY,
the Wife of WILLIAM DOWELL); Witness JOHN WILLIAMS Clerk of our said Court this 7th day
of January 1796, & in the 20 year of the Commonwealth
   Prince William County to wit, In Obedience to the within, we the Subscribers have
caused to come before us the within named MOLLY DOWELL and have examined her privately, (the return of the execution of the privy Examination of MOLLY DOWELL); Given under
our hands & seals this 7th day of January 1796   ALEXR. LITHGOW
                                                        WM. BARNES

   At a Court continued and held for Prince William County the 5th day of April 1796
This Deed from WILLIAM DOWELL & MOLLY his Wife to JEREMIAH DOWELL was proved
by the Oaths of ALEXANDER LITHGOW, WILLIAM BARNES and JOHN WILLIAMS, and together with a Dedimus for the privy examination of the feme returned executed,
ordered to be recorded   Teste JOHN WILLIAMS, Cl Cur

p.   (On margin: Exd. & delivered to JOHN WATSON the 20th day of Septr. 1796)
658   KNOW ALL MEN by these presents that I WILLIAM SMITH of Town of DUMFRIES
        County of Prince William for the sum of One hundred and Ten pounds current
money to me in hand paid by CUMBERLAND WILSON of Town & County aforesaid by
these presents for myself my heirs do release remise and discharge the said CUMBER-
LAND WILSON his heirs from all right title interest and demand in Law & Equity which I
have unto two tracts of land lying in County aforesaid; containing Two hundred and
Thirty acres conveyed to said CUMBERLAND WILSON by HUGH DAVIS and JANE his Wife
by Deed bearing date the Eighteenth day of November in year one thousand seven hundred and ninety four which Two hundred and Thirty acres of land was by a Deed of
Mortgage bearing date the Sixteenth day of October one thouand seven hundred and
ninety four conveyed by HUGH DAVIS & JANE his Wife to WILLIAM SMITH to secure the
payment of One hundred and five pounds current money of Virginia with legal Interest
thereon from the date of the said Deed until paid; on Twenty fifth day of December in
year one thousand seven hundred and ninety five; And I WILLIAM SMITH do further
acknowledge that I have received the aforesaid sum of money with legal Interest on the
same for which the aforesaid Two hundred and thirty acres of land was mortgaged of
Mr. WM. DAVIS, by his Father WILLIAM DAVIS; In Witness whereof I have hereunto set
my hand and affixed my seal this Twenty second day of February one thousand seven
hundred and ninety six
Sealed and Delivered in presence of
        THOMAS SCOTT,   JOHN FRISTOE,   WILLIAM SMITH
        JOHN WILLIAMS,   THOMAS CHAPMAN
    At a Court continued and held for Prince William County the 5th day of April 1796
This Deed from WILLIAM SMITH to CUMBERLAND WILSON was acknowledged by the said
SMITH to be his act and deed and ordered to be recorded
                    Teste JOHN WILLIAMS, Cl Cur

pp.   THIS INDENTURE made and entered into this Thirty first day of March in year
659-   of our Lord one thousand seven hundred and ninety six Between ARCHIBALD
660   CARR of Town of DUMFRIES County of Prince William of one part and CARTY
        WELLS of County of Prince William of other part; Witnesseth that ARCHIBALD
CARR for the sum of Sixty pounds current money to him in hand paid by CARTY WELLS,
do by these presents bargain sell and confirm unto CARTY WELLS his heirs all that tract
of land lying in County aforesaid adjoining a tract of land conveyed to CARTY WELLS by
said ARCHIBALD CARR on the seventh day of December one thousand seven hundred
and ninety five, which tract of land is bounded, Beginning at two red Oaks and two Dogwoods on North Fork of QUANTICO RUN, being corner to the tract of land conveyed by
said CARR to said WELLS as aforesaid, thence down said Run and binding therewith So.
53 Et. 43 poles, thence So. 36d. Wt.18 poles, thence So. 22d Wt. 14 poles to a white Oak at
the mouth of a small Branch or Valley, then leaving the Run So. 48d. 30m. Wt. 56 poles
to a Hickory sapling, thence No. 22d. Wt. 36 poles to a Stake between two Spanish Oaks,
thence No. 48d. Wt. 75 poles to a red Oak, thence No. 22d. Wt. 18 poles to a Chesnut Oak
and Hickory, corner to said WELLS, then with his line No. 48d. 30m. Et. 139 poles to the
beginning, including Thirty acres be the same more or less and all houses profits with
the appurtenances; To have and to hold unto CARTY WELLS his heirs; And ARCHIBALD
CARR for himself his heirs doth warrant and for ever defend the bargained premises
unto CARTY WELLS his heirs against all claims of any person; In Witness whereof the
said ARCHIBALD CARR hath hereunto set his hand and affixed his seal the day month
and year first within written

Sealed & Delivered in presence of
    WILLIAM SMITH, PHILIP DAWE,   ARCHD: CARR
    WILLIAM CARR, EZEKIEL DONNELL,
    JOHN WILLIAMS
At a Court continued and held for Prince William County the 5th day of April 1796
This Deed from ARCHIBALD CARR to CARTY WELLS was proved by the Oaths of PHILIP
DAWE, WILLIAM SMITH & JOHN WILLIAMS, and ordered to be recorded
              Teste JOHN WILLIAMS, Cl Cur

pp.   (On margin: Examd. & Deld. April 7th 1797, J. WMS:)
660-   THIS INDENTURE made and entered into this 5th day of April in year of our Lord
661   one thousand seven hundred and ninety six Between ARCHIBALD CARR of Town
        of DUMFRIES County of Prince William of one part and THOMAS JACOB of Town &
County aforesaid of other part; Witnesseth that ARCHIBALD CARR for the sum of Thirty
three pounds current money to him in hand paid by THOMAS JACOB do by these presents bargain sell & confirm unto THOMAS JACOB his heirs all that tract of land lying in
County aforesaid containing Sixteen acres and an half more or less adjoining Thirty
acres of land conveyed by ARCHIBALD CARR to CARTY WELLS on the thirty first day of
March one thousand seven hundred and ninety six and bounded, Beginning at a
Spanish Oak sapling in the dividing line between said ARCHIBALD CARR and DANIEL
CARR, runing thence No. 22d. Wt. 36 poles to a red Oak, thence No. 48 1/2d. Et. 75 poles to
a Stake between two Spanish Oaks, thence So. 22d. Et. 36 poles to a Hickory saplin inter-
secting with the line between ARCHIBALD CARR and CARTY WELLS, thence So. 48 1/2d.
West 75 poles to the beginning, containing Sixteen acres and an half of land be the
same more or less, the said tract of land is part of a larger tract of land which was conveyed by JOHN TAYLOE and ANN his Wife to ARCHIBALD CARR by Deed bearing date the
ninth day of October in year one thousand seven hundred and ninety five; and duly
recorded among the Records of the County Court of Prince William, And all houses profits and appurtenances; To have and to hold the bargained premises unto THOMAS
JACOB his heirs and ARCHIBALD CARR for himself his heirs do warrant and for ever
defend the aforesaid premises unto THOMAS JACOB and his hiers against all claims; In
Witness whereof the said ARCHIBALD CARR hath hereunto set his hand and affixed his
seal the day month and year first within written
Sealed and Delivered in presence of
    EDWD. DENEALE,   ARCHD: CARR
    WILLIAM SMITH, JOHN W. WIGGENTON
At a Court contd. and held for Prince William County the 5th day of April 1796
This Deed from ARCHIBALD CARR to THOMAS JACOB was proved by the Oaths of EDWARD
DENEALE, WILLIAM SMITH & JOHN W. WIGGINTON and ordered to be recorded
           Teste JNO. WILLIAMS, Cl Cur

pp.   THIS INDENTURE made and entered into this Fourth day of September in year of
661-   our Lord one thousand seven hundred and ninety five Between JOHN WILLIAMS
663   and JANE his Wife of County of Prince William of one part and LUDWICK STHULE
       of County aforesaid of other part; Witnesseth that JOHN WILLIAMS and JANE his
Wife for the sum of One hundred pounds current money to them in hand paid by LUD-
WICK STHULE, do by these presents bargain sell and confirm unto LUDWICK STHULE and
his heirs all those two lotts of land lying in Town of DUMFRIES and County aforesaid,
which were conveyed to JOHN WILLIAMS by MORRIS COX and CATHARINE his Wife by
Deed of Bargain and Sale bearing date the twenty fourth day of October one thousand

seven hundred and eighty nine and to MORRIS COX by JOHN LANGFITT by Deed bearing
date the Sixth day of October 1785; both which recited Deeds are duly recorded among
the Records of aforesaid County Court; And also all the remainder of a Lott in the aforesaid Town numbered Forty which lies between the OLD COUNTY ROAD and those part of
said Lott No. 40 sold and conveyed to a certain JAMES NOLAND and a certain JOHN
ANDERSON by aforesaid MORRIS COX, who conveyed the said part to JOHN WILLIAMS by
Deed before recited; To have and to hold the bargained premises unto LUDWICK STHULE
his heirs and JOHN WILLIAMS and JANE his Wife their heirs do warrant and for ever
defend the bargained premises unto LUDWICK STHULE and his heirs against the claim
of any person; In Witness whereof said JOHN WILLIAMS and JANE his Wife have hereunto set their hands and affixed their seals the day month and year first within written
Sealed and Delivered in presence of

WM. SMITH, PHILIP DAWE,   JOHN WILLIAMS
GEO: LANE, JOHN FRISTOE,   JANE WILLIAMS
JOSEPH GILBERT SENR.

The Commonwealth of Virginia to ALEXANDER LITHGOW, WM. BARNES and JOHN LAW-
SON Gentlemen, Greeting; Whereas (the Commission for the privy Examination of JANE, the
Wife of JOHN WILLIAMS); Witness JOHN WILLIAMS, Clerk of our said Court the fourth day
of September 1795 and in the 20th year of the Commonwealth
   Prince William County, to wit. In Obedience to the within, we the Subscribers hve
caused to come before us the within named JANE WILLIAMS and have examined her
privately (the return of the execution of the privy Examination of JANE WILLIAMS); Given under
our hands and seals this 31st day of March 1795   WM. BARNES
                                                         J. LAWSON
   At a Court continued and held for Prince William County the 5th day of April 1796
This Deed from JOHN WILLIAMS and JANE his Wife to LUDWICK STHULE was acknowledged by said JOHN WILLIAMS and (together with a Dedimus for the privy examination
of the feme returned executed) ordered to be recorded
                        Teste JOHN WILLIAMS, Cl Cur

pp.   THIS INDENTURE made and entered into this Fourth day of September in year of
663-   our Lord one thousand seven hundred and ninety five Between LUDWICK
664   STHULE of County of Prince William of one part and JOHN WILLIAMS of County
        aforesaid of other part; Witnesseth that LUDWICK STHULE for the sum of One
hundred pounds current money to him in hand paid by JOHN WILLIAMS, do by these
presents bargain sell and confirm unto JOHN WILLIAMS and his heirs all those parcels
of lotts lying in Town of DUMFRIES which JOHN WILLIAM and JANE his Wife conveyed
to LUDWICK STHULE by Deed bearing date the aforesaid Fourth day of September one
thousand seven hundred and ninety five, and all houses advantages with the appurtenances; To have and to hold the bargained premises unto JOHN WILLIAMS and his heirs
and LUDWICK STHULE for himself & his heirs doth warrant and for ever defend the bargained premises unto JOHN WILLIAMS against all claims, Provided Nevertheless and it is
the meaning of these presents that if LUDWICK STHULE his heirs do pay unto JOHN WIL-
LIAMS his heirs the full sum of Seventeen pounds Six shillings and eight pence specie
with legal interest thereon from the date hereof upon the first day of November next
ensuing, Also the further sum of fifty pounds specie with legal Interest thereon from
the date hereof on the thirty first day od December which shall be in the year one
thousand seven hundred and ninety six, That then this Deed shall cease and become
void, otherwise to stand and remain in full force power and virtue. In witness whereof
the said LUDWICK STHULE hath hereunto set his hand and affixed his seal the day and
year first within written

Sealed and Delivered in presence of
    PHILIP DAWE, WM. SMITH,   LUDWICK STHULE
    JOHN FRISTOE,   JOSEPH GILBERT JUNR.
  At a Court continued na held for Prince William County the 5th day of April 1796
This Deed of Mortgage from LUDWICK STHULE to JOHN WILLIAMS was acknowledged by
said STHULE to be his act and deed and was thereupon admitted to Record
               Teste JOHN WILLIAMS, Cl Cur

pp.   THIS INDENTURE made the 25th day of March one thousand seven hundred &
664-   ninety six Between DAVID BLAND, Grandson & Heir at Law of JAMES BLAND
665   deced., of County of Prince William of one part and WILLOUGHBY TEBBS of said
        County of other part; Witnesseth that DAVID BLAND for the sum of Five hundred
Dollars to him in hand paid by WILLOUGHBY TEBBS by these presents doth bargain &
sell unto WILLOUGHBY TEBBS all those lands and tenements within the County of Prince
William on which said DAVID now liveth lying in QUANTICO NECK formerly called COCK
PIT POINT NECK containing now by estimation about two hundred and ten acres the
same being formerly granted by Patent dated the thirteenth day of August one thou-
sand seven hundred and Eleven to FRANCIS STONE & WILLIAM & JAMES BLAND, Grand
Father to said DAVID, which land was devised (by said JAMES BLAND by Will dated the
22d day of February 1755 and recorded in said County the 22d day of March 1796), to said
DAVID BLAND and BENJAMIN BLAND or the Surviver; together with all the rest of his
Estate (the said land being first purchased by JAMES BLAND of said STONE and WILLIAM
BLAND or their parts thereof) Begining at a marked Locust standing on a Valley falling
into a Branch of POWELLS CREEK & extending thence South 85d. West 59 poles to a
marked Hickory standing on a Hill side, thence North 66d. Wt. 101 po. to another
Hickory standing on a Hill side, thence North 35 West 62 poles to a small Hickory standing in the head of a Valley, thence West 78 poles to a Great white Oak standing on top
of a Hil, thence South 19 Et. 98 poles to a small Pine on a Hill side, thence So. 17 Et. 56
poles to a small Hickory sapling standing on a Hill side and near a large Spanish Oak,
thence So. 39 Et. 40 poles to a small black Oak sapling standing on a narrow Ridge,
thence So. 55 Et. 220 poles to a small black Oak standing on the Top of a Ridge, thence No.
2 Et. 216 poles to the begining Locust; containing as before estimated except Thirty five
acres out of the tract conveyd by said BLAND to JOHN CURRY & now in the possession of
the Widow of the said CURRY; Also one other tract of land lying on OCCOQUAN RUN
granted to said JAMES BLAND at or near what is now called DAVIS's FORD, Also one
other tract of land in TARAPIN FOREST formerly called PETER OARs, or otherwise OREs
Old Field, which several tracts of land said DAVID doth bargain & sell unto WILLOUGHBY
TEBBS free and clear from all incumbrances, And DAVID BLAND his heirs against all
persons will warrant and defend. In Witness whereof DAVID BLAND hath hereunto set
his hand and seal the day month & year first above written
Sealed & Delivered in presence of
    ALLEN BLAND, DAVID W. SCOTT,   DAVID BLAND
    WM. FARROW, HENSON RENO,
    DANIEL TEBBS, JOHN O"CONNOR
  At a Court continued & held for Prince William County the 5th day of April 1796
This Deed from DAVID BLAND to WILLOUGHBY TEBBS was proved by the oaths of
WILLIAM FARROW, HENSON RENO & DAVID WILSON SCOTT and ordered to be recorded
              Teste JOHN WILLIAMS, Cl Cur

p.   I HEREBY Assign all my right and title to a Preemption Right lying on the
666   Waters of LICKING CREEK to WILLIAM FARROW of Prince William County, the
        same being due to me for a Cabbin Improvement in the DISTRICT of KENTUCKY
in the year 1775-6. In Witness whereof as a party to these presents, I have hereunto set
my hand & seal this 21st day of November 1793 at the Town of DUMFRIES, County aforesaid, The same being for value received
Witness WILLOUGHBY TEBBS,   NAT: TRIPLETT
        ADAM GARDENHIRE
    At a Court continued and held for Prince William County the 5th day of April 1796
This Deed of Assignment from NATHANIEL TRIPLETT to WILLIAM FARROW was proved
by the Oaths of ADAM GARDENHIRE and WILLOUGHBY TEBBS and ordered to be recorded
                    Teste JOHN WILLIAMS, Cl Cur

pp.   (On margin: Examined & Delivered the 27th day of April 1796, J. WILLIAMS)
666-   TO ALL PERSONS to whom this present writing shall come, Greeting. I BENJA-
667   KING of County of LOUDOUN for divers good causes and considerations me there-
        unto moving and for the tender regard and affection which I bear unto my Son,
WILLIAM KING, do by these presents grant transfer and make over unto said WILLIAM
KING one half of a tract of land lying in County of Prince William on the Branches of
OCAQUAN, which I purchased of ABELL HAZLERIG and others, Deed bearing date 1764,
and bounded; Beginning at a Hickory near the head of a Branch in BROWNs line, thence
with said line S. 64d. Et. 176 po: to a Spanish Oak by side of a Marsh, thence So. 9d. E. 112
po: to a white and red Oak sprouts, thence So. 75d. Wt. 130 po. to a Gum, corner to
SAMUEL KING, thence No. 6d. Wt. 180 po. to the beginning, including 140 acres, To have
and to hold the parcel of land unto WILLIAM KING his heirs, hereby warranting and
defending him the said WILLIAM KING his heirs from all suits at Law or controversies
brought by any person; In Witness whereof I have hereunto set my hand and seal this
11th day of April one thousand seven hundred and ninety four
Sign'd Seal'd and delivered in presents off
        JOHN STONESTREET, SYLVESTER GRIMES,   BENJAMIN his mark + KING
        WILLIAM his mark X GRIMES
        JAMES his mark X KITCHEN
    At a Court held for Prince William County the 1st day of December 1794
This Deed from BENJAMIN KING to WILLIAM KING was proved by the Oaths of JOHN
STONESTREET and SYLVESTER GRIMES and ordered to be certified;
                    Teste ROBT. GRAHAM, Cl Cur
    At a Court continued and held for the said County the 5th day of April 1796
This Deed was fully proved by the Oath of WILLIAM GRIMES and ordered to be recorded
                    Teste JOHN WILLIAMS, Cl Cur

pp.   (On margin: Examd. & Delivered April 14th 1796, J. WMS.)
667-   THIS INDENTURE made this Eighteenth day of March in year of our Lord one
669   thousand seven hundred and ninety six Between ALEXANDER HENDERSON, JOHN
        GIBSON and JAMES REID of Town of DUMFRIES, County of Prince William of one
part and WILLIAM TYLER and GEORGE LANE of the County aforesaid of other part;
Whereas ALEXANDER HENDERSON, JOHN GIBSON and JAMES REID or any two of them by a
Decree of the Worshipful Court of Prince William County pronounced on the 6th day of
August in the year one thousand seven hundred and ninety five between JOHN CANNON
Plaintiff and COLIN CAMPBELL Defendant, were authorized and directed to sell at Public
Auction for ready money two lotts of land, the property of said COLIN CAMPBELL, lying

in Town of DUMFRIES and described by the numbers Thirty Eight and Forty Three, and
to convey the said premises to the purchaser or purchasers thereof; And Whereas said
ALEXANDER HENDERSON, JOHN GIBSON and JAMES REID on the Fourth day of November
in the year 1795 (having given notice as in the Decree is directed) did agreeable thereto publickly set up the said two lots of land for sale and WILLIAM TYLER for himself and
the said GEORGE LANE bid the sum of Four hundred pounds current money for the two
lotts of land which being the highest bid make for the two lotts the same were accordingly struck off to the said WILLIAM TYLER and GEORGE LANE. Now This Indenture
Witnesseth that ALEXANDER HENDERSON, JOHN GIBSON and JAMES REID by virtue of the
before mentioned Decree and for the sum of Four hundred pounds current money to
them in hand paid by WILLIAM TYLER and GEORGE LANE, by these presents do bargain
and sell unto WILLIAM TYLER and GEORGE LANE and their heirs all the right title and
demand which either of them have either in Law or Equity to the two lotts of land
which two lotts of land were confeyed to COLIN CAMPBELL by Deeds of Lease and Release
from WILLIAM BRENT and HANNAH his Wife bearing date the 20th & 21st days of
October one thousand seven hundred and eighty seven; To have and to hold the two
lotts of land unto WILLIAM TYLER and GEORGE LANE their heirs, And ALEXANDER
HENDERSON, JOHN GIBSON and JAMES REID for themselves and their heirs the two lotts
of land unto WILLIAM TYLER and GEORGE LANE their heirs against the claim of all
persons will warrant and forever defend. In Witness whereof the said ALEXANDER
HENDERSON, JOHN GIBSON and JAMES REID have hereunto set their hands and affixed
their seals the day and year first within written
Signed Sealed and Delivered in presence of
    JAMES JAMES,   JAMES JOHNSTON,   ALEXR: HENDERSON
    JOHN McCREERY, ESME SMOCK   JOHN GIBSON
                                    JAMES REID

    At a Court continued and held for Prince Wm. County the 5th day of April 1796
This Deed from ALEXANDER HENDERSON, JOHN GIBSON and JAMES REED, Commissioners,
to WILLIAM TYLER and GEORGE LANE was proved by the Oaths of JAMES JAMES, JAMES
JOHNSTON and JOHN McCREERY and ordered to be recorded
              Teste JOHN WILLIAMS, Cl Cur

pp.   THIS INDENTURE made and entered into this Fourth day of February in year of
669-   our Lord one thousand seven hundred and ninety six Between WILLIAM FAR-
670   ROW and SARAH his Wife of County of Prince William of one part and SIMON
           LUTTRELL and THOMAS CHAPMAN, Executors and Trustees of WILLIAM CARR
deced., of County aforesaid of other part; Witnesseth that WILLIAM FARROW and SARAH
his Wife for the sum of Eight hundred and thirteen pounds, three shillings and one
penny to them in hand paid by SIMON LUTTRELL and THOMAS CHAPMAN, do by these
presents bargain sell and confirm unto SIMON LUTTRELL and THOMAS CHAPMAN their
heirs to the use as expressed in the Will of said WILLIAM CARR deced., one preemptive
Right lying in the State of KENTUCKY and Waters of LICKING BRANCH granted to WIL-
LIAM FARROW, also two tracts of land lying in County of Prince William near the Town
of DUMFRIES whereon said FARROW now lives, the first containing about three hundred and fifty acres and the other three hundred acres, adjoining each other, the lands
having been recovered of ALLEN MACRAEs Executors, Together with all houses with the
appurtenances; To have and to hold the bargained premises unto SIMON LUTTRELL and
THOMAS CHAPMAN, Executors and Trustees of WILLIAM CARR deced., and WILLIAM FAR-
ROW and SARAH his Wife their heirs doth warrant and forever defend the bargained
premises against the claims of any person; In Witness whereof the said WILLIAM

FARROW and SARAH his Wife have hereunto set their hands and seals the day and year first written
Signed Sealed and Delivered in the presence of
    WY. TEBBS,   LUKE CANNON,   WILLIAM FARROW
    WM. SMITH,   SAML. HOWISON,   SARAH FARROW
    RICHARD BROOKE
   At a Court continued and held for Prince William County the 5th day of April 1796 This Deed from WILLIAM FARROW and SARAH his Wife to SIMON LUTTRELL and THOMAS CHAPMAN, Executors and Trustees of WILLIAM CARR deced., was proved by the Oaths of WILLIAM SMITH, RICHARD BROOKE and SAMUEL HOWISON and ordered to be recorded
               Teste JOHN WILLIAMS, Cl Cur

pp.   THIS INDENTURE made and entered into this Eighteenth day of December in
670-   year of our Lord one thousand seven hundred and ninety five Between WIL-
672   LIAM ROBERTSON and JANE his Wife of County of Prince William of one part and
GEORGE SELECTMAN of County aforesaid of other part; Witnesseth that WILLIAM ROBERTSON and JANE his Wife for the sum of Sixty pounds current money of Virginia to said WILLIAM ROBERTSON in hand paid by GEORGE SELECTMAN, do by these presents bargain sell and confirm unto GEORGE SELECTMAN and his heirs all that tract of land lying in County aforesaid on the Branches of WHORES CREEK and the BEAVER DAM containing One hundred and two acres as granted to JAMES PEAKE by Patent bearing date the Eighth day of September 1788; and sold and conveyed by JAMES PEAKE and CONSTANT his Wife and Attorney, COLLINS GRAY and LEVINAH his Wife to LEVI SCOTT by Deed bearing date the 15th day of February 1791, and sold and conveyed by said LEVI SCOTT and ELIZABETH his Wife to ANN PEACHY by Deed bearing date the seventh day of December 1791; and sold and conveyed by RAWLEIGH P. DOWNMAN and ANN his Wife (formerly the aforesaid ANN PEACHY), to WILLIAM ROBERTSON by Deed bearing date the 21st day of October 1794; which tract is bounded; Beginning at a Chesnut Oak near a large path in the Edge of the Wood cutting, corner to TAYLOE, thence with his line N. 57 Wt. 123 po: to a black Oak in COCKEs line, thence leaving TAYLOE and binding with COCK So. by Et. 130 po. to a white Oak in the edge of a Glade by MOSSes Line, No. 55 Et. 130 po: to the aforesaid TAYLOEs line, thence along his line No. 36 Wt. 86 po. to the beginning, and all houses profits with the appurtenances of every kind; To have and to hold the bargained premises unto GEORGE SELECTMAN and his heirs; And WILLIAM ROBERTSON and JANE his Wife and their heirs do warrant and forever defend the bargained premises unto GEORGE SELECTMAN and his heirs against all claims; In Witness whereof the said WILLIAM ROBERTSON and JANE his Wife hath hereunto set their hands and affixed their seals this Second day of March one thousand seven hundred and ninety six
Signed Sealed & Delivered in presence of
    DANIEL DAUGHERTY, JNO: FISHER,   WILLIAM ROBERTSON
    HENRY SELECTMAN, DANL. DAUGHTERY JANE her mark + ROBERTSON
    JONATHAN WILLETT
   At a Court contd. and held for Prince Wm. County the 5th day of April 1796 This Deed from WILLIAM ROBERTSON and JANE his Wife to GEORGE SELECTMAN was proved by the Oaths of JOHN FISHER, HENRY SELECTMAN JUNR. and DANIEL DAUGHERTY and together with a Dedimus for the privy examination of the feme returned executed ordered to be recorded   Teste JOHN WILLIAMS, Cl Cur
   The Commonwealth of Virginia to ALEXANDER LITHGOW, WILLIAM BARNES and JOHN LAWSON Gentlemen, Greeting, Whereas (the Commission for the privy Examination of JANE, the Wife of WILLIAM ROBERTSON); Witness JOHN WILLIAMS Clerk of our said Court this 18th

day of December 1795 and in the 20th year of the Commonwealth
 Prince Wm. County, to wit: In obedience to the within, we the Subscribers have caused
to come before us the within named JANE ROBERTSON and examined her privily (the
return of the execution of the privy Examination of JANE ROBERTSON,) Given under our hands
and seals this 18th day of Decr. 1795   ALEXR. LITHGOW
                                                                WM. BARNES

pp.   THIS INDENTURE made and entered into this (blurred out) December in year of
673-   our Lord one thousand seven hundred and ninety five Between WILLIAM
674   ROBERTSON (by HENRY FEWELL his Attorney in fact) and JANE ROBINSON, Wife
           of said WILLIAM ROBINSON of County of Prince William of one part and GEORGE
SELECTMAN of County aforesaid of other part; Witnesseth that WILLIAM ROBERTSON and
JANE his Wife, for the sum of Sixty pounds current money of Virginia to HENRY FEWELL
the said WILLIAM ROBERTSONs Attorney in fact in hand paid by GEORGE SELECTMAN, do
by these presents bargain sell and confirm unto GEORGE SELECTMAN his heirs all that
tract of land lying in County aforesaid, on the Branches of WHORES CREEK and the
BEAVER DAM, containing One hundred and Ten two acres (Patent to JAMES PEAKE, the
various conveyances until WILLIAM ROBERTSON, and the description of the bounds of the land as in
the foreing Indenture) To have and to hold the bargained premises unto GEORGE SELECT-
MAN and his heirs; And WILLIAM ROBERTSON (by HENRY FEWELL his said Attorney in
Fact) and JANE ROBERTSON and their heirs the bargained premises do warrant and for
ever defend unto GEORGE SELECTMAN and his heirs against all claims; In Witness
whereof the said HENRY FEWELL hath hereunto set his hand and affixed the Seal of the
aforesaid WILLIAM ROBERTSON on the day month and year first within written and the
aforesaid JANE ROBINSON hath also hereunto set her hand and affixed her seal the same
day and year
Signed Sealed and Delivered by the said HENRY FEWELL
 Attorney in Fact for said WM. ROBERTSON and by sd.
JANE ROBERTSON in presence of us
        ALEXR. LITHGOW, JOHN WILLIAMS,   WILLIAM ROBERTSON by
        THOMAS CHAPMAN, DANL. DAUGHERTY   HENRY FEWELL his Atty. in fact
        WM. BARNES, DANIEL DAUGHERTY,   JANE her mark ✚ ROBERTSON
        JOHN FISHER, ROBERTSON GRAY,   WILLIAM ROBERTSON
        HUGH DAVIS
 At a Court contd. and held for Prince William County the 5th day of April 1796
This Deed from WILLIAM ROBERTSON (executed by HENRY FEWELL his Attorney in fact)
and JANE ROBINSON, Wife of said WILLIAM ROBERTSON, to GEORGE SELECTMAN was
proved by the Oaths of WILLIAM BARNES, JOHN WILLIAMS and DANIEL DAUGHERTY and
ordered to be recorded   Teste JOHN WILLIAMS Cl Cur

pp.   THIS INDENTURE made the fifth day of October one thousand seven hundred
674-   and ninety five Between JOHN FAIRFAX and MARY his Wife of County of
677   MONONGALIA and WILLIAM FAIRFAX and NANCY his Wife of County of Prince
           William of one part and SAMUEL JACKSON of County of Prince William of other
part; Witnesseth that JOHN FAIRFAX and MARY his Wife and WILLIAM FAIRAX and
NANCY his Wife for the sum of One hundred and Fifty pounds specie to (them) in hand
paid by SAMUEL JACKSON, by these presents doth bargain sell and confirm unto
SAMUEL JACKSON his heirs all that tenement of land lying in County of Prince William
and on the head dranes of the CROOKED BRANCH of OCAQUAN and bounded, Beginning at
a Chesnut Oak on COCKRILLs MOUNTAIN, corner to HENRY PEAKE, then with his line No.

20 Et. 60 po: to a Stake in said line, then No. 76d. Et. 113 po: to a red Oak and box Oak, then So. 11d. Et. 169 po: to a red Oak, corner to BLANCETT in PEAKs Line, then with said line So. 63d. Wt. 195 po: to a Popular in a Branch corner to PEAKs Heirs, then with the line of said Heirs No. 83, Et. 85 po: to a red Oak saplin and an Ash in a Branch, then No. 38 Wt. 78 po. to a Barron Ridge, then with the line of HENRY PEAKs Younger Patent No. 65d. Et. 200 po. to a red Oak, then No. 22d. Et. 14 po. to the beginning, containing Two hundred and fifty acres, it being part of a tract of land granted to WILLIAM VEALE in 1777 and conveyed to ALEXANDER HENDERSON by said VEALE in 1779, and from said HENDERSON to RODHAM BLANCHARD in 1788 and from said BLANCHARD to WILLIAM FAIRFAX as Executor to his Father's Last Will and Testament in 1794, and who devised the said Two hundred and fifty acres to his Son, JOHN FAIRFAX, party to these presents; Together with all houses profits commodities and appurtenances; To have and to hold the tenement and premises unto SAMUEL JACKSON his heirs and JOHN FAIRFAX and MARY his Wife and WILLIAM FAIRFAX and NANCY his Wife and their heirs against all persons to SAMUEL JACKSON his heirs shall warrant and forever defend by these presents; In Witness whereof the said JOHN FAIRFAX and MARY his Wife and WILLIAM FAIRFAX and NANCY his Wife hath hereunto set their hands and seals the day and year first above written Signed Sealed and Delivered in presence off

JAMES MUSCHETT,	JOHN FAIRFAX
WM. W. DUNNINGTON,	MARY FAIRFAX
MUNGO HANCOCK,	WILLIAM FAIRFAX
CHARLES TYLER JUNR., JOHN MUSCHETT	NANCY FAIRFAX

The Commonwealth of Virginia to THOMAS BUTLER and EDWARD JONES Gentlemen, Greeting, Whereas (the Commission for the privy Examination of MARY, the Wife of JOHN FAIRFAX); Witness JOHN WILLIAMS Clerk of our said Court this sixth day of October 1795 and in the 20th year of the Commonwealth   JOHN WILLIAMS

(The recording of the return of the execution of the privy examination of MARY FAIRFAX is made in the margin of the book and much of it is hidden by a black line; it is dated the 10th day of July 1795 and signed by THOMAS BUTLER and EDWARD JONES.)

Received this fifth day of October 1795, One hundred & fifty pounds specie being the consideration mentioned for the within land & premises
Teste JAMES MUSCHETT,   JOHN FAIRFAX
    MUNGO HANCOCK, CHARLES TYLER JUNR.

At a Court held for Prince William County the 4th day of April 1796 This Deed and the Receipt thereon endorsed from JOHN FAIRFAX and MARY his Wife and WILLIAM FAIRFAX and NANCY his Wife to SAMUEL JACKSON was proved by the Oath of JAMES MUSCHETT (the feme NANCY FAIRFAX being first privily examined and thereto consenting) and ordered to be certified; And at a Court continued and held for the said County the fifth day of April in the same year; The said Deed and Receipt were fully proved by the Oaths of MUNGO HANCOCK and CHARLES TYLER JUNR. and (together with a Dedimus for the privy Examination of MARY FAIRFAX returned executed) ordered to be recorded   Teste JOHN WILLIAMS, Cl Cur

pp. 677-680   THIS INDENTURE made this Eleventh day of February in year of our Lord one thousand seven hundred and ninety two Between MASON FOLEY of County of PARSON in State of NORTH CAROLINA of one part and PHILIP DAWE of County of Prince William of other part. Whereas MASON FOLEY by his certain Letter of Attorney bearing date the fifth day of November one thousand seven hundred and seventy one and duly recorded in the County Court of Prince William on the same day, did appoint his Brother, JAMES FOLEY, of said County his true and lawful Attorney for

him and in his name to sue out of the Secretaries Office a Writ in the nature of an ad quod damnun and thereby to proceed to dock the intail of One hundred and fifty acres of land be the same more or less of which said MASON FOLEY was seized as tenant in fee tail by devise from his Father, JOHN FOLEY, deced., and after the due execution of the said Writ, did direct and empower the said JAMES FOLEY to sell the land for his said MASON's benefit, and in his name to make seal and deliver any Deed of Bargain and Sale or other legal conveyance for the same; And Whereas JAMES FOLEY by virtue of the said Letter of Attorney did proceed and in a legal manner dock the intail of said tract of land and by a Deed bearing date the twenty fifth day of November one thousand seven hundred and ninety four duly recorded in said County for the sum of One hundred and Twenty seven pounds, Ten shillings current money therein mentioned did bargain sell and convey the One hundred and fifty acres of land more or less to PHILIP DAWE his heirs; Now This Indenture Witnesseth that MASON FOLEY as well for the sum of One hundred and twenty seven pounds, Ten shillings current money by PHILIP DAWE to JAMES FOLEY, his Attorney in fact, in hand paid, as to confirm the aforesaid Deed made by JAMES FOLEY to PHILIP DAWE and also for the sum of Five shillings specie to him said MASON in hand paid by PHILIP DAWE by these presents doth grant and confirm unto PHILIP DAWE his heirs all the before mentioned tract of land containing One hundred and fifty acres be the same more or less which tract of land was granted by Patent bearing date the 9th day of November 1698 to a certain JOHN WALLIS, who assigned the said grant to a certain JAMES MANN, who by his last Will and Testament duly recorded in STAFFORD County Court devised the tract of land to his two Daughters, MARGARET and URSLEY, and MARGARET having intermarried with JOHN FOLEY, the Grandfather of said MASON and said URSLEY having intermarried with a certain WILLIAM GRIGSBY, they by Deeds of Lease and Release dated 1740 and duly recorded in County Court of Prince William conveyed their part of said tract of land to said JOHN FOLEY, Father of said MASON, from whom the whole tract passed and descended to his Son, JOHN FOLEY, the Father of said MASON, who by his last Will and Testament duly recorded in the County aforesaid, on the 25th day of May 1761, devised the tract of land to his Son, the said MASON FOLEY, party to these presents; the said tract of land by a Survey thereof made by SAMUEL BYRNE contains One hundred and Fifty three acres and three quarters of an acre and the boundaries thereof are as follows, Beginning at a white Oak upon a Ridge in THOMAS GREGGs his line (now DOCT: GEORGE GRAHAMs) and running thence No. 10d. Wt. 168 poles to a red Oak in Poysen Field & then Wt. 10d. So. 146 po: to a red Oak, thence So. 10d. Et. 168 poles to GREGGs his line, finally along GREGGs line to the beginning white Oak, and all waters water courses and appurtenances to said tract of land belonging unto PHILIP DAWE his heirs; And MASON FOLEY his heirs by these presents forever warrant & defend the tract of land unto PHILIP DAWE his heirs against the claim of every person; In Witness whereof the said MASON FOLEY hath hereunto set his hand and affixed his seal the day and year first within written
Sealed and Delivered in presence of
    WILLIAM SMITH, THOS: CHAPMAN,   MASON FOLEY
    WALKER TURNER, MOSES DAULTON,
    WILLIAM FARRELL SENR.
  At a Court held for Prince William County the 4th day of April 1796
This Deed from MASON FOLEY to PHILIP DAWE was proved by the Oaths of THOMAS CHAPMAN and WILLIAM SMITH and ordered to be Certified; And at a Court continued and held for said County the fifth day of April in the year aforesaid, the said Deed was fully proved by the Oath of WALKER TURNER and ordered to be recorded
               Teste JOHN WILLIAMS, Cl Cur

p.   (On margin: Examd. & deld. RD. B. ALEXANDER per note the 10th July 1797, W. H.)
680   THIS INDENTURE made this 1st day of November in year of our Lord one thou-
           sand seven hundred and ninety five Between THOMAS WHITING and POLLY
WHITING his Wife of one part and FRANCES BROWN of other part; Witnesseth that THO-
MAS WHITING and POLLY his Wife for sum of Four hundred and Eighty pounds current
money of Virginia to them in hand paid, by these presents doth bargain and sell unto
FRANCES BROWN and her heirs all that tract of land called BUSHY PARK lying in County
of Prince William comprehending at this time a piece of land exchanged for with JOHN
ARMISTEAD deced., and containing in the whole by estimation Four hundred acres be
the same more or less reference being had for the boundaries and contents to the Sur-
veyes which have been made thereof heretofore; To have and to hold the said land with
all its appurtenances to said FRANCES and her heirs; And said THOMAS and POLLY his
Wife against the claims of every person shall warrant and forever defend; In Testimony whereof the said THOMAS and POLLY his Wife have subscribed their names and
affixed their seals this day and year above
Signed Sealed and Delivered in presence of
        RHD. B. ALEXANDER,   JOHN CAMPBELL,   THOMAS WHITING
        M: WHITING, ALEXR: SCOTT, EDMD. BROOKE
     At a Court continued and held for Prince Wm. Coty. the 5th day of April 1796
This Deed from THOMAS WHITING to FRANCES BROWN was proved by the Oaths of ED-
MUND BROOKE, JOHN CAMPBELL and MATTHEW WHITING and ordered to be recorded
                         Teste JOHN WILLIAMS, Cl Cur

pp.   THIS INDENTURE made this Eighth day of (blotted) in year of our Lord one thou-
681-   sand seven hundred and ninety five Between MARGARET TYLER, Administratrix
682   of all the goods chattels rights and credits of JOHN TYLER, Late Sheriff of Prince
           William County, deced., of one part and JAMES JOHNSTON of Town of DUMFRIES in
the County aforesaid of other part; Whereas a Fieri facias was sued out of the General
Court on a Judgment obtained by the Commonwealth against JOHN LINTON for sum of
Eight hundred and twenty pounds, Sixteen shillings and three pence, and One hundred
and Five pounds of tobacco and Fifty shillings for costs directed to the Sheriff of Prince
William County, And Whereas JOHN TYLER then Sheriff of Prince William by COLIN
CAMPBELL his Deputy levied the aforesaid Execution on the land and Negroes of the said
JOHN LINTON and made the following return; "Exd. on Land and Negroes and sold part
thereof for L. 112..15..0; the balance not sold for want of buyers," by said Judgment and
Execution of Record in the General Court; And Whereas said MARGARET TYLER as
Administratrix of JOHN TYLER, late Sheriff of Prince William County and by virtue of
the aforesaid Execution did expose to sale at public auction according to Law the aforesaid land and Negroes taken by virtue of the aforesaid Execution and which remained
unsold as aforesaid, at which public sale two lots of ground lying in Town of DUMFRIES
laid down by the numbers Forty One and Forty Two, being part of the property on
which the said execution was levied and was set up to be sold to the highest bidder at
which public sale JAMES JOHNSTON bid for the two lotts the sum of Two hundred and
Thirty one pounds current money, which being the highest bid made for the two lotts
the same were accordingly struck off to JAMES JOHNSTON; Now This Indenture Witnesseth that MARGARET TYLER, Administratrix of JOHN TYLER, late Sheriff of Prince William County, in consideration of the premises and of the sum of Two hundred and Thirty
one pounds current money in hand paid by JAMES JOHNSTON, by these presents doth
bargain and sell unto JAMES JOHNSTON his heirs the two lotts or parcels of Ground in
Town of DUMFRIES numbered Forty One and Forty Two which two lotts of ground were
sold & conveyed by JOHN MACRAE and WILLOUGHBY TEBBS, Directors and Trustees of the

Town of DUMFRIES, to aforesaid JOHN LINTON by Deed bearing date the 27th day of May in year one thousand seven hundred and Eighty eight; And all houses improvements and appurtenances; To have and to hold the two lotts or parcels of Ground with all the appurtenances unto JAMES JOHNSTON his heirs; In Witness whereof the said MARGARET TYLER, Administratrix of JOHN TYLER, late Sheriff of Prince William County, hath hereunto set her hand and affixed her Seal the day and year first before written
Signed Sealed & Delivered in presence of

CECILID ANN TYLER, MARY CAMPBELL,   MARGARET TYLER, Admrx.
M. HARRISON JUNR., WILLIAM TYLER,   of JOHN TYLER deced.
GEORGE GRAY TYLER

At a Court held for Prince William County the 7th day of September 1795
This Deed from MARGARET TYLER, Administratrix of JOHN TYLER deced., to JAMES JOHNSTON was proved by the Oath of MATTHEW JOHNSTON JUNR. and ordered to be Certified; And at a Court continued and held for said County the 5th day of April 1796, the said Deed was fully proved by the Oaths of WILLIAM TYLER and GEORGE GRAY TYLER and ordered to be recorded   Teste JOHN WILLIAMS Cl. Cur.

pp.   THIS INDENTURE made this 9th day of (blotted) year of our Lord one thousand
683-   seven hundred and ninety six Between PETER HANSBROUGH JUNR. and ANNE
686   FRANCES his Wife of County of Prince William of one part and BERNARD HOOE
             JUNR. of County aforesaid of other part; Witnesseth that PETER HANSBROUGH for
sum of One thouand seven hundred and sixty seven pounds current money of Virginia to PETER HANSBROUGH paid by said BERNARD HOOE; by these presents doth bargain sell and confirm unto BERNARD HOOE and his heirs a tract of land lying in County of Prince William and Parish of Dittengin containing Five hundred and seventy nine acres be the same more or less bounded, Beginning at a Water Oak in the head of a Meadow formerly called THE DUCK POND, being a corner of DOCTR: GRAHAMs Land, and running No. 19d. 41m. Wt. 122 po: to a large red Oak, corner to WILLIAM BROWN, thence So. 31d. 52m. Wt. 30 po: to a Spanish Oak on East side of a large Branch called WINTERS UPPER BRANCH, thence down the Branch the several courses and meanders thereof to a corner tree in the Fork of a Branch, being the corner tree to MARK THARPs Lott of Land, it being a Water Oak, thence running up a Branch of WINTERS BRANCH the several meanders thereof (it being MARK THARPs land) to a large Water Oak, corner tree to MARK THARPs and JOHN STEALs Lotts of land, thence along the said JOHN STEALs line N. 82 E. 150 po: and 7 links to a Spanish Oak another of the said STEALs corners, thence No. 61 Et. 106 poles to an Oak another of said STEALs corners on the main MOUNTAIN ROAD, thence running the same course with the line of BENJAMIN THOMAS's Lott now under Lease to him to a large white Oak, thence through said THOMAS's Lott to the line of DOCT: GRAHAM then with said GRAHAMs line No. 71d. 8m. Wt. 321 6/10 po. to the beginning, Together with all houses and appurtenances and all right title and demand of PETER HANSBROUGH and ANNE FRANCES his Wife unto BERNARD HOOE JUNIOR his heirs; And PETER HANSBROUGH and ANNE FRANCES his Wife and from the claim of every person shall forever by these presents defend; In Testimony whereof said PETER HANSBROUGH and ANNE FRANCES his Wife hath hereunto set their hands and affixed their seals
Signed Sealed & Delivered acknowledged in presence of

CHARLES EWELL, WILLIAM TYLER   P. HANSBROUGH JR.
ROBT. H. HOOE, WILLIAM CARR   ANNE F. HANSBROUGH
HANCOCK LEE, H. D. HOOE

BE IT REMEMBERED that whereas SALLEY CARTER hath instituted an Suit against the within mentioned PETER HANSBROUGH JUNR. (which is now pending before the Court of Appeals) for the within mentioned land, that in case said SALLEY CARTER should

recover the sd. Land from said HANSBROUGH that thereupon this Bargain and Sale doth
dissolve and that it is not the intention or meaning of the contracting parties to these
presents that said PETER HANSBROUGH doth or shall warrant the within mentioned
lands against the claim of said SALLEY CARTER or any person claiming under her,
Signed by the parties at the time of executing the within Deed to with the 9th of March
1796 In presence of CHS. EWELL,

      ROBT. H. HOOE, HANCOCK LEE,   P. HANSBROUGH JR.
      WM. TYLER, WILLIAM CARR   BERND. HOOE JUNR.

  The Commonwealth of Virginia to CHARLES EWELL, ROBT. H. HOOE and ALEXANDER
BRUCE Gentlemen Greeting; Whereas (the Commission for the privy Examination of ANNE
FRANCES, the Wife of PETER HANSBROUGH JUNR.) Witness JOHN WILLIAMS Clerk of our said
Court this 20th day of March 1796 and in the 20th year of the Commonwealth

  Prince William County to wit; In Obedience to the within we the Subscribers have
caused to come before us the within mentioned ANNE FRANCES HANSBROUGH and have
examined her privily (the return of the execution of the privy Examination of ANNE FRANCES
HANSBROUGH): Given under our hands this 10th day of March 1796

                       CHS: EWELL,
                       ROBT. H. HOOE

  At a Court continued and held for Prince Wm. Coty the 5th day of April 1796
This Deed and the Memorandum thereon endorsed from PETER HANSBROUGH JUNR. and
ANNE FRANCES his Wife to BERNARD HOOE JUNR. was proved by the Oaths of WILLIAM
TYLER, CHARLES EWELL and WILLIAM CARR and together with a Dedimus for the privy
examination of the feme returned executed, ordered to be recorded

              Teste   JOHN WILLIAMS, Cl Cur

pp.   KNOW ALL MEN by these presents that we LEVI SCOTT and ELIZABETH SCOTT,
686-   Wife of said LEVI of CHARLES County in the State of MARYLAND, for the sum of
688   Sixty one pounds Four shillings current money of Virginia to us in hand paid
        by ANNE PEACHY of County of Prince William, by these presents do bargain sell
and confirm unto ANNE PEACHY and her heirs all that tract of land lying in County of
Prince William on the Branches of HOOES CREEK and the BEAVER DAM, containing One
hundred and two acres as granted to JAMES PEAKE by Patent bearing date the eighth
dayu of September one thousand seven hundred and Eighty eight and sold by JAMES
PEAKE and CONSTANT his Wife and ANTHONY COLLINGS GRAY and LEVINAH his Wife to
said LEVI SCOTT by Deed of Bargain and Sale bearing date the fifteenth day of February
in year one thousand seven hundred and ninety one, being bounded, Beginning at a
Chesnut Oak near a large Path in the edge of the Wood Cutting Corner to TAYLOE, thence
with his line North fifty one degrees West one hundred and twenty three po: to a black
Oak in COCKs line, thence leaving TAYLOE and binding with COCK South by East two
hundred and forty six poles to a white Oak in the Edge of a Glade by MOSS's Line North
fifty five degrees East one hundred and thirty poles to the aforesaid TAYLOEs line,
thence along his line No. thirty six degrees West eighty six poles to the beginning, To
have and to hold the aforesaid tract of land with the appurtenances unto ANNE PEACHY
and her heirs; And LEVI SCOTT and ELIZABETH his Wife their heirs to said ANN PEACHY
and her heirs against the claims of all persons do warrant and defend; In Witness
whereof the said LEVI SCOTT and ELIZABETH his Wife have hereunto set their hands and
seals this seventh day of December in year of our Lord one thousand seven hundred
and ninety one
Signed seled and delivered in presence of
      JOHN MACRAE, WM. DOWNMAN,   LEVI SCOTT
      ANTHONY C. GRAY   ELIZABETH SCOTT

The Commonwealth of Virginia to JOHN MACRAE, WILLIAM DOWNMAN and ALEXANDER
LITHGOW Gentlemen Greeting. Whereas (the Commission for the privy Examination of ELIZA-
BETH, the Wife of LEVI SCOTT); Witness ROBERT GRAHAM Clerk of our said Court the 7th
day of December in the 16th year of the Commonwealth 1791   ROBT. GRAHAM
   Prince William County Sct. In Obedience to the within, we the Subscribers have
caused to come before us the within mentioned ELIZABETH SCOTT and have examined
her privately (the return of the execution of the privy Examination of ELIZABETH SCOTT); Given
under our hands and seals this 7th day of December 1791
                                        JNO: MACRAE
                                        WM. DOWNMAN
   At a Court held for Prince William County the 6th day of February 1792
This Deed from LEVI SCOTT and ELIZABETH his Wife to ANN PEACHY was proved by the
Oaths of JOHN MACRAE and WILLIAM DOWNMAN & ordered to be certified.
                   Teste ROBT. GRAHAM, Cl Cur
   At a Court continued and held for said County the 5th day of April 1796
This Deed was fully proved by the Oath of ANTHONY C. GRAY and (together with a Dedi-
mus for the privy examination of the feme returned executed) ordered to be recorded
                   Teste JOHN WILLIAMS, Cl Cur

pp.   (On margin: Examd. & deld. Apl. 27th 1797)
688-   THIS INDENTURE made this 31st day of March one thousand seven hundred and
689   ninety five Between HENRY LEE Esqr., and ANNE LEE his Wife of County of WEST-
         MORELAND of one part and CUMBERLAND WILSON of Town of DUMFRIES in the
County of Prince William, Merchant, of other part; Witnesseth that HENRY LEE and
ANNE LEE his Wife for the sum of Five shillings current money to them in hand paid by
CUMBERLAND WILSON by these presents do bargain sell and confirm unto CUMBERLAND
WILSON his heirs Four acres of Arable Marsh lying on North side of QUANTICO CREEK
being part of a larger quantity of Marsh and Highland Patented and purchased by Colo:
BERTRAND EWELL of Colo. WILLIAM FITZHUGH of State of MARYLAND, by Deeds of Lease
and Release and a Patent from the Proprietors Office and by said EWELL sold and con-
veyed to Capt. WILLIAM TEBBS, and by said TEBBS to THOMAS ATTWELL, who by Deeds of
Lease and Release dated the 8th and ninth days of July 1783 conveyed the same Marsh
Land to said HENRY LEE, which last mentioned Deeds are duly recorded among the
Records of the aforesaid County, said Four acres of Marsh hereby conveyed are bounded
Beginning at a box Oak, the beginning corner of a quantity of Marsh belonging to the
Heirs of ISRAEL FOLSOM deced., standing on or near the edge of the Marsh and running
No. 75d. 30m. Et. 17 po: to a black Walnut standing on the high land then So. 67d. Et. 22
po: to a Stone on the high land, thence So. 30d. Et. 19 1/2 po: to another Stone in the
Marsh, thence So. 80d. Wt. 32 1/2 po: to another Stone in the Marsh and line of said
FOLSOM, thence with his line No. 30d. Wt. 31 po: to the beginning; containing Four acres
of arable Marsh, Also one other tract of Marsh Land adjoining the aforesaid tract containing two acres and three quarters of an acre and conveyed to HENRY LEE on the
eighth day of June one thousand seven hundred and Eighty five by the aforesaid THO-
MAS ATTWELL and ANN his Wife; And all houses water courses orchards profits and
appurtenances to the same in any wise appurtaining; To have and to hold the two tracts
of Marsh Land unto CUMBERLAND WILSON his heirs; And HENRY LEE and ANNE his Wife
and their heirs do by these presents warrant and defend the two tracts of Marsh Land
unto CUMBERLAND WILSON against the claim of all persons; In Witness whereof the
said HENRY LEE Esqr. and ANN his Wife hath hereunto set their hands and affixed their
seals the day and year within written

Sealed and Delivered in presence of
    H. ROSS, DAVID BOYLE,   HENRY LEE
    WILLIAM LINTON   ANNE LEE
At a Court held for Prince William County the 4th day of May 1795
This Deed from HENRY LEE Esqr. and ANNE his Wife to CUMBERLAND WILSON was proved
by the Oaths of DAVID BOYLE and WILLIAM LINTON and ordered to be certified; And at a
Court continued and held for the said County the Sixth day of April 1796, this Deed was
fully proved by the Oath of HECTOR ROSS and ordered to be recorded
                  Teste JOHN WILLIAMS Cl Cur

p.   (On margin: Examd. & Deld. M. HARRISON JR., Atto. for WASHINGTON, Janry.
690   6th 1798)
     THIS INDENTURE made the Sixth day of April in year of our Lord one thousand
seven hundred and ninety two Between MARY BURWELL of Prince William County in
Virginia, Widow, of one part and BUSHROD WASHINGTON Esqr. and THOMAS PORTER,
Merchants, both of Town of ALEXANDRIA, of other part; Witnesseth that in consideration of Five shillings Sterling to MARY BURWELL in hand paid by BUSHROD WASHING-
TON & THOMAS PORTER, by these presents doth bargain and sell unto BUSHROD
WASHINGTON & THOMAS PORTER all that tract of land situate in County of Prince William whereon said MARY BURWELL now lives, containing One thousand and Twenty six
acres; To have and to hold the land with the appurtenances during the full term of one
whole year to the intent to enable the said MARY BURWELL to grant release and convey all the premises and the reversion threof to BUSHROD WASHINGTON & THOMAS
PORTER their heirs to such uses and in such manner as MARY BURWELL doth now
intend shortly to grant release and convey the same by Indenture intended to bear date
the day next after the day of the date of these presents; In Witness whereof the said
MARY BURWELL hath hereunto set her hand and seal the day and year above written
Sealed and delivered in presence of
    JAMES THOMSON, WILLIAM GRAHAM,   MARY BURWELL
    JOHN THOMSON
At a Court held for Prince William County the 2d. day of May 1796
This Deed from MARY BURWELL to BUSHROD WASHINGTON and THOMAS PORTER was
proved by the Oaths of JAMES THOMSON, JOHN THOMSON and WILLIAM GRAHAM and
ordered to be recorded   Teste JOHN WILLIAMS, Cl Cur

pp.   (On margin: Lre. of Atto: examd. & deld. to BLANCETT 2d April 1797, N. COX)
691-   KNOW ALL MEN by these presents that I CALEB BUTLER of FAYETTE County and
692   State of KENTUCKY for divers good causes and considerations me thereunto
     moving by these presents appoint my Brother in Law and trusty friend, ASA
BLANSETT of Prince William County my true and lawfull Attorney for me and in my
name to transact all my business, collect all debts, legacies or devises or other demands
due to me with the State of Virginia but more especially to demand and if necessary sue
for recover and receive of the persons in whose hands the same may be vested all
monies goods or chattels lands or tenements due to me as Legatee devisee or legal re-
presentative of my deceased Mother in Law, CATHARINE MARTIN, late of Prince William County deced., hereby declaring what my said Attorney may do in the premises as
valid and binding as if transacted by myself; Given under my hand and seal this Eighth
day of March 1796   CALEB BUTLER
FAYETTE County Sst. This day personally appeared before me, JAMES TROTTER, one of
the Justices of the Peace for County aforesaid, CALEB BUTLER who acknowledged the
foregoing Letter of Attorney to be his act and deed for the purposes therein specified;

Given under my hand this 8th day of March 1795   JAMES TROTTER
   STATE of KENTUCKY, To all to whom these presents shall come, Greeting; Know ye that
JAMES TROTTER Esquire whose name is subscribed to the Instrument of hereto and was
at the time of subscribing the same a Justice of the Peace in and for FAYETTE County
duly appointed and commissioned and full faith and credit is and ought to be given to
his Certificate and other official acts
   In Testimony whereof ISAAC SHELBY Esquire, Governor of said State hath hereunto set
his hand and caused the Seal of the State to be affixed at FRANKFORT on the eighth day
of March in year of our Lord one thousand seven hundred and ninety six
                                        ISAAC SHELBY
          By the Governor. JAMES BROWN, Secretary
   At a Court held for Prince William County the 2d. day of May 1796
This Power of Attorney from CALEB BUTLER to ASA BLANSETT was presented to the Court
and (together with the Certificates of JAMES TROTTER Esqr. and the Governor of KEN-
TUCKY thereto annexed) ordered to be recorded
                        Teste JOHN WILLIAMS, Cl Cur

pp.   (On margin: Examd. & Deld. JAMES SMITH Septr. 29th 1796, J. WMS: Cl Cur)
692-   THIS INDENTURE made this Twelfth day of November in year of our Lord one
693   thousand seven hundred and ninety three Between TRAVIS DAVIS and FANNEY
         his Wife of NELSON County and State of KENTUCKY of one part, CUMBERLAND
WILSON of Prince William County of other part; Witnesseth that TRAVIS DAVIS and
FANNEY his Wife for the sum of One hundred and twenty pounds specie to them in hand
paid by CUMBERLAND WILSON by these presents have bargained and sold unto CUM-
BERLAND WILSON his heirs a right and title of One hundred and Thirty acres of land
(lying in Prince William County) be the same more or less in QUANTICO NECK near
POWELLS CREEK, the said land being prt of HOSINGTONs Patent, and purchased by ISAAC
DAVIS deced., Father to said TRAVIS, of WILLIAM BLAND IN 1763, and bounded, Beginning at a marked Pine in the Division between this land and the land formerly held by
BENJAMIN BLAND, and extending thence North East 150 pole to WARDENs Dividing Line,
then So. Et. 130 po. to the land formerly held by JOHN CAMPBELL, then So. Wt. 150 po. to
HOSINGTONs Back Line, then with said back line No. Wt. 130 po: to the beginning, To
have and to hold the One hundred and thirty acres of land unto CUMBERLAND WILSON
his heirs free and clear from all incumbrances whatsoever; And TRAVIS DAVIS and
FANNEY his Wife their heirs by these presents shall warrant and forever defend; In
Witness whereof the said TRAVIS DAVIS and FANNEY his Wife hath hereunto set their
hands and seals the day month and year first above written
Sealed & Deliver'd in presents of
      JNO: KINCHELOE, WM. DAVIS.   TRAVIS DAVIS
      JOHN KINCHELOE JUNR.,   FANNEY DAVIS
      J. H. HOOE as to TRAVIS DAVIS,
      ROBT. H. HOOE as to TRAVIS DAVIS
   At a Court held for Prince William County the 2d. day of December 1793
This Deed and the Receipt thereon endorsed from TRAVIS DAVIS and FANNEY his Wife to
CUMBERLAND WILSON were proved by the Oaths of JOHN KINCHELOE and WILLIAM
DAVIS and ordered to be certified;   Teste ROBERT GRAHAM, Cl Cur
   At a Court held for Prince William County the 2d. day of May 1796
This Deed was fully proved by the Oaths of JOHN KINCHELOE JUNR. and ROBERT H. HOOE
and ordered to be recorded   Teste JOHN WILLIAMS, Cl Cur

pp.   KNOW ALL MEN by these presents that I SAMPSON LEACHMAN of County of
693-   Prince William for the sum of One hundred and fifty pounds to me in hand paid,
694   by these presents do bargain sell and deliver unto WILLIAM CUNDIFF one Negro
          man named Elliss, one Sorrel Mare and Coalt, one sorrel horse, six head of cattle,
eleven head of hogs, three beds and furniture, one chest of drawers, two tables, three
pewter dishes; To have and to hold the above mentioned property to him and his heirs
and said SAMPSON LEACHMAN and his heirs the above said property to WILLIAM CUN-
DIFF and his heirs shall warrant and forever defend by these presents; In Witness
whereof I have hereunto set my hand and seal this Thirtyeth day of April one thousand
seven hundred and ninety six
Sealed and Delivered in presence of
     JOSEPH BUTLER,   SAMPSON LEACHMAN
     WILLIAM MATTISON
     At a Court held for Prince William County the 2nd day of May 1796
This Bill of Sale and Receipt from SAMPSON LEACHMAN to WILLIAM CUNDIFF was acknowledged by said LEACHMAN to be his act and deed and ordered to be recorded
                         Teste JOHN WILLIAMS, Cl Cur

pp.   (On margin: Examd. & Deld. Mr. VAL: PEERS for Mr. NEWMAN the 6th Septr. 1796)
694-   THIS INDENTURE made this 27th day of January in the year of our Lord one
696   thousand seven hundred and ninety four Between JOHN B. ARMISTEAD of
          CAROLINE County in State of Virginia of one part and THOMAS NEWMAN of
Prince William County of other part; Witnesseth that for sum of Seven hundred and
Twenty four pounds current money to him the said JOHN B. ARMISTEAD in lhand paid
by VALENTINE PEERS of LOUDOUN County as well as for the farther sum of Five shillings
currency to said JOHN B. ARMISTEAD in hand paid by THOMAS NEWMAN, doth by these
presents bargain sell and confirm unto THOMAS NEWMAN his heirs three certain tracts
of land lying in Prince William County to wit, One tract now in the tenure of EDWARD
ROGERS and under Lease for Three Lives at the yearly rent of Fifteen poudns per
annum containing Two hundred and twelve acres; One other tract held by WILLIAM
MITCHELL for Fifteen years, containing One hundred and two acres at the yearly rent
of Twelve pounds, And one other tract held by SAML. OWENS for Fifteen years containing Two hundred and twenty six acres at the yearly rent of Twenty five pounds currency; To have and to hold the said three tracts of land with all improvements and
rents issues and profits arising therefrom to THOMAS NEWMAN his heirs freed and dis-
engaged from all manner of incumbrances, said JOHN B. ARMISTEAD hath full right to
convey the same in special Trust however and to this true intent that whereas JOHN B.
ARMISTEAD as Guardian and Trustee for his Brother, ADDISON ARMISTEAD, hath this
day bargained and sold unto VALENTINE PEERS a certain tract of land in Prince William County being a prt of his said Brother, ADDISONs, land containing per Survey
Three hundred and sixty two acres for the sum of Seven hundred and twenty four
poudns currency, And Whereas the said ADDISON being now a minor cannot convey the
same to said PEERS, now if said ADDISON when he shall attain to and be of full age in
Law or within six months thereafter on demand of said PEERS or his assigns convey to
said PEERS his heirs with general Warranty and satisfactory security against all claims
in fee simple estate in and to said tract of his, ADDISONs land, then THOMAS NEWMAN
shall forthwith reconvey and restory unto JOHN B. ARMISTEAD the hereby granted
premises as if this Deed had not been made; In Testimony whereof and for due perfor-
mance of all and singular the several covenants and engagements herein contained
and expressed, the said parties have hereunto put their hands and seal the day and year
first within written

Signed Sealed acknowledged & delivered in presence of us
JOHN McCLANACHAN,   )   JOHN B. ARMISTEAD
NICH: PEERS, RICHD: GILL) as to J. B. Armistead   THOS: NEWMAN
EDMD. BROOKE, BENJA: G. ORR)
NICHOLAS PEERS   ) as to Thomas Newman
   At a Court held for Prince William County the 1st day of September 1794
This Deed in Trust from JOHN B. ARMISTEAD to THOMAS NEWMAN was proved by the Oath
of NICHOLAS PEERS as to the execution thereof by both parties and ordered to be certi-
fied; And at a Court held for said County the 6th day of October 1794,. This Deed was
acknowledged by THOMAS NEWMAN to be his act and deed & ordered further Certified;
And at a Court contd. and held for the said County the 8th day of December 1795, the said
Deed was proved by the Oath of JOHN McCLANACHAN as to the execution thereof by
ARMISTEAD and ordered to be further certified;   Teste ROBERT GRAHAM, Cl Cur
   At a Court held for the said County the 2nd day of May 1796
This Deed was fully proved by the Oath of RICHARD GILL and ordered to be recorded
                     Teste JOHN WILLIAMS, Cl Cur

pp.   (On margin: Examd. & deld. ARRINGTON WICKLIFF, Admor. of MOSES WICKLIFF
696-   deced. 28th Augt. 1799, W. HOWISON)
698   THIS INDENTURE made this Thirteenth day of February in year of our Lord one
         thousand seven hundred and ninety six Between ARRINGTON WICKLIFF and
CATY his Wife of County of Prince William and ROBERT WICKLIFF and SARAH his Wife of
FAIRFAX County of one part and MOSES WICKLIFF of County of Prince William of other
part; Witnesseth that ARRINGTON WICKLIFF and CATY his Wife and ROBERT WICKLIFF
and SARAH his Wife for the sum of One hundred and Thirty five pounds specie in hand
paid by MOSES WICKLIFF, by these presents have bargained and sold unto MOSES WICK-
LIFF his heirs all that tract of land containing Two hundred acres be the same more or
less situate in County of Prince William lying in the Fork of BULL RUN and BUCKHALL
BRANCH and is part of two tracts of land, one taken up by THOMAS DAVIS of STAFFORD
County in the year 1730, the other by WANSFORD ARRINGTON about the year 1713; the
said DAVIS's part was given to OWEN OWENS by said DAVIS in 1744, the said OWENS sold to
BENJAMIN WICKLIFF of FAIRFAX County, said BENJAMIN WICKLIFF dying without Will
the said land falling to said ARRINGTON, party to these presents; who is Heir at Law of
said BENJAMIN WICKLIFF deced., the other part was given to said ROBERT WICKLIFF,
party to these presents, by his Grandfather, ROBERT WICKLIFF deced. who married the
aforesaid WANSFORD ARRINGTONs Daughter, who was an Heiris, and is bounded, Beginning on BULL LRUN at the mouth of BUCKHALL BRANCH, then up BULL RUN and
binding therewith No. 43d. Et. 94 po:, then No. 12d. Wt. 15 po;, then No. 52d. Wt. 150 po;
then No. 60d. Wt. 152 po: to the mouth of Branch, then No. 77d. Wt. 12 po., then No. 26d.
Wt. 42 po: then No. 14d. Wt. 42 po; then No. 33d. Et. 22 po. to the mouth of another Branch
which divides this land from the land sold by CHARLES WICKLIFF to THOMAS BIRD, then
up the said Branch and binding therewith No. 11d. 30m. Wt. 8 po., then No. 81d. Wt. 14
po., then So. 70d. Wt. 44 po., then No. 78d. Wt. 25 po., to a red Oak corner to said BIRD,
then So. 24d. Et. 22 po., to a white Oak on a Ridge, then So. 87d. Wt. 41 po. to a Stake in
HOOE's Field near the head of a small Branch, then Et. 147 po., with HOOEs line to a box
Oak now dead in MOSLEYs line, formerly DAVIS, then Et. 20 po., to a dead red Oak on a
Ridge, then S. 6d. Et. 59 po. (directions and distances continue for three more lines without land
marks or names) to the begining and the beginning corner of the aforesaid WANSFORD
ARRINGTONs Tract, Together with all houses profits and appurtenances to said Two
hundred acres of land belonging; free and discharged from all incumbrances; In Witness whereof the said ARRINGTON WICKLIFF and CATY his Wife and ROBERT WICKLIFF

and SARAH his Wife to this present Indenture of Bargain and Sale hath hereunto set
their hands and seals the day month and year first above written
Signed Sealed and Delivered in presence of

JNO: KINCHELOE,   JNO: KINCHELOE JUNR.   ARRINGTON WICKLIFF
ELIJAH WICKLIFF,   MOSES WICKLIFFE JUNR.   CATY WICKLIFF
ROBT. H. HOOE to ROBT. WICKLIFF acknowd.   ROBERT WICKLIFF
                                               SARAH WICKLIFF

At a Court held for Prince William County the 2d day of May 1796
This Deed and the Receipt thereon endorsed from ARRINGTON WICKLIFFE and CATY his
Wife and ROBERT WICKLIFF and SARAH his Wife to MOSES WICKLIFF, was proved (as to
the execution thereof by ROBERT WICKLIFF) by the Oaths of ROBERT H. HOOE, JOHN
KINCHELOE JUNR. and MOSES WICKLIFF JUNR., and the same being acknowledged by
ARRINGTON WICKLIFF to be his acts and deeds were ordered to be recorded
Teste JOHN WILLIAMS, Cl Cur

pp.   THIS INDENTURE TRIPARTITE made the seventh day of April in year of our
699-   Lord Seventeen hundred and ninety two Between MARY BURWELL of Prince
701   William County, Widow, of the first part; BUSHROD WASHINGTON Esqr. and THO-
           MAS PORTER, Merchts., of the Town of ALEXANDRIA of the second part and
ROGER PRESCOTT of State aforesaid Gent. of third part; Whereas the better to enable said
MARY BURWELL to grant and convey unto BUSHROD WASHINGTON and THOMAS PORTER
and their heirs upon the Trusts and Confidences nevertheless herein after mentioned,
said MARY BURWELL by Indenture of Bargain and Sale bearing date the day next before
the day of the date of these presents for the consideration of Five shillings did bargain
and sell unto BUSHROD WASHINGTON and THOMAS PORTER One thousand and Twenty six
acres of land situate in County of Prince William whereon said MARY BURWELL now
resides with the appurtenances thereunto belonging; To have and to hold the One thousand and Twenty six acres of land sold unto BUSHROD WASHINGTON and THOMAS PORTER
or assigns from the date of the recited Indenture unto the term of one whole year by
force and virtue of said Indenture and of the Statute for transferring uses into possession the said BUSHROD WASHINGTON and THOMAS PORTER are actually possessed of the
one thousand and twenty six acres of land and thereby capable of taking the freehold
and inheritance of the same by release; And Wheras a MARRIAGE is intended by Gods
permission to be shortly had and solemnized between said ROGER PRESCOTT and said
MARY BURWELL; Now This Indenture Witnesseth that MARY BURWELL by and with the
consent and agreement of ROGER PRESCOTT, testified by his being made a party to these
presents, by these presents doth release unto BUSHROD WASHINGTON and THOMAS POR-
TER their heirs all the said One thousand and twenty six acres of land; And this Indenture further Witnesseth that MARY BURWELL for the consideration aforesaid hath
bargained and sold unto BUSHROD WASHINGTON and THOMAS PORTER all her slaves both
old and young, male and female, which she is now possessed of and entitled to together
with the future increase of said females; To have and to hold the said land and slaves
and the future increase of the female slaves unto BUSHROD WASHINGTON and THOMAS
PORTER their heirs upon trust and confidence that until said intended marriage had
and solemnized, in trust, for MARY BURWELL and her heirs and shall permit her to
receive and take the rents issues and profits thereof, And after the intended marriage
had and solemnized then permit ROGER PRESCOTT to have and take the rents issues and
profits of the lands and hire of said slaves and their increase during his natural life
and after the death of said ROGER, if he shall be survived by said MARY, then again to
permit said MARY to take the issues and profits of said land and slaves; In Witness
whereof the parties to these presents have hereunto set their hands and seals the day

month and year first within written
Sealed and Delivered in the presence of
    JAMES THOMSON,   MARY BURWELL
    WM. GRAHAM, JOHN THOMSON   R. PRESCOTT
  At a Court held for Prince William County the 2nd day of May 1796
This Deed of Settlement to uses from MARY BURWELL and ROGER PRESCOTT to BUSHROD
WASHINGTON and THOMAS PORTER was proved by the Oaths of JAMES THOMSON, WIL-
LIAM GRAHAM and JOHN THOMSON the witnesses thereto, and ordered to be recorded
                      Teste JOHN WILLIAMS, Cl Cur

p.   KNOW ALL MEN by these presents that I CHARLES HARDEN of Prince Wm. Coun-
701   ty do for favours received gratisly give from me my heirs to ROLLEY HARDIN of
         County aforesaid the goods and chattles, to wit, one bay hors five years old about
thirteen hands high no barnd; one Sorril Mare Colt three years old with a blais in its
face and three white feet about thirteen hand two inches high, also one red Cow an Calf
markt. with a Crap in the left ear an Swallow Fork in the rite; and both her horns sawed
of, also one ditto same mark with a white face, also one heefer Couler as above and
mark, one black ditto with a white face the same mark, also eleven hogs one yeare old
markt. with the same mark of the above Cattle, and twenty two pigs unmarkt., also two
feather beads and furniter an Sixteen lbs. of Pewter, also one linning wheale and won
woollen ditto; the above articles I do give gratisly to the above ROLLEY HARDEN his
heirs as his own property to convey bargain and sell as he shall think proper; As Witness my hand and seal this 6th day of March 1796
Sind. Sead. and deverd. in the presents of
    MOSES LYNN, EBINEZAR ATHEY,   CHARLES HARDING
    JOHN WILLIAMS
  At a Court held for Prince William County the 2d. day of May 1796
This Deed of Gift from CHARLES HARDING to ROLLEY HARDING was acknowledged by the
said CHARLES HARDING to be his act and deed and ordered to be recorded
                      Teste JOHN WILLIAMS, Cl Cur

pp.   KNOW ALL MEN by these presents that whereas I have a tract of land situate in
701-   the State of KENTUCKY on the Waters of LICKING, estimated and supposed to con-
702   tain One thousand acres; And Whereas some disputes have arisen respecting the
         bounds and title of said lands, And Whereas my trusty friend, WILLIAM FARROW,
is going to aforesaid County and have agreed to take such steps and measures as will
effectually secure and perfect my right and title to the aforesaid Land, now to the end
that said FARROW may be lawfully impowered to act in the premises and to carry my
intention and wishes in full effect respecting the aforesaid lands, I hereby authorize
and impower and appoint him my lawful Attorney and Agent to take all lawful ways in
establishing my right and title to the lands; In Testimony whereof I have hereunto set
my hand and affixed my seal this Second day of May in year of our Lord one thousand
seven hundred and ninety six
                      GEORGE KING
  At a Court contd. and held for Prince William County the 3d. day of May 1796
This Letter of Attorney from GEORGE KING to WILLIAM FARROW was acknowledged by
the said KING and orderd to be recorded   Teste JOHN WILLIAMS, Cl Cur

pp.   THIS INDENTURE made this fourth day of November in year of our Lord one
702-   thousand seven hundred and ninety five Between CATESBY GRAHAM, Devisee of
703   ELIZABETH GRAHAM deced. of one part and WILLIAM GRAHAM, also a Devisee of

ELIZABETH GRAHAM of other part; Witnesseth that CATESBY GRAHAM for the sum of
Five shillings to him in hand paid by WILLIAM GRAHAM, by these presents doth bargain sell and confirm unto the said WILLIAM, all his part right title and Interest in a
certain parcel of land Leased by said ELIZABETH GRAHAM of MARTIN COCKBURN by
Indenture bearing date the fourth day of June in year of our Lord one thousand seven
hundred and ninety two; lying in Prince William County and bounded as by reference
to said Indenture will appear; his interest in which tract of land among other things
was devised by the said ELIZABETH GRAHAM to CATESBY GRAHAM, JENNEY GRAHAM
and WILLIAM GRAHAM, which being as yet undivided, CATESBY GRAHAM doth relinquish to WILLIAM GRAHAM; To have and to hold the parts and Interest of said CATESBY
in the aforesaid devised tenement to WILLIAM GRAHAM his heirs during the term of
lives which said Tenement was originally leased by ELIZABETH GRAHAM of MARTIN
COCKBURN, and CATESBY GRAHAM his interest in the devised premises to said WILLIAM
shall warrant and forever defend; In Testimony whereof said CATESBY GRAHAM hath
hereunto affixed his name and seal the day and year above mentioned
Signed Sealed & Delivered in presence of
        MARTIN J. HANCOCK, ELIJAH GRAHAM,   CATESBY GRAHAM
        VAL: PEERS, NICHS: PEERS
    At a Court continued and held for Prince William County the 8th day of December 1795
This Deed from CATESBY GRAHAM to WILLIAM GRAHAM was proved by the Oaths of
MARTIN J. HANCOCK and VALENTINE PEERS and ordered to be certified; And at a Court
continued and held for said County the third day of May 1796, the Deed was acknow-
ledged by said CATESBY GRAHAM to be his act and deed & ordered to be recorded
                    Teste JOHN WILLIAMS, Cl Cur

pp.   THIS INDENTURE made this Tenth day of December in year of our Lord one
703-   thousand seven hundred and ninety five Between JAMES ROACH of Town of
704   DUMFRIES County of Prince William and ANNE ROACH his Wife of one part and
         DAVID WILSON SCOTT of the Town & County aforesaid of other part; Whereas
JOSHUA BARKER of the Town and County aforesaid by one Indenture of Lease under his
hand and.   duly recorded among the Records of the aforesaid County Court on the
seventh day of September one thousand seven hundred and eighty nine for the consideration therein mentioned did demise granted and to farm lett unto JAMES ROACH his
heirs a certain lott of Ground lying in Town of DUMFRIES bounded, Beginning at the
upper Corner of DUMFRIES WAREHOUSE and running thence to MESSRS. POPE and HUN-
TERs Lotts, thence with their Lotts to SARAH EWELLs Lott, (now in the occupation of
COLIN CAMPBELL) thence with SARAH EWELLs lott of land to the Street next the Creek,
thence with said Street to the beginning; To hold to said JAMES ROACH and ANN ROACH
his Wife and JOHN THOMAS ROACH his Son and longest liver of them by the yearly rent
of Ten pounds current money of Virginia and performing the several agreements in
said Lease; Now This Indenture Witnesseth that JAMES ROACH and ANNE his Wife in
consideration of the sum of Thirty five pounds current money to them in hand paid, by
these presents have sold and set over unto DAVID WILSON SCOTT his heirs all the lott of
Ground in Town of DUMFRIES leased as aforesaid by JOSHUA BARKER to JAMES ROACH;
In Witness whereof JAMES ROACH and ANNE his Wife have hereunto set their hands and
affixed their seals the day and year first before written
Sealed and Delivered in the presence of
        WALKER TURNER,   JAMES ROACH
        GEORGE WEAVER, HORATIO BLANCETT   ANNE ROACH
    At a Court held for Prince William County the 4th day of Jany. 1796
This Deed of Assignment of Lease from JAMES ROACH and ANNE his Wife to DAVID

WILSON SCOTT was proved by the Oath of HORATIO BLANCETT and ordered to be Certified;
And at a Court contd. and held for said County the 5th day of April 1796, was further
proved by the Oath of WALKER TURNER and ordered to be further certified; And at a
Court continued and held for said County the 3d. day of May 1796, this Deed was fully
proved by the Oath of GEORGE WEAVER and ordered to be recorded
                    Teste JOHN WILLIAMS, Cl Cur

pp.   THIS INDENTURE made the 29th day of May in year of our Lord one thousand
705-   seven hundred and ninety two Between ELIZABETH SCOTT, Relict of JAMES SCOTT
706   deced., in County of FAUQUIER of one part and THOMAS HARRISON of Prince Wil-
           liam County of other part; Witnesseth that ELIZABETH SCOTT for the sum of
Three hundred pounds to her in hand paid before the execution of these presents; doth
bargain sell and confirm unto THOMAS HARRISON his heirs all that tract of land lying
on CEDAR RUN in County of Prince William and adjoining the land of said THOMAS HAR-
RISON being the one half of a tract of land late the property of SETH HARRISON deced.,
and of which said ELIZABETH SCOTT became possessed as a Coheir and one of the Repre-
sentatives of said SETH HARRISON deced. and is bounded, Beginning at a small marked
Elm in line of HARRISON and HARRISON, thence No. 83 1/2 Et. 216 po. to the line of HAR-
RISON and WHITLEDGE to a small marked red Oak, thence with said line to a large white
Oak standing on the bank of CEDAR RUN and corner tree of HARRISON and WHITLEDGE,
thence up the Run with the meanders thereof to a large Sugar tree, corner to aforesaid
HARRISON and HARRISON, thence leaving the Run with said line to the beginning;
containing One hundred and forty eight acres as surveyed by HENRY D. HOOE in the
Division made between said ELIZABETH SCOTT, THOMAS SCOTT and THOMAS HARRISON
and their Wives as representatives of the aforesaid SETH HARRISON deced. and lying
below the lands allotted to said THOMAS HARRISON, together with all profits and privi-
liges to said land belonging; To have and to hold the before mentioned lands unto THO-
MAS HARRISON and to his heirs; And ELIZABETH SCOTT and her heirs shall forever
herafter warrant and defend the hereby granted land to THOMAS HARRISON and his
heirs against the claims of all persons; In Witness whereof she hath hereunto set her
hand and affixed her Seal the day and date before written
Signed Sealed and Delivered in presence of
        LAWRENCE ASHTON,   JNO: P. HARRISON,   ELIZATH: SCOTT
        ALEXR: SCOTT,   THOMAS SCOTT,
        MATTHEW HARRISON JR., LANGH: DADE
   At a Court held for Prince William County the 7th day of April 1793
This Deed from ELIZABETH SCOTT to THOMAS HARRISON was proved by the Oaths of MAT-
THEW HARRISON JR. and LANGHORNE DADE and ordered to be Certified
                    Teste ROBERT GRAHAM, Cl Cur
   At a Court continued and held for said County the third day of May 1796
The said Deed was fully proved by the Oath of THOMAS SCOTT and ordered to be recorded
                    Teste JOHN WILLIAMS, Cl Cur

pp.   WE WHOSE NAMES are hereto subscribed do promise to pay to the President and
706-   Directors of the QUANTICO COMPANY the sum of Fifty Dollars for every share of
708   Stock in said Company set opposite to our respective names in such manner and
           proportion and at such times as shall be determined by the said President and
Managers in pursuance of an Act of the General Assembly of this Commonwealth
intituled "An Act for opening and improving the Navigation of QUANTICO CREEK in
County of Prince William. Witness our hands this (blank) day of March 1796

SUBSCRIBERS NAMES	NO. SHARES SUBSCRIBED
JESSE EWELL	Eleven shares
JAMES & GEORGE DENEALE	Twelve shares
TIMOTHY BRUNDIGE	Six shares
THOMAS CHAPMAN	Six shares
BERNARD GALLAGHER	Six shares
JAMES MUSCHETT	Five shares
PHILIP DAWE	Five shares
JOSEPH GILBERT	Five shares
WILLIAM LINTON	Two shares
JAMES HAYES	Two shares
ALEXANDER LITHGOW	Three shares
JOHN LAWSON	Two shares
ADAM COOKE	One share
MATTHEW HARRISON JR.	One share
LUKE CANNON	Three shares
GALVAN DeBERNOUX	Five shares
NATHANIEL C. HUNTER	One share
TOWNSHEND DADE	One share
ALEXANDER BRUCE	One share
WILLIAM BEALE	One share
WILLIAM McDANIEL	One share
THOMAS LEE	One share
DANIEL C. BRENT	Two shares
GERRD. ALEXANDER JR.	One share
JOHN POPE	Two shares
WILLIAM CARR	Five shares
JOHN CARR	Three shares
THOMAS THORNTON	Two shares
JOHN OVERALL	One share
GEORGE GRAHAM Doctr.	One share
GEORGE LANE	Two shares
JAMES GUINNETT	Two shares
DAVID W. SCOTT.	Two shares
JOHN FRISTOE	Two shares
JOHN WILLIAMS	One share
CHARLES EWELL	Three shares
JAMES SMITH	Five shares
JESSE EWELL JR.	Two shares
	117 shares

We the Subscribers, Commissioners appointed by an Act of Assembly for receiving Subscription to the QUANTICO COMPANY do hereby certify that we did open Subscription Books agreeable to the aforementioned Act of Assembly, that the aforegoing Subscribed shares were made as the Law directs and that the same is a true copy of the Books and Subscriptions received by said Commissioners.
Given under our hands at DUMFRIES this sixth day of June 1796

JOHN LAWSON,   JAMES DENEALE
JAMES MUSCHETT   PHILIP DAWE

At a Court contd. and held for Prince William County the seventh day of June 1796 This List of Subscribers to the QUANTICO COMPANY was presented to the Court and ordered to be recorded   Teste JOHN WILLIAMS, Cl Cur

pp. THIS INDENTURE made this seventh day of June in year of our Lord one thou-
708- sand seven hundred and ninety six Between ALEXANDER LITHGOW and JOHN
710 LAWSON Esqr. both of Town of DUMFRIES and County of Prince William, and
Commissioners under the Decree hereinafter mentioned of one part and THOMAS
SWANN at present of Town of ALEXANDERIA of other part; Whereas a certain ANN
MASON now deced., was in her life time seiz'd of a tract of land containing Five hundred
acres situate in County of Prince William and in the Parish of Hamilton, it being part of
a greater tract or Pattent of Land of Seven hundred and fifty acres granted to one JOHN
PEAKE on the twenty third day of October in year of our Lord one thousand seven
hundred and Twenty eight and purchased by the said ANN MASON of JOHN PEAKE as will
appear by Deeds of Lease & Release bearing date the twenty first and twenty second
days of April one thousand seven hundred and thirty eight; and duly recorded in County of Prince William, And said ANN MASON having by her Last Will and Testament
directed that the said land among other things to be sold by her Executors for the payment of her debts and the surplus if any to be divided between her Grand Children,
SAMUEL SELDEN and MARY SELDEN, And it appearing that there was a small sum only
due to the Executors of Colo. GEORGE MASON deced., for which the said Land was liable,
and that the surplus arising from the sale thereof belong'd to the Representatives of
said MARY SELDEN, the County Court of Prince William at their November Term last
decreed that said lands should be sold at publick sale for cash to the highest bidder for
the purpose of discharging the said claim and to be applied to the use of the representatives of said MARY SELDEN and appointed ALEXANDER LITHGOW and JOHN LAWSON together with RICHARD GRAHAM or any two of them to make said sale and execute a Deed to
the purchaser of the land, And ALEXANDER LITHGOW and JOHN LAWSON having pursuant to their authority aforesaid sold the land to the highest bidder for cash and said
THOMAS SWANN having become the purchaser thereof at the price of Six hundred and
Ten pounds; NOW THIS INDENTURE WITNESSETH that ALEXANDER LITHGOW and JOHN
LAWSON as well in pursuance of their authority as Commissioners as also for the sum of
Six hundred and Ten pounds to them in hand paid by THOMAS SWANN do bargain and
sell unto THOMAS SWANN and his heirs the aforesaid tract containing five hundred
acres together with all houses profits commodities to tract of land belonging; In
Witness whereof the said ALEXANDER LITHGOW and JOHN LAWSON have hereunto set
their hands and affix'd their seals the day and year first before written
Seal'd and Delivered in presence of
(no witnesses recorded) ALEXANDER LITHGOW
JOHN LAWSON
Received of Mr. ALEXANDER LITHGOW and JOHN LAWSON the sum of Six hundred and
ten pounds it being the amount of the consideration within mentioned and directed by
the decree within mentioned to be paid to the Complainant or any of them
THO: SWANN, one of the Complainants
June 7th 1796
At a Court continued and held for Prince William County the 10th day of June 1796
This Deed from ALEXANDER LITHGOW and JOHN LAWSON, Commissioners appointed by a
Decree of the said Court to THOMAS SWAN, and the receipt thereon from THOMAS SWANN
to said Commissioners were acknowledged by the parties and ordered to be recorded
Teste JOHN WILLIAMS, Cl Cur

pp. (On margin: Exd. & Deld. July 29th 1799 to Mr. DUVAL, W. H.)
710- THIS INDENTURE made this twenty ninth day of November one thousand seven
713 hundred and Eighty eight Between THOMAS ARRINGTON and MARY his Wife of
County of FAUQUIER, Planter, of one part and JAMES NISBETT of County of Prince

William, of other part; Witnesseth that THOMAS ARRINGTON and MARY his Wife for the sum of Eighty pounds current money, by these presents do bargain sell and confirm unto JAMES NISBETT his heirs a certain tract of land lying in County of Prince William containing One hundred acres be the same more or less which said tract of land was granted by Deed from the Proprietors Office to WILLIAM HARRISON and LEWIS MARK-HAM, the said THOMAS ARRINGTON by sundry mesne conveyances being now possessed thereof; the same is bounded, Beginning at a Pine corner to the land of JAMES NISBETT and running from thence South fifty eight degrees East ninety two poles to the line of Colo. GEORGE MASON, thence with his line to a white Oak the corner of Colo. THOMAS BLACBURNs land, thence with his line to a white Oak, corner to said NISBETTs land, thence with his line to the beginning; And all woods water courses profits and appur-tenances; To have and to hold the lands unto JAMES NISBETT his heirs; And THOMAS ARRINGTON and his heirs by these presents shall warrant and for ever defend; said THOMAS ARRINGTON hereby reserves for himself his heirs one acre of the granted land where the GRAVE YARD at present is; In Witness whereof the said THOMAS and MARY ARRINGTON have hereunto set their hands and affixed their seals the day and year first above written

Sealed and Delivered in presence of
     WILLIAM DOWNMAN, THOMAS MADDUX,   THOMAS ARRINGTON
     JOSEPH NELSON, RICHARD MADDUX   MARY her mark X ARRINGTON

The Commonwealth of Virginia to FRANCIS TRIPLETT, MARTIN PICKETT and BENJAMIN SHACKLEFORD Gentlemen, Greeting, Whereas (the Commission for the privy Examination of MARY, the Wife of THOMAS ARRINGTON); Witness ROBERT GRAHAM Clerk of our said Court the second day of May 1789   ROBERT GRAHAM

FAUQR: County, to wit; By virtue of this Writ to us directed we have privately exa-mined the sd. MARY ARRINGTON (the return of the execution of the privy examination of MARY ARRINGTON); Witness our hands and seals this 21d. day of May 1789
     FRANCIS TRIPLETT
     B. SHACKLEFORD

At a Court held for Prince William County the 1st day of June 1789
This Deed and the Receipt thereon from THOMAS ARRINGTON and MARY his Wife to JAMES NISBETT (a Dedimus for the privy Examination of the feme being returned executed) were proved by the Oath of WILLIAM DOWNMAN and ordered to be Certified; And at a Court held for said County the 4th day of July 1796, the said Deed and Receipt were fully proved by the Oaths of THOMAS MADDUX and RICHARD MADDUX and ordered to be recorded   Teste JOHN WILLIAMS, Cl Cur

pp.   KNOW ALL MEN by these presents that we CATHARINE DOUGLAS SENIOR, MAR-
713-   GARET DOUGLAS and CATHARINE DOUGLAS JUNIOR in that part of the Kingdom
717   of Great Britain called Scotland for divers good causes us thereunto moving by
    these presents do make and appoint ALEXANDER HENDERSON of DUMFRIES in County of Prince William within the Territory of the United States of America our true and lawful Attorney to treat with any person whatsoever for selling or disposing of in fee simple the following tenements; One tract of land lying on BRETON in Prince Wil-liam County and Territory of the United States of America which was by Deeds of Lease and Release bearing date the first and second days of May in year Seventeen hundred and Sixty seven conveyed by a certain ROBERT BRENT and ANN his Wife to CATHARINE DOUGLAS SENIOR (party to these presents) as Executrix and GEORGE BRENT, ALEXANDER HENDERSON, JOHN RIDDELL and WILLIAM CARR as Executors of a certain JAMES DOUG-LAS, late of Prince William County deceased to the uses expressed in the Will of said

said JAMES DOUGLAS, And also one other tract of land situated in County of STAFFORD which was by Deeds bearing date the twelfth and thirteenth days of February Seventeen hundred and Sixty seven duly recorded among the Records of STAFFORD County conveyed by ELIZABETH STROTHER, JOHN WALLER and MARY his Wife to said CATHARINE DOUGLAS SENIOR, Executrix and the said GEORGE BRENT, ALEXANDER HENDERSON, JOHN RIDDELL and WILLIAM CARR Executors of said JAMES DOUGLAS to the uses expressed in the Will of JAMES DOUGLAS and all right title interest both legal and equitable of all or either of us as Tenants in Dower, joint tenants, tenants in Common or in severally of in or to the parcels of land we do by these presents constitute ALEXANDER HENDERSON our true and lawful Attorney to treat with any person for the sale of all or any Negro or other slaves, stock, plantation utensils or personal estate of whatsoever nature it may be; In Witness whereof we the said CATHARINE DOUGLAS SENIOR, MARGARET DOUGLAS and CATHARINE DOUGLAS JUNIIOR have hereto affixed our hands and seals this Twenty seventh day of February in year one thousand seven hundred and ninety six

Signed Sealed & acknowledged in the presence of
ARCHD: HENDERSON,   CATHARINE DOUGLAS SENR.
ANDREW MITCHELL,   MARGARET DOUGLAS
                                         CATHARINE DOUGLAS JR.

(This Power of Attorney is followed by Certificates of JOHN HALL, Notary Publick dwelling in the City of GLASGOW in the County of LANERK in that part of Great Britain called Scotland, dated the twenty seventh day of February one thousand seven hundred and ninety six; of JOHN DUNLOP Esquire Lord Provost and Chief Magistrate of the City of Glasgow attesting JOHN HALL to be a Notary Public dated the same day; And the Certificate of ANDREW MITCHELL of City of GLASGOW a subscribing Witness attesting the hand writing of CATHARINE DOUGLAS SENIOR, MARGARET DOUGLAS and CATHARINE DOUGLAS JUNIOR; sworn to the twenty seventh day of February one thousand seven hundred and ninety six).

At a Court held for Prince William County the fourth day of July 1796
This Letter of Attorney from CATHARINE DOUGLAS SENIOR, MARGARET DOUGLAS and CATHARINE DOUGLAS JUNR. to ALEXR. HENDERSON together with the Certificates of the Acknowledgement thereof, were ordered to be recorded
Teste JOHN WILLIAMS, Cl Cur

pp.   (On margin: Examd. & Deld. Mr. PHILIP DAWE, J. WMS:)
717-   THIS INDENTURE made the 26th day of June in year of our Lord one thousand
719   seven hundred and ninety three Between THOMPSON RANDOLPH of County if
           Prince William of one part and THOMAS LEE, President, THOMAS HARRISON,
PHILIP DAWE, ROBERT HOOE, WILLIAM HELM and EDWARD CARTER, Commissioners for the Poor of the County of other part; Witnesseth that THOMPSON RANDOLPH for the sum of One hundred and forty three pounds nineteen shillings to him in hand paid by said Commissioners, by these presents doth bargain sell and confirm unto (the Commissioners) all that parcel of land lying in County of Prince William on the Waters of QUANTICO and bounded; Beginning at a white Oak by a Branch corner to PRESLY COX, thence along his line N. 84 1/2 Wt. 86 po. to a white Oak, corner to the REVD. MR. SCOTT, thence along his line N. 65 Wt. 142 po: to a Poplar by a Branch, thence No. 20 wt. 67 po: to a white Oak on a Hill side, thence No. 75 Wt. ( ) po. to a black Oak, thence leaving SCOTT and binding with RIDLEY, N. 66 Et. 118 po. to a Hickory corner to said RANDOLPHs own land, thence binding with his own lines S. 52 Et. 158 po. to a white Oak on a stony point, thence No. 60 Et. 66 ploles to a Hickory and red Oak beginning corner to said RANDOLPH and CHARLES CORNWELL, thence with said CORNWELL No. 6 E. 54 po: to a white Oak by a Branch in GEORGE ASH's line, thence with ASH's line So. 52 E. 194 po: to a black Oak his corner,

thence S. 3 E. 20 po. to a Stake in BERRYMANs line, thence along it S. 14 Wt. 18 po. to a
Stake in DAVIS's line, thence binding with DAVIS N. 77 Wt. 39 po. to a Peach tree, thence
N. 12 Wt. 60 po., to a white Oak and red Oak, thence No. 70 Wt. 105 po. to a fallen white
Oak, thence S. 6 Wt. 14 po. to a Beech on the Run side, thence to the beginning, contai-
ning Two hundred and Sixty one acres and three quarters of an acre which land was
granted to THOMPSON RANDOLPH by BEVERLEY RANDOLPH Esqr. Governor of Virginia
by Deed bearing date the 21st day of November 1791; Together with all houses woods and
emoluments to the same belonging; To have and to hold the hereby granted land to (the
President and Commissioners above named) In Witness whereof the said THOMPSON RAN-
DOLPH hath hereunto set his hand and affixed his seal the day and date above written
Signed Sealed acknowledged & Delivered in presence of
        DAVID JAMESON,   THOMPSON RANDOLPH
        JAMES GRIGSBY, GEORGE COPPIN,
        CUTHBERT HARRISON JUNR.
    At a Court held for Prince William County the seventy day of October 1793
This Deed from THOMPSON RANDOLPH to the Commissioners for the Poor was proved by
the Oath of DAVIS JAMESON and ordered to be certified;
                    Teste ROBERT GRAHAM, Cl Cur
    At a Court held for Prince William County the sixth day of July 1795, This Deed from
THOMPSON RANDOLPH to the Commissioners of the Poor was further proved by the Oath
of GEORGE COPIN and ordered to be further certified; And at a Court continued and held
for the said County the fifth day of July 1796, This same Deed was fully proved by the
Oath of JAMES GRIGSBY and ordered to be recorded
                    Teste JOHN WILLIAMS, Cl Cur

pp.   (On margin: Examd. & Deld. Apl. 14th 1797, N. COX).
719-   THIS INDENTURE made this seventeenth day of June Anno Domini one thousand
721   seven hundred and ninety six Between FRANCES BOTTS of County of CULPEPER of
          one part and JAMES HOLLIDAY of County of Prince William of other part;
Whereas FRANCES BOTTS and BENJAMIN BOTTS are entitled to and seized in common of
the tract of land whereon said HOLLIDAY now lives in County of Prince William and
which tract of land is bounded by lines described in a certain Deed of Indenture made
and executed by SETH BOTTS deceased on the sixteenth day of June one thousand seven
hundred and Seventy five and now of Record in County Court of Prince William, to his
Son, JOSHUA BOTTS, for the said land (the said FRANCES BOTTS's Estate therein being one
third part of the said tract of land during the term of her natural live in right of Dower
and said BENJAMIN BOTTS the other two parts of said land and the remainder of said
FRANCES BOTTS's after her death; And Whereas BENJAMIN BOTTS hath covenanted with
said HOLLIDAY that he will convey to him the said HOLLIDAY his said two parts and the
remainder of the other part vesting after the death of said FRANCES BOTTS in fee simple
whenever said BENJAMIN BOTTS shall be thereunto required by said HOLLIDAY, after
the Twenty seventh day of April one thousand seven hundred and ninety seven, said
HOLLIDAY paying said BENJAMIN BOTTS at the same time the sum of Two hundred
pounds, wherefore the inconveniences which are likely to arise from such divided
possession render it the interest of the parties that said FRANCES BOTTS should also dispose of her Estate in the aforesaid land to said JAMES HOLLIDAY; NOW THIS INDENTURE
Witnesseth that FRANCES BOTTS for the sum of Forty pounds to her in hand paid by
JAMES HOLLIDAY by these presents do bargain and sell unto JAMES HOLLIDAY his heirs
the whole of her one third part of the land; To have and to hold the one third part of
said land during the natural life of said FRANCES BOTTS unto JAMES HOLLIDAY his heirs;
In Witness whereof the said FRANCES BOTTS hath hereunto set her hand and seal the

day and year first above written
Sign'd Seal'd and delivered in the presence of
     BENJ: BOTTS, DANIEL TRIPLETT,   FRANCES BOTTS
     EDMUND BURKE, PETER COSPER
  At a Court held for CULPEPER County the 20th day of June 1796
This Indenture of Bargain and Sale from FRANCES BOTTS to JAMES HOLLIDAY was proved
by the Oaths of DANIEL TRIPLETT, EDMUND BROOKE and PETER COSPER, witnesses there-
to and ordered to be recorded   Teste JOHN JAMESON, Cl Cur
  At a Court continued and held for Prince William County the fifth day of July 1796
This Deed from FRANCES BOTTS to JAMES HOLLIDAY was presented to the Court and with
the Probate of the Proof thereof, ordered to be recorded
                Teste JOHN WILLIAMS, Cl Cur

p.   THIS INDENTURE made and entered into this 5th day of July 1796 by NATHANIEL
722   ELLICOTT, Witnesseth that said ELLICOTT by these presents doth liberate and
      imancipate a mulatto woman by the name of Emmy and for ever quits all claim
to her and forever discharges her from his service. In Testimony whereof the said
ELLICOTT hath hereunto set his hand and affixed his seal the day and year first written
In presence of THOMAS SCOTT,
     M. HARRISON JR.   NATHL. ELLICOTT
  At a Court continued and held for Prince William County the 5th day of Julyl 1796
This Deed of Freedom from NATHANIEL ELLICOTT to a mullato woman named Emmy was
acknowledged by the said ELLICOTT and ordered to be recorded
            Teste JOHN WILLIAMS, Cl Cur

pp.   THIS INDENTURE made and entered into this sixth day of June in year of our
722-   Lord 1796 Between Captain RICHARD SCOTT BLACKBURN of one part and JACOBUS
724   LANGHYER of County of Prince William of other part; Witnesseth that said
      RICHARD SCOTT for sum of Four hundred and Fifty pounds in hand paid by sd.
JACOBUS by these presents do bargain & sell unto said JACOBUS his heirs all that MILL
and tract of land containing One hundred acres deeded and conveyed to said RICHARD
SCOTT by his Father, Colo. THOMAS BLACKBURN by Deed dated the 9th March 1790
recorded in the County Court of Prince William being part of a larger tract granted to
RICHARD BLACKBURN by Patent bearing date the 28th day of May 1739, which hundred
acres are bounded, Beginning at a Stump on the East side of the Old Mill, corner to JOHN
TYLER and said BLACKBURN's Original Patent, thence to run up the and binding therewith untill it comes to PETER SMITH's line, thence with said line to the Corner to be
established for said SMITH and EDWARD HARVEY, then So. Easterly to the beginning,
Together with all houses Mills Mill Seats water courses and appurtenances of every
kind; To have and to hold the land of one hundred acres, Mill and appurtenances unto
said JACOBUS; And RICHARD SCOTT BLACKBURN his heirs doth warrant and forever defend the afsd. land Mill and appurtenance unto said JACOBUS against all claims; In Witness whereof the said RICHARD SCOTT BLACKBURN hath signed sealed and delivered this
Deed the day and year first written
In presence of JAMES MUSCHETT,   R. S. BLACKBURN
     CHARLES TYLER JR., WALTER ASHMORE,
     JOHN MUSCHETT
  At a Court continued and held for Prince William County the 5th day of July 1796
This Deed from RICHARD S. BLACKBURN to JACOBUS LANGHYER was proved by the Oaths
of JAMES MUSCHETT, CHARLES TYLER and JOHN MUSCHETT and ordered to be recorded
            Teste JOHN WILLIAMS, Cl Cur

pp.   THIS INDENTURE made and entered into this seventh day of June in yar 1796
724- Between THOMAS BLACKBURN and CHRISTIAN his Wife of County of Prince Wil-
726   liam of one part and JACOBUS LANGHYER of same County of other part; Witnesseth that said THOMAS and CHRISTIAN in consideration of thirty seven pounds
specie in hand paid to them by JACOBUS LANGHYER by these presents do bargain and
sell unto said JACOBUS his heirs one certain tract of land containg One hundred and
Eighteen acres and a half with a Mill threon situate in afsd. County being a part of a
larger tract granted by Patent to RICHARD BLACKBURN deced., and the said One
hundred and eighteen acres and a half are bounded, Beginning at A., a gut making into
BROAD RUN where Mr. JOHN TYLERs deced., corner stood, thence with his line North
28d. Wt. 136 poles to B., supposed to be another of said TYLERs corners, thence North 64d.
East 60 poles to C., another of his corners, thence North 16d. West 152 pole to D., a large
white Oak, also corner to said TYLER, thence South 58d. West to E., a Stake in an old Field,
thence South 35d. East 127 poles to F., four Beaches growing from one root, standing on
the North side of BROAD RUN at the beginning of a high stony hill, thence down said
Run binding therewith to the beginning, containing One hundred and eighteen and a
half acres pursuant to a Survey thereof made by WILLIAM CUNDIFF as will appear by a
platt by him made signed by his own name and dated the 6th May 1796; Together with
all Mills, Mill Seats water courses and all appurtenances of every kind; To have and to
hold the One hundred and eighteen acres and a half of land with said Mill, Mill Seats
and water courses unto said JACOBUS his heirs and sd. THOMAS and CHRISTIAN his Wife
theirs heirs agree with said JACOBUS his heirs to warrant and defend for ever against
all claims of all persons; In Testimony whereof said THOMAS and CHRISTIAN his Wife
have hereunto subscribed their names and affixed their seals and delivered this Deed
the day and year first written

In presence of J. LAWSON,   THOMAS BLACKBURN
       WM. BARNES, KITTY BLACKBURN   CHRISTIAN BLACKBURN
       CHARLES TYLER JR., JAMES MUSCHETT

The Commonwealth of Virginia to WILLIAM BARNES, JOHN LAWSON and JAMES SMITH
Gentlemen, Greeting. Whereas (the Commission for the privy Examination of CHRISTIAN, the
Wife of THOMAS BLACKBURN); Witness JOHN WILLIAMS Clerk of our said Court this 7th day
of June 1796 and in the 20th year of the Commonwealth   JOHN WILLIAMS

Prince William County, to wit, In Obedience to the within, we the Subscribers have
caused to come before us the within named CHRISTIAN and have examined her privately (the return of the execution of the privy Examination of CHRISTIAN BLACKBURN); Given under
our hands and seals this 7th day of June 1796   WILLIAM BARNES
                                           J. LAWSON

At a Court continued and held for Prince William County the 5th day of July 1796
This Deed from THOMAS BLACKBURN & CHRISTIAN his Wife to JACOBUS LANGHYER (a
Dedimus for the privy examination of the feme being returned executed) was proved by
the Oaths of JOHN LAWSON, CHARLES TYLER and JAMES MUSCHETT and ordered to be
recorded   Teste JOHN WILLIAMS, Cl Cur

pp.   THIS INDENTURE made this first day of November in year of our Lord one thou-
727- sand seven hundred & ninety four Between HENRY LEE Esqr. of County of WEST-
728   MORELAND of one part and ISAAC McPHERSON of Town of ALEXANDRIA County of
FAIRFAX of other part; Witnesseth that HENRY LEE for sum of Thirty eight
pounds current money of Virginia to said HENRY LEE in hand paid by ISAAC McPHER-
SON by these presents doth bargain sell & confirm unto ISAAC McPHERSON his heirs a
tract of land lying upon OCCOQUAN RIVER in County of Prince William bounded, Begin-

ning on the River at the place where two Birches formerly stood, being the upper corner to PETYTONS TRACT, and the lower Corner of EWELLs and runing thence down the
said River and binding therewith South fifty eight degrees East twenty eight poles,
thence South sixty seven and a half degrees East forty one poles to two red Oaks, one
now down, corner to a tract of land formerly granted to GEORGE MASON, and now property of the Heirs of TAYLOE and THORNTON, thence along the line of said tract cor-
rected South eleven degrees and a half West one hundred & seventy eight poles to an
old marked Poplar standing near the head of a small Branch, corner of said tract and
corner to PEYTONS TRACT, thence to the beginning, containing Thirty seven acres
which was granted unto said HENRY LEE his heirs by Patent under the hand and seal of
the said State and the hand of JAMES WOOD, Lieutenant Governor thereof bearing date
the fifth day of October one thousand seven hundred and ninety three; And all houses
profits commodities & appurtenances; To have and to hold the said tract of land unto
ISAAC McPHERSON his heirs; And HENRY LEE and his heirs the tract of land unto ISAAC
McPHERSON his heirs shall warrant and for ever defend by these presents; In Witness
whereof the said parties have hereunto set their hands and seals the day and year first
beforementioned
Sealed and Delivered in presence of
    HZH: SMOOT, CHARLES PAGE,   HENRY LEE
    EDWARD HARPER
    At a Court of Hustings Contd. & held for the Town of ALEXA: 21st May 1796
This Deed and Receipt from HENRY LEE to ISAAC McPHERSON were proved by the Oaths
of HEZEKIAH SMOOT, CHARLES PAGE and EDWARD HARPER to be the act and deed of the
said HENRY LEE which is ordered to be certified to the County Court of Prince William
               Teste P. WAGENER, Cl Cur
    At a Court continued and held for Prince William County the fifth day of July 1796
This Deed and Receipt and the Certificate of Proof thereof were ordered to be recorded
               Teste JOHN WILLIAMS, Cl Cur

pp.   (On margin: Examd. & deld. April 27th 1797, N. COX)
728-   THIS INDENTURE made this first day of January one thousand seven hundred
730   and ninety six Between JOHN LANGFITT of Town of DUMFRIES County of Prince
       William of one part and DANIEL FORGIE of same Town & County of other part;
Witnesseth that JOHN LANGFITT in consideration of the Rents and Covenants herein
after reserved and containing of the part DANIEL FORGIE or assigns to be paid and performed, by these presents doth Lease set and to farm let unto DANIEL FORGIE all that
part of a lott or half acre of ground nearly opposite to the Lott on which the said
LANGFITT now Dwells, laid down in a Platt & Survey of said Town by the number Forty &
which was conveyed to said LANGFITT by Deed from JOHN ANDERSON and SUSANNA his
Wife bearing date the sixth day of June one thousand seven hundred and ninety one
and duly recorded among the Records of said County Court; To have and to hold the part
of a Lott or half acre of land and premises with the appurtenances unto DANIEL FORGIE
& assigns from the day of the date hereof during the full term of Fifteen years next
ensuing; paying therefore yearly during the term unto JOHN LANGFITT his heirs the
Rent of Nine pounds specie current money of Virginia, the first payment thereof to
begin and be made on the first day of January which shall be in the year One thousand
seven hundred & ninety seven and also paying all Taxes that now is or may be imposed
on said premises; In Witness whereof the said parties to these presents have hereunto
set their hands and affixed their seals the day month and year first within written

Signed Sealed and Delivered in presence of   JOHN LANGFITT
                                                              DANIEL FORGIE

Memo. It is further covenanted that if DANIEL FORGIE shall erect or cause to be
erected any Meat House or other Out House or Houses on the premises and said JOHN
LANGFITT shall not think proper to allow him for such buildings, then said DANIEL
FORGIE have liberty to removed the said buildings off said premises to whatever place
he may think proper; Witness my hand and seal the date first mentioned
Teste JOHN WILLIAMS, GEO: LANE   JOHN LANGFITT
        DAVID WILSON SCOTT
        JOSEPH GILBERT, JOHN FRISTOE
    At a Court held for Prince William County the fourth day of July 1796
This Lease from JOHN LANGFITT to DANIEL FORGIE was proved by the Oaths of JOSEPH
GILBERT and JOHN WILLIAMS and ordered to be Certified; And at a Court continued for
said County the fifth day of July 1796; this same Lease was fully proved by the Oath of
GEORGE LANE and ordered to be recorded   Teste JOHN WILLIAMS, Cl Cur

pp.   THIS INDENTURE made this 8th day of May in year of our Lord one thousand
730-   seven hundred & ninety Between PETER FRANCIS TRENIS & HANNAH TRENIS his
732   Wife of Town of DUMFRIES in County of Prince William of one part and CHARLES
         EWELL of said County of other part; Witnesseth that PETER FRANCIS TRENIS and
HANNAH his Wife for sum of Fifty eight pounds current money of Virginia to them in
hand paid by CHARLES EWELL said PETER FRANCIS TRENIS and HANNAH his Wife doth
bargain sell and confirm unto CHARLES EWELL his heirs all that tract of land lying in
County of Prince William between the Main Road as leads to QUANTICO WAREHOUSES &
the BEAVER DAM RUN, the land of said CHARLES EWELL & Mr. GALVANs given & conveyed by BERTRAND EWELL to PETER FRANCIS TRENIS & HANNAH his Wife by Deed the
21st March 1785 & appears on an exact survey Fifty eight acres of land Beginning for
the said land at the sd. Main Road in the sd. CHARLES EWELLs line, running from thence
with his line to the head of the COOL SPRING BRANCH, No. 30 Et. 46 poles, thence down
the meanders of said Branch to the BEAVER DAM RUN, thence up said Run and binding
therewith to the mouth of the COAL PITT BRANCH where Mr. GALVAN binds, thence
along his line So. 81 West 106 poles to his corner on said Main Road, thence down the
Main road binding therewith 127 poles to the beginning, containing fifty eight acres;
Together with all houses profits mills comodities & appurtenances belonging; To have
and to hold the Fifty eight acres of land unto CHARLES EWELL his heirs; In Witness
whereof said PETER FRANCIS TRENIS & HANNAH TRENIS his Wife hath hereunto to this
present Indenture of Bargain & Sale sett their hands and seals the day month and year
first written
Signed Sealed and Delivered in presence of
        JAMES JAMES,   JNO: MACRAE,   P. F. TRENIS
        JOSEPH JAMES
    At a Court held for Prince William County the 5th day of July 1790
This Deed with the Receipt thereon from PETER FRANCIS TRENIS & HANNAH his Wife to
CHARLES EWELL was proved by the Oath of JAMES JAMES and ordered to be Certfied; At a
Court continued and held for Prince William County the 3d day of May 1791, This Deed
was further proved by the Oath of JOSEPH JAMES & ordered to be further certified;
                    Teste RT. GRAHAM, Cl Cur
    And at a Court continued & held for the same County the 5th day of July 1796
This Deed was fully proved by the Oath of JOHN MACRAE and ordered to be recorded
                    Teste JOHN WILLIAMS, Cl Cur

pp.   THIS INDENTURE made the ninth day of October in year of our Lord one thou-
732- sand seven hundred and ninety five Between JOHN TAYLOE & ANN his Wife of
734   County of RICHMOND of one part and LUKE CANNON & FRANCIS CANNON, both of
       Prince William County of other part; Witnesseth that JOHN TAYLOE and ANN his
Wife for sum of Three hundred pounds current money of Virginia to them in hand paid
by LUKE CANNON & FRANCIS CANNON, by these presents doth bargain & sell unto LUKE
CANNON & FRANCIS CANNON their heirs a certain tract of land lying in County of Prince
William on the Waters of QUANTICO RUN, bounded, Beginning at a large Mulberry tree
on South side of North Fork of QUANTICO RUN, extending then up said run and binding
therewith No. 10.30 Wt. 18 po. to a white Oak sapling on said Run side, thence So. 76 Wt.
90 po: to a marked red Oak near a small Branch, thence up said Branch No. 63 Wt. 20 po.
to a marked Hickory sapling and Dogwood Bush, thence So. 52.15 Wt. 225 po. to a heap of
Stone in the out line of the Patent, thence with that line So. 25 Et. 221 po. to a Stake on
South side of South Fork of QUANTICO RUN, thence No. 37 Et. 320 po: to the first station
including by a late survey Three hundred acres, and all trees tithes commons profits
and appurtenances belonging; To have and to hold the tenement and all the premises
unto LUKE CANNON & FRANCIS CANNON their heirs and JOHN TAYLOE and ANN his Wife
their heirs the premises against all persons to said LUKE CANNON & FRANCIS CANNON
their heirs shall warrant and for ever defend by these presents; In Witness whereof
the said JOHN TAYLOE & ANN his Wife have hereunto set their hands and seals the day
and year first above written
Signed Sealed and Delivered in presence of us
      WILLIAM CARR; THOMAS TRIPLETT,   JOHN TAYLOE
      JAMES WALLACE, VINCENT REDMAN,   ANN TAYLOE
      WM. BEALE JR., WILLIAM GORDEN
   The Commonwealth of Virginia to ROBERT WORMELEY CARTER, GEORGE LEE TURBER-
VILLE & VINCENT REDMAN Gentlemen, Greeting, Whereas (the Commission for the privy
examination of ANN, the Wife of JOHN TAYLOE); Witness JOHN WILLIAMS Clerk of our said
Court the 3d day of October 1795 and in the 20th year of the Commonwealth
   RICHMOND County, to wit, In Obedience to the within, we the Subscribers have caused
to come before us the within named ANN TAYLOE and have examined her privily (the
return of the execution of the privy examination of ANN TAYLOE); Given under our hands and
seals this 9th day of October 1795   GEORGE LEE TURBERVILLE
                            VINCENT REDMAN
  At a Court held for Prince William County the 7th December 1795
This Deed from JOHN TAYLOE and ANN his Wife to LUKE CANNON and FRANCIS CANNON
were proved by the Oaths of THOMAS TRIPLETT & WILLIAM CARR (and together with a
Dedimus for the privy examination of the feme returned executed) were ordered to be
Certified; And at a Court held for the same County September 5th 1796; This Deed was
fully proved by the Oath of WILLIAM BEALE JUNR. and ordered to be recorded
            Teste JOHN WILLIAMS, Cl Cur

pp.   TO ALL PEOPLE to whim this present intended written Writting shall come,
734- Know ye that I JAMES HATHAWAY SENR. of County of FAUQUIER and Parish of
735   Hamilton have as well for the natural love and affection that I have and bare
      unto my Son, JAMES HATHAWAY JUNR. of aforesaid County as divers other good
causes and valuable considerations me thereunto moving by these presents doth give
bargain sell & confirm unto my Son, JAMES HATHAWAY JUNR. & his heirs a certain
tract of land lying in County of Prince William, it being the tract of land purchased by
me of a certain CHARLES STEWART, the quantity of acres, boundaries &c. will appear by
said CHARLES STEWARTs Deed to me, with all houses orchards and all things necessarily

belonging is hereby vested in said JAMES HATHAWAY JUNR., and his heirs; Also the ten
Negro slaves hereafter mentioned, Vizt., Jack, Moses, David, Tom, Ellen, Winney,
Mary, Jamima, George & Rebeckah, and all future increase of the female slaves; To
have and to hold unto JAMES HATHAWAY JUNR. and his heirs likewise 3 Mares and their
future increase, all the black Cattle, sheep, hoggs & plantation utensils &c., which
belong to the aforesaid tract of land; In Testimony whereof I said JAMES HATHAWAY
SENR. have to these presents interchangeably set my hand and affixed my seal this 22d
day of January in year of our Lord one thousand seven hundred and ninety six
Signed Sealed & Delivered in presence of
          JAMES WALLACE SENR.,   JAMES HATHAWAY SENR.
          EDWARD ROGERS, JAMES WALLACE JUNR.
     At a Court held for FAUQUIER County the 22d. day of February 1796
This Indenture was proved to be the act & deed of said JAMES HATHAWAY SENR. by the
Oaths of JAMES WALLACE SENR., EDWARD ROGERS & JAMES WALLACE JUNR., witnesses
thereto, and ordered to be certified;   Teste F. BROOK. C. F. C.
     At a Court held for Prince William County the 5th day of September 1796
This Deed from JAMES HATHAWAY SENR. to JAMES HATHAWAY JUNR. with the Certifi-
cate of Proof thereon were ordered to be recorded
                                             Teste JOHN WILLIAMS, Cl Cur

pp.   THIS INDENTURE made this first day of September in year of our Lord one thou-
735-   sand seven hundred & ninety six Between ADDISON BOLES ARMISTEAD of Prince
738   William County of one part and JAMES NEWMAN of same County of other part;
          Witnesseth that ADDISON BOLES ARMISTEAD for the sum of Five shillings cur-
rent money of Virginia to him in hand paid by JAMES NEWMAN, by these presents doth
bargain & sell unto JAMES NEWMAN a certain tract of land situate in afsd. County it
being part of a tract of land formerly the property of JOHN ARMISTEAD deceased, which
by his Will he devised to several of his Sons as it will thereby more fully appear; the
said tract of land lies on the CATAMOUNT or South Branch of BULL RUN and is bounded,
Beginning at a white Oak standing on North side of the CATAMOUNT BRANCH being
likewise a corner to BERNARD HOOE SENR., thence down the Run and binding thereon
the several courses to the Junction of the North & South Fork of the CATAMOUNT,
thence up North Fork or STEEP BOTTOMED BRANCH the several courses to a white Oak in
the DEEP BOTTOMED BRANCH corner likewise to B. HOOE, thence So. West 150 po. being
aline dividing the land of ADDISON BOLES ARMISTEAD between BERNARD HOOE & JAMES
NEWMAN to the beginning on the CATAMOUNT BRANCH, containing Twenty five acres,
And all houses orchards profits & appurtenances; To have and to hold the lands hereby
conveyed unto JAMES NEWMAN his heirs during the full term of one whole year paying
therefore the rent of one pepper corn on Lady Day next if lawfully demanded to the
intent that by virtue of these presents and of the Statute for transferring uses into
possession said JAMES NEWMAN may be in actual possession of the premises & be thereby enabled to accept a release of the reversion & inheritance thereof; In Witness
whereof sd. ADDISON BOLES ARMISTEAD have hereunto set his hand & seal the day and
year first above written
Signed Sealed & Delivered in presence of us
          BERND. HOOE SENR.   ADDISON B. ARMISTEAD
          GARNER his mark + FORTUNE,
          THOMAS NEWMAN, THOMAS P. HOOE,
          WM. CUNDIFF, JOHN DEBELL
     At a Court held for Prince William County the 5th day of September 1796
This Lease from ADDISON B. ARMISTEAD to JAMES NEWMAN was proved by the Oaths of

BERNARD HOOE SENR., GARNER FORTUNE & WILLIAM CUNDIFF and ordered to be
recorded   Teste JOHN WILLIAMS, Cl Cur

        THIS INDENTURE made the second day of September in year of our Lord one
thousand seven hundred and ninety six Between ADDISON BOLES ARMISTEAD of Prince
William County of one part & JAMES NEWMAN of aforesd. County of other part; Witnesseth that for the sum of Sixty three pounds current money of Virginia to ADDISON
BOLES ARMISTEAD in hand paid by JAMES NEWMAN, by these presents doth bargain sell
release & confirm unto JAMES NEWMAN (in his actual possession now being by virtue
of a bargain & sale to him thereof made and by force of the statute for transferring
uses into possession) and his heirs a certain tract of land situate in County of Prince
William, (the previous ownership, the descent by Will and the description of the bounds of the land
repeated as in the foregoing Lease); To have and to hold the land hereby conveyed unto
JAMES NEWMAN his heirs free and clear from all incumbrances whatsoever; And
ADDISON B. ARMISTEAD and his heirs the premises unto JAMES NEWMAN and his heirs
shall warrant and for ever defend by these presents; In Witness whereof the said
ADDISON B. ARMISTEAD have hereunto set his hand and affixed his seal the day and
year first above written
Signed Sealed and Delivered in presence of us
        BERND. HOOE SENR.   ADDISON B. ARMISTEAD
        GARNER his mark + FORTUNE,
        THOMS: NEWMAN, THOS: P. HOOE,
        WM. CUNDIFF, JOHN DEBELL
    At a Court held for Prince William County the 5th day of September 1796
This Release & the Receipt thereon from ADDISON BOLES ARMISTEAD to JAMES NEWMAN
was proved by the Oaths of BERNARD HOOE SENR., GARNER FORTUEN & WM. CUNDIFF &
ordred to be recorded   Teste JOHN WILLIAMS, Cl Cur

p.   THIS INDENTURE made and entered into this fifth day of Septr. in year of our
738   Lord one thousand seven hundred and ninety six Between ROBERT LUTTRELL of
        County of Prince William of one part and SIMON LUTRELL of County of Prince
Wm. of other part; Witnesseth that ROBERT LUTRELL for the sum of Two hundred and
Sixteeen pounds current money of Virginia to him in hand paid by SIMON LUTRELL do
by these presents bargain and sell unto SIMON LUTRELL and to his heirs part of that
tract of land which THOMAS NORMAN deceased devised to EDWARD NORMAN & THOMAS
NORMAN, and which tract THOMAS NORMAN SENR. purchased of CHELTON, Beginning at
F., a large marked white Oak, thence Southerly 51 degrees West 210 poles to G., a new
marked line about 8 poles from a marked Black Oak, thence along the new marked line
North 260 to D., a Stake in an Old Field in the Out Line of the tract, thence along the Out
Line North 72 degrees 30m. East 165 poles to E., the corner missing, then South 3 degrees
East 171 poles to the beginning; containing 216 acres more or less with all houses
profits with the appurtenances of every kind; To have and to hold the premises unto
SIMON LUTRELL his heirs against the claim of any person; In Witness whereof ROBERT
LUTRELL hath hereunto set his hand and seal the day and year first written
Signed Sealed and Delivered in the presence of
        GEO: LANE, ALEXANDER LITHGOW,   ROBERT LUTTRELL
        ROBT. H. HOOE, WILLIAM CARTER
    At a Court held for Prince William County the 5th day of Septr. 1796
This Deed from ROBERT LUTTRELL to SIMON LUTTRELL was acknowledged by the said
ROBERT LUTTRELL & ordered to be recorded Teste JOHN WILLIAMS, Cl Cur

pp.   THIS INDENTURE made this Twenty fifth day of February in year of our Lord
739- one thousand seven hundred and ninety six Between SARAH PURCELLE,
740   THOMAS, JAMES, GEORGE, CHARLES & BETSEY PURCELLE of County of Prince
William of one part and WALTER COE of said County of other part; Witnesseth
that SARAH PURCELLE, THOMAS, JAMES, GEORGE, CHARLES & BETSEY PURCELLE for the
sum of Ninety five pounds specie current money of Virginia to them in hand paid by
WALTER COE, by these presents doth bargain sell and confirm unto WALTER COE his
heirs one tract of land lying in the Forks of CEADER and BROAD RUNs and known by the
name of PURCELLEs LOWER LOTT, said Lott supposed to contain One hundred acres of
land being part of a tract belonging to the Commonwealth of Virginia and commonly
distinguished by "BRISTOES TRACT," Together with all houses improvements profits and
appurtenances to the same belonging; To have and to hold the said leased tract of land
unto WALTER COE and his heirs; And SARAH PURCELLE, THOMAS, JAMES, GEORGE,
CHARLES & BETSEY PURCELLE & their heirs shall warrant and forever defend by these
presents; In Witness whereof the above named SARAH PURCELLE, THOMAS, JAMES,
GEORGE, CHARLES & BETSEY PURCELLE have hereunto set their hands and affixed their
seals

Signed Sealed & acknowledged in presence of

THOS: LEACHMAN,   SARAH hir mark ✝ PURCELL
ENOCK his mark ✝ SIMS,   THOMAS PURCELL
WM. his mark ✝ GRAY   JAMES PURCELL
                                     CHARLES PURCELL
                                     BETSEY her mark ✝ PURCELL

At a Court held for Prince William County the 5th day of September 1796
This Deed of Assignment from SARAH POWELL, THOMAS, JAMES, GEORGE, CHARLES &
BETSEY PURCELL to WALTER COE was proved by the Oaths of THOMAS LEACHMAN, ENOCK
SIMMS & WM. GRAY & ordered to be recorded
                    Teste JOHN WILLIAMS, Cl Cur.

        KNOW ALL MEN by these presents that we SARAH PURCELLE, THOMAS, JAMES,
GEORGE, CHARLES, & BETSEY PURCELLE are held and firmly bound unto WALTER COE in
the penal sum of Two hundred pounds specie current money of Virginia to which pay-
ment well and truly to be made we bind ourselves our heirs firmly by these presents; In
Testimony whereof we have this 25th day of February 1796 set our hands & seals
THE CONDITION of the above obligation is such that whereas the above bound SARAH
PURCELLE, THOMAS, JAMES, GEORGE, CHARLES & BETSEY PURCELLE have this day sold
and by Deed indented conveyed unto WALTER COE one lott of land in the Forks of CEDER
and BROAD RUNs, and it is suggested that JOHN PURCELLE & WILLIAM PURCELLE, Sons of
SARAH & Brothers of the other parties and SALLEY PURCELLE, Daughter of SARAH &
Sister to the other parties have & at a future day may set up a claim to the said lott of
land; Now it is that should either said JOHN WILLIAM or SARAH PURCELLE jointly or
severally or by their certain Attorney their heirs assert any claim & recover any part
of the aforesaid premises, then said SARAH PURCELLE, THOMAS, JAMES, GEORGE,
CHARLES & BETSEY PURCELLE are to hold harmless & reimburse the said WALTER COE the
damages he may sustain by such recovery, Then this obligation to be void else to
remain in full force and virtue

Witness THOS: LEACHMAN,   SARAH her mark ✝ PURCELL
        ENOCK his mark ✝ SIMMS,   THOMAS PURCELL
        WM. his mark ✝ GRAY   JAMES PURCELL
                                CHARLES PURCELL
                                BETSEY her mark ✗ PURCELL

(Note. There is no signature for GEORGE PURCELL at the end of the Deed or end of the Bond.)
At a Court held for Prince William County the 5th day of September 1796
This Bond from SARAH PURCELL, THOMAS, JAMES, GEORGE, CHARLES & BETSEY PUR-
CELL to WALTER COE was proved by the Oaths of THOMAS LEACHMAN, ENOCK SIMMS &
WM. GRAY & ordered to be recorded Teste JOHN WILLIAMS, Cl Cur

pp.   THIS INDENTURE made this Twenty first day of May in year of our Lord one
741-   thousand seven hundred and ninety six Between JOHN BIGGS & ELIZABETH his
743   Wife of Prince William County of one part and GEORGE GRAHAM, Practitioner of
          Phisic in Town of DUMFRIES of other part; Witnesseth that JOHN BIGGS & ELIZA-
BETH his Wife for the sum of Eighty nine pounds, Two shillings current money of Virginia to them in hand paid by GEORGE GRAHAM, by these presents do bargain & sell
unto GEORGE GRAHAM One hundred and Thirty two acres of land be the same more or
less lying on MOLES BRANCH on North side of OCCOQUAN in County of Prince William
and bounded, Beginning at a white Oak, corner to GEORGE GRAHAM & WILLIAM DAVIS,
thence N. 24 E. 145 po: to a large Poplar another corner of said GRAHAM, thence No. 3.
W. 106 po. to four red Oak saplins, thence S. 27 E. 186 poles to a box Oak on a Ridge,
thence N. 62 E. 66 poles,then No.22 30m. E. 42 poles to a white Oak Stump near a blazed
Hiccory, thence S. 13 E. 36 poles to a Beech on said OCCOQUAN, then up said OCCOQUAN &
binding therewith S. 45 W. 85 poles, then So. 13 W. 32 poles, then S. 8. 30m. Wt. 100 poles
to a white Oak, corner to said GRAHAM, then with his line S. 80 W. 98 poles to the beginning, including One hundred and Thirty two acres which tract of land contains a tract
of land granted to JOHN DUNKAN by Patent bearing date the twelfth day of September
1731 & conveyed by said DUNKAN to JAMES FOLEY, & conveyed by JAMES FOLEY to JOHN
BIGGS by Deeds of Lease & Release dated the third & fourth of September 1779 and
recorded among the records of the County of Prince William, & also contains a tract of
land granted to said JOHN BIGGS by Patent bearing date the twelfth day of December one
thousand seven hundred and ninety one; To have and to hold the aforesaid tracts of
land unto GEORGE GRAHAM his heirs clearly & absolutely exonerated from all incumbrances; And JOHN BIGGS & ELIZABETH his Wife against the claim of all persons will for
ever warrant and defend. In Witness whereof we have hereunto set our hands and
seals the day & year first above written
Signed Sealed and Acknowledged in presence of
        ROBT. H. HOOE, CHS. EWELL,   JOHN BIGGS
        JOSHUA his mark X BIRD   ELIZABETH BIGGS
        WILLIAM WISHART,
        RD. H. FOOTE, JOHN McCREERY
The Commonwealth of Virginia to ROBERT HOWSON HOOE & CHARLES EWELL Gentlemen
Greeting, Whereas (the Commission for the privy Examination of ELIZABETH, the Wife of JOHN
BIGGS); Witness JOHN WILLIAMS Clerk of our said Court the fourth day of January 1796
and in the 20th year of the Commonwealth   JOHN WILLIAMS
Prince William County, to wit; In obedience to the within, we the Subscribers have
caused to come before us the within named ELIZABETH BIGGS and examined her pri-
vately (the return of the execution of the privy examination of ELIZABETH BIGGS); Given under
our hands and seals this 21st day of May 1796   ROBT. H. HOOE
                                                      CHS: EWELL
At a Court held for Prince William County the 5th day of Septr. 1796
This Deed & Receipt thereon from JOHN BIGGS and ELIZABETH his Wife to GEORGE
GRAHAM were proved (the Deed) by the Oaths of ROBT. H. HOOE, CHS. EWELL & JOHN
McCREERY, (& the Receipt) by JOHN McCREERY & (together with a Dedimus for the

privy Examination of the feme returned executed) ordered to be recorded
Teste JOHN WILLIAMS, Cl Cur

(The end of Prince William County Deed Book Y, 1791-1796, published by the Antient Press in two books, Deed Abstracts of Prince William County, Virginia 1791-1794; and Deed Abstracts of Prince William County Virginia 1794-1796).

COLQUHOUN. James (Walter (of Dumbries -11), 12, 15, 16.
COMBS. John 2.
COMMISSIONERS for the POOR. Listed 123.
COOK. Adam 8, 120.
COOPER. Benjamin 19, (voter -54, 55).
COPIN/COPPIN. George 124; William Junr. (voter -54, 56).
CORNWELL. Charles (voter -54), 123; Charles Junr. (voter -53); Francis 39, (voter -56, 57); Francis Senr. (voter -54); Jesse (voter -54, 55); Peter 12; Samuel 8, 68, 69; Sarah 12.
COSPER. Peter 125.
COUNTIES: Caroline 114; Culpeper 20, 124, 125; Fairfax 16, 27, 49, 65, 113, 126; Fauquier 7, 14, 36, 38, 51, 62, 69, 75, 76, 87-89, 96, 119, 121, 129, 130; Frederick 32, 63, 97; Loudoun 87, 102; Montgomery 30; Northumberland 70; Richmond 36, 37, 41, 58, 81-83, 129; Stafford 4, 24, 25, 32, 37, 42, 51, 62, 85, 113, 123; Westmoreland 33, 34, 110, 126.
COX. Catharine 99; John (voter -53); Morris 99, 100; Nathaniel 93, 97; Presly 123.
CREEKS. Hooes 49, 66, 110; Little 79; Powell 11, 101, 113; Quantico 28, 35, 51, 86, 87, 111, 119; Whores 33, 34, 64, 104, 105.
CROUCH. William 95.
CRUPPER. Richard 11.
CUMPTON. Alexander 9.
CUNDIFF. William (voter -54, 56, 57), 80, 114, 126, 130, 131.
CURRY. John 101.
CURTIS. -58; Chichester 59, 60; Lettice 59, 60.

DADE. Henry C. 1, 14, (voter -54); Langhorne 44, 46-48, (voter -53, 55), 62, 77, 78, 96, 119; Townshend (voter-53, 55, 56), 120.
DAROCH. John 1, 11, 35, 36.
DAUGHERTY. Barbara 64; Daniel 33-35, (voter -53, 55), 64, 66, 104, 105.
DAULTON. Moses 95, 107.
DAVIS -124; Benson 44, (voter -53, 55); Cornelius 20, 45, 46; Elizabeth 48, 49, 67, 68; Fanney (of Nelson Co., Ky. -113); Henry 90, 91; Hugh 23, 26, 27, 44-46, (voter -54), 90, 91, 98, 105; Isaac 11, 20, 45, 45; Isaac (deced. -44) 45, 113; Jane 23, 45, 46, 98; Jean 44, 45; John 45, (voter -56); John Senr. (voter -53); Joshua 90; Mary 45, 46, (Wickliff -90), 91; Moses (voter -53, 54); Presley 45, 46; (contd.)

DAVIS. (contd.) Richard (voter -53); Simon 9, 17; Thomas 16, 17, 43, 69; Thomas Senr. (voter -53, 55); Thomas (of Stafford Co. -115); Travis 44, 45, 46, 48, (of Nelson Co., Ky. -113); Warren 45, 46; William 21, 26, 44, 46, 48, (voter -56, 57), 67, 68, 98, 113, 133; William Junr. 44-46; William (deced. -48); William (Son of Isaac, voter -54, 55).
DAWE/DAUGH. Philip 2, 3, 23, 24, 26, 27, 39, 44, 46, (voter -53, 55, 56), 67, 99-101, 106, 107, 120, 123.
DEBELL. John 130, 131.
DENEALE. Edward 99; George 94, 120; James (voter -55), 65, (Mill -92), 94, 120.
DERMOTT. James R. 61; Mary (Spence) 61.
DIGGS. Thomas (Gent., Fauquier Co. -88).
DOGAN. Henry (voter -53).
DONNELL. Ezekiel 24, (voter -54), 87, 89; John 87.
DOUGHERTY. Daniel 34, 104.
DOUGLASS. Catharine Junr. (of Scotland -122), 123; Catharine Senr. (of Scotland -122), 123; James 72-74; James (deced. -122), 123; Margaret (of Scotland -122), 123.
DOWDALL. Thomas (voter 53, 56, 57).
DOWELL. Isaac 97, Jermiah (voter -53), 57, 97; John (deced., date Will recorded -97); Molly (of Frederick Co. -97); William (of Frederick Co. 97).
DOWNMAN. Ann 104; Rawleigh P. 104; William 110; (Gent. -111), 122.
DOWNTON. Richard 36.
DULANY. Benjamin 76.
DUMFRIES: District Court 31, 87; Fairfax Street 1, 8, 25; Princess Street 1, 7, 7; Town of 7, 8, 11, 15, 18, 20, 25, 26, 40-43, 47, 62, 63, 67, 72-74, 76, 84, 87, 91, 98-100, 102, 103, 108, 109, 111, 121, 123, 127, 128, 133; Water Street 7, 84, 87.
DUNAWAY. Ezekiel 78.
DUNKAN. John 133.
DUNNINGTON. William 52; William W. 93, 106.
DUNSCOMB. Andrew (Gent., Richmond City -34), 35.
DUVAL. Senett (voter -56, 57); William (voter -53).
DYAL/DIAL/DOYLE. Charles 12, 13; Sarah (Calvert) 12, 13.
DYE. Amos (voter -53); John 27, 28, (voter -53, 55).

EDMONDS. Elias 62, 63.
EDRINGTON. John 33, (voter -53, 55, 56).
EDWARDS. Haden 51; John (voter -53).
ELLICOTT. Elizabeth (Daughter of John -81);
  John (late of Town of Baltimore, deced. -81);
  Nathaniel 65, 66, 80, 81, 125.
ERWIN. William 34, 35.
ESPIE. Corner 41.
EVANS. Jesse 36.
EWELL. Bertrand 111, 128; Charles (Gent. -6),
  13, 32, 36, (voter -56, 57), 77-79, 90, 91, 109,
  110, 120, 128, 133; Charlotte 13, 14; James
  (Gent. -6), 7, 14,38; James Senr. (voter -54, 56);
  Jesse 95, 120; Jesse Junr. 1, 8, 120; Jesse
  Senr. (Gent.-13), 14, 36, (voter -53), 72, 73;
  Sarah 118.

FAIR. Cleman 68.
FAIRFAX. Hezekiah 21, (voter -54, 56, 57);
  John 21, (of Monongalia Co. -105), 106; Mary
  (of Monongalia Co. -105), 106; Nancy 103,
  106; Sarah 21; William 20-22, (voter 54,
  56), 105, 106; William (deced. -20), 21,22.
FALKNER. Thomas (deced. -18).
FALLIN. Elizabeth 12, 15.
FARRELL. William Senr. 107.
FARROW. Isaac 10, 11, 18, (voter -54, 56);
  Sarah 103, 104; William (voter -54, 57), 92, 93,
  101-104, 117.
FENWICK. Edward 65, 66.
FERGUSON. John (voter -53, 57).
FEWELL. Henry 105.
FIELDER. Samuel 39, (voter -54, 55);
  William 39.
FISHER. Amos 64; John 34, 35, 64, 104, 105;
  Thomas 64.
FITZHUGH -29; John (voter -53), (Esqr. -95);
  John Thornton (Esqr. -24), (voter -56, 57);
  Philip 95; William (voter -55);
  William (Coll;, of Maryland -111).
FLORANCE. Elizabeth 9; George 8, 9, 17, 52,
  (voter -54, 56), 67, 68; George June. (voter
  -56); George Senr. (voter -54, 55); James 52,
  (voter -54, 55, 56); Joseph 8, 9, 17, 67, 86;
  Mary 86; William 8, 9, 17, 86.
FOLEY. James 2, 3, 20, 21, 46, (voter -53, 56,
  57), 106, 107, 133; John 3; John (deced.-107);
  Margaret (Mann) 107; Mary 2, 3; Mason (of
  North Carolina) 2, 3, (of Parson Co., N. C., 106),
  107.

FOLSOM. Israel (deced. -84, 111); Sarah 84.
FOOTE. Richard 24; (voter -53); Richard
  H. 133; Richard Senr, (voter -56).
FORBES. David (deced. -43); Hugh 43;
  Murray 43.
FORGIE. Daniel (of Dumfries -127), 128.
FORTUNE. Garner 130, 131.
FOSTER. Chloe (of Fauquier Co. -37), 38, 39;
  James 18, 38, 52, (voter -53, 56), 71, 72;
  John (of Fauquier Co. -37), 38, 39; Joshua
  (voter -54, 56; William 18, (voter -56);
  William Senr. (voter -54); William (deced. -71).
FOUSHEE. John 30.
FOX. Amos 12.
FOXWORTHY. William 13.
FRENCH. Stephen (voter -54, 56).
FRISTOE. Franky (of Dumfries -91); John 12,
  33, 63, (of Dumfries -91), 98, 100, 101, 120,
  128; John Junr. 33; William 33.
FRYER. John (voter -53); John Senr. (voter -56).

GAINES. Rowland 25.
GALLAGHER. ( )ard (voter -53); Bernard 69, 70,
  120.
GALLAHUE. Derby 11.
GALLOWAY. John 35.
GALVAN. Mr. 128.
GARDENHIRE. Adam 102.
GARDINER. James 80.
GERRARD. William 89.
GIBSON. John (Mercht.-3), 4-6, 40, 43, (voter -53,
  55, 56), 63, 64, 83, (of Dumfries -92), 102, 103.
GILBERT. Joseph 23, 24, 27, (voter -53, 57),
  84, 120, 128; Joseph Senr. 100, 101.
GILL. Richard 115.
GORDON. William 37, 129.
GRAHAM. Catesby 117, 118; Elijah 118;
  Elizabeth (deced. -117), 118; George 24, 48,
  (voter -53), 65, 66, (Doctor -107), 109, 120,
  123; James (voter -53); Jenney 118;
  Richard 11, (Gent. 31), 121; Robert (Clerk of
  Court -1), (voter -53, 55); Salley (of Fauquier
  Co. -7), 51, 52, 62, 63; Walter (of Fauquier Co.
  -7), 51, 52, 62, 63, 69, 70; William 112, 117,
  118.
GRANT. Daniel 88, 89; Joseph 88; William
  (Gent.-6), 85, 86; William Senr. (voter -53, 56,
  57).
GRAY. Anthony (voter -54); Anthony C. 79;
  Collins-104; Anthony Collings-110) 111; (contd)

GRAY (contd.) Levinah 104, 110; Robertson 105;
William 132, 133.

GRAYSON. Benjamin (deced. -95); George
Washington 71; Mary 61; Robert 16, 45;
Spence 60, 61, (Revd. -94), 95; Susanna 60.

GREEN. Elijah (voter -54); James (voter -54),
58; Thomas (voter -53).

GREENHOW. John (Gent. of Richmond City -34),
35.

GREGG. Thomas 107.

GRIEVES. Daniel (voter -54); Nathaniel (voter
-54, 55).

GRIGORY. Benjamin 89, 90.

GRIGSBY. Benjamin (voter -55); Elizabeth 94;
James 16, 23, 27, 37, 38, (voter -54), 124;
Redman 94; Ursley (Mann) 107; William 107.

GRIMES. Sylvester 102; William 102.

GRIMSTEAD. Ann 66, 67; James (voter -53, 56);
James Senr. 66, 67. John (voter -53, 56), 66, 67.

GUIONETT. James (voter -53), 120.

GWATKINS. James (voter -54).

HALLEY. James 11.

HALOST. Richard 37, 85.

HAMILTON. Barton 46.

HAMMITT. John 14, 32, (voter -57), 75.

HAMRICK. Seiers 59, 60.

HANCOCK. Martin J. 118; Mungo 10, 11,
28-30, 36, 63, 68, 81, 94, 106.

HANSBROUGH. Ann Frances 107, 110;
Peter Junr. 4, (voter -54), 79, 109, 110.

HARDING/HARDIN. Charles 117; Edwd: 52,
(voter -53); Rolley 117.

HARPER. Edward 127.

HARRIS. Thomas (voter -54, 56, 57).

HARRISON B. 41; Benjamin (of Fauquier Co.
-88), 89, 90; Burdet 12; Burr 46, 47;
Cuthbert 46, 47; Cuthbert Junr. 124;
George 47; John P. 119; Mary (of Fauquier Co.
-88), 89, 90; Mathew (Gent. -6); Mathew Junr.
22, 23, 40, 43, 47, 67, 109, 112, 119, 120, 125;
Seth (deced. -119); Thomas 5, (Revd. -6), 12,
(Sheriff -22), 23, 54, 119, 123; William 122.

HART. Catharine 6, 7; Leonard 6, 7;
Thomas (voter -54, 55, 56); William (voter
-53, 55).

HARVEY. Edward 125.

HATHAWAY. James Junr. (of Fauquier Co. -129),
130; James Senr. (of Fauquier Co.-129), 130.

HAYES. James 40, 43, 95, 120; Janes Junr. 24.

HAZLERIG. Abell 102.

HEDGES. Grief 52; John 7, 38, (voter -55);
John Junr. (voter -55); Mary (Marriage -16).

HELM. Thomas (Gent., Fauquier Co. -62), 123;
William (voter -53, 55, 56).

HENDERSON. Alexander 4-6, 15, 20, (Esqr. -40),
42, 43, (voter -55), 70, 102, 103, 106, (of Dumfries -122), 123; Archd: 123; John G. 92;
William 84.

HERNDON. James White 42.

HESLOP. John G. 58.

HEWES. Abram 49, 64, 65.

HEWITT. Rachel 68.

HIGHWARDEN. John 39.

HILL. Rossill 14.

HILLYARD. Nathaniel 37.

HIXON/HICKSON. William 9, 17, 24, 25,
(voter -54, 55).

HOFF. Moore 6, 38, 39, (voter -53, 56, 57).

HOLBORNE. William (of Richmond Co. -58).

HOLLADAY/HOLLIDAY. James 71, 124, 125.

HOLLEY. Henry 10.

HOLSCLAW/HOLTZCLAW -36, 59.

HOMES. James 89, 90.

HOOE. -115; Bernard (Gent.-6), 38, 39, (voter
-53, 55), 76, 77, 130, 131; Bernard Junr.
(voter -53, 55), 109, 110; Henry Dade 47,
(voter -56), 79, 109, 110, 119; Howson 32,
(Gent. -75); Howson Junr. (voter -54, 55), 79,
80; Howson Senr. (voter -54, 55); Jane 79, 80;
J. H. 113; John 5, (voter -55), 79; Robert
Howson (voter-53), 109, 110, 113, 116, 131, 133;
Robert H. (Gent. -90), 91; Thomas P. 130, 131;

HOOMES. Thomas Senr. (voter -53, 56, 57).

HOOPER. Thomas 2.

HOPE. Henry 59, 60.

HORTON. Snowden (voter -54, 57; William (of
Stafford Co. -42).

HOWARD. W: 96.

HOWISON. Alexander 12; Samuel 67, 104;
Stephen 21, (voter -53, 56).

HUBER/HUPBER. George (voter -53, 56), 91.

HUGHES. Margaret 1, 2; William 1, 2.

HUME(S). Alexander 52, (voter -54, 55);
Frances 52.

HUNTER -118; Nathaniel (voter -53, 57, 58);
63, 120.

HUSKINS. William 61.

HUTCHINSON. Benjamin 18; Isaac 88;
John (Birthday noted -94); Robert 18, 19.

TRIPLETT (contd.) James 9; Nat: 7, 102; Nathaniel 8; Nath: Hedgman 19, 20, 51; Thomas 82-84, 97, 129.

TRONE/TROANE. Peter 4, (voter -53, 55).

TROTTER. James (Justices of Fayette Co. in Kentucky -112, 113).

TURBERVILLE. George Lee (Gent., Richmond Co. -82), 83, 129.

TURNBULL. Henry 13, (voter -55).

TURNER. Walker 3, 107, 118, 119.

TYLER. Benjamin (voter -54, 55, 56); Cedilid Ann 109; Charles 13, 41, 42, (voter -54), 59, 60, 74, (Gent. -77), 80, 84, 85; Charles Junr. 10, 11, 29, 30, 66, 106, 125, 126; George Gray 50, (voter -54), 61, 67, 85, 109; Henry 38, 37, (voter -54); John (Gent. -6), 7, 60,125; John (deced. -67), 108, 126; Margaret 67, 68, 108, 109; William 1, 8, 14, 15, 25, 39, 50, (voter -54), 67, 68, 102, 103, 109, 110.

VEALE. William 20, 106.

WALKER. Henry 4.

WALLACE/WALLIS. James 82-84, 129; James Junr. 130; James Senr. 130; John 107.

WALLER. John 123; Mary 123.

WARD -79.

WARDEN -113; Asa (of Charles Co., Maryland -11); Richard (deced. -11).

WAREHOUSE: Quantico 14, 68-70, 128.

WASHINGTON -52, 71; Bushrod (Esqr., Mercht. of Alexandria -112), 116, 117; Henry (Gent. -38), (voter -54, 57, 58); 73, 77, 78, 80; Lund Junr. 60, 61; Susanna (Spence) 60.

WATERS. John Junr. (voter -53, 57); John Senr. (voter -56); Phillamon 10.

WATSON. John 12, 98; Samuel 58, (Minister Metodist Episcopal Church -78).

WEAVER. George (voter -54), 118, 119.

WEBSTER. James (voter -54, 57).

WELLS. Benjamin 16, 38; Carty (voter -53), 85, 86, 92, 98, 99.

WERT. Conrad (voter -54).

WHEELER. Benjamin (voter -53, 55), 80; Nathan (voter -53); Richard (voter -53).

WHITE. James (voter -56, 57).

WHITECOTTON. George 78; Nancey 78.

WHITING -31; M. 19, 108; Matthew (voter -55, 56); Peter Beverley 19; Polly 108; Thomas 108.

WICKLIFFE. ( )ington (voter -53), Arrington (voter -57), 68, 115, 116; Benjamin 90, (of Fairfax Co., deced. -115); Caty 115, 116; Charles 115; Elijah 116; ( )ts. (voter -53, Moses (voter 056, 57), 75, 76, 115, 116; Moses Junr. 116; Nathaniel (died without Will -90), Robert 75, (of Fairfax Co. -115); Robert (deced. -115); Sarah (of Fairfax Co. -115), 116.

WIGGINTON. Benjamin (voter -55); James 22, 23, 52, (voter -54), 86; John W. 87, 94, 99.

WILKINSON. John (voter -54, 57).

WILLCOCKS. John 20, (voter -57, 58).

WILLETT. Jonathan 104.

WILLIAMS. George 7, (voter -53, 57, 58), 63; Isaac 41; J. 1; Jane 99, 100; John 2-4, 7, 12, 19, 20, 23, 24, 26, 27, 36, (appointed Clerk of Court -40), 43, 44, 46, 52, (voter -54), 62-64, 67, 77, 78, 84, 87, 93, 94, 96-100, 105, 117, 120, 128.

WILSON. Cumberland 26, 44, 45, 72, 74, (of Dumfries -98), 111-113.

WINDSOR. Sampson (voter -55).

WISHART. William 76, 133.

WOOD. James (Lt. Governor of Virginia -127) Jane 4; John 13; John (of Charles Co., Maryland, deced. -4).

WOODCOCK. John S. (Gent., Frederick Co. -33).

WOODYARD. Leonard (voter -53); John (voter -54, 57, 58.

WRIGHT/WRITE. John 18, (voter -53, 56); Richard 10; William (voter -56); William Senr. (voter -53, 56).

WROE. Benjamin (voter -53, 56); Richard (voter -53, 55).

WYATT. James (voter -54); William (voter -53); William Edward (Gent. -60).

YOUNG. Edwin 47; Original (Gent. -90).